W9-ACP-674

GOOD NEWS STUDIES

Consulting Editor: Robert J. Karris, O.F.M.

Volume 25

The Letters of Paul

An Introduction

Charles B. Puskas, Jr.

A Michael Glazier Book
THE LITURGICAL PRESS
Collegeville, Minnesota

Acknowledgments

The author and publisher are grateful for the permission to reprint the following:

Pages 139–149 and 191–203 of Charles B. Puskas, AN INTRODUCTION TO THE NEW TESTAMENT, Peabody, Mass.: Hendrickson Publishers, 1989.

Pages 14–23 of GALATIANS by Hans Dieter Betz, copyright © 1979 Fortress Press. Used by permission of Augsburg Fortress.

Pages 4–8, 55–63 from LETTERS IN PRIMITIVE CHRISTIANITY by William Doty, copyright © 1973 Fortress Press. Used by permission of Augsburg Fortress.

Pages 98–103 of A CHRONOLOGY OF PAUL'S LIFE by Robert Jewett, copyright © 1979 Fortress Press. Used by permission of Augsburg Fortress.

A Michael Glazier Book published by The Liturgical Press

Cover design by David Manahan, O.S.B. Detail of manuscript, Carolingian Bible, Bibliotheque Nationale, Ms. Lat. 1, Paris.

1 2 3 4 5 6 7 8 9

Library of Congress Cataloging-in-Publication Data

Puskas, Charles B.
The letters of Paul : an introduction / Charles B. Puskas.
p. cm. — (Good news studies ; v. 25)
"A Michael Glazier book."
Includes bibliographical references and indexes.
ISBN 0-8146-5690-0
1. Bible. N.T. Epistles of Paul—Introductions. I. Title.
II. Series.
BS2650.2.P87 1993
227′.06—dc20 92-46909
CIP

Contents

Abbreviations

Abbreviations of biblical books, ancient texts, periodicals, and reference works are derived from *The Society of Biblical Literature Members Handbook* (1992), "Instructions for Contributors," 209–226. Consult Bibliography for information on additional titles.

ABD	*The Anchor Bible Dictionary.* 6 vols. Eds., D.N. Freedman, et al. New York: Doubleday, 1992.
Ante-Nicene	*The Ante-Nicene Fathers: Translations of the Writings of the Fathers down to A.D. 325*, 10 vols., eds. A. Roberts, et al. Buffalo, NY, 1884–86; repr. Grand Rapids: Eerdmans, 1951.
Austin, *Hellenistic World*	M. M. Austin, *The Hellenistic World from Alexander to the Roman Conquest,* Cambridge University Press, 1981.
Barrett, *NTB*	C. K. Barrett, ed., *The New Testament Background*: Selected Documents, Harper. Torchbooks. New York: Harper & Row, 1961.
Bauer, *Orthodoxy*	W. Bauer, *Orthodoxy and Heresy in Earliest Christianity*, trans. & ed. by R. Kraft, et. al., from 1934 Ger. ed. Philadelphia: Fortress Press, 1971.
BC	F. J. Foakes-Jackson and K. Lake, eds. *The Beginnings of Christianity Part I. The Acts of the Apostles,* 5 vols. London: Macmillan & Co., 1920–33; reprint ed., Grand Rapids: Baker Book House, 1979.

Bruce, *Book of Acts*	F. F. Bruce, *The Book of Acts.* NIC. Grand Rapids: Eerdmans, 1952.
Charlesworth, *Pseudepigrapha*	J. H. Charlesworth, *The Old Testament Pseudepigrapha,* 2 vols. Garden City, N.Y.: Doubleday, 1983, 1985.
Eusebius, *H.E.*	Eusebius Pamphilus, *Ecclesiastical History* (written ca. 305–24 A.D.). Trans. C. F. Cruse, 1850, Grand Rapids: Baker Book House, 1955 repr.
GBS	*Guides to Biblical Scholarship.* Philadelphia; Minneapolis: Fortress Press.
Hennecke, *NTA*	E. Hennecke, *New Testament Apocrypha*, 2 vols., ed., W. Schneemelcher, trans. by R. McL. Wilson, et al. Philadelphia: Westminster Press, 1963, 1965.
Hengel, *Judaism & Hellenism*	M. Hengel, *Judaism and Hellenism*, 2 vols. trans. J. Bowden. Philadelphia: Fortress Press, 1974.
IDB	*The Interpreter's Dictionary of the Bible*, G. A. Buttrick, ed., 4 vols. New York/Nashville: Abingdon Press, 1962.
IDBSup	*The Interpreter's Dictionary of the Bible Supplementary Volume*, K. Crim, ed. Nashville: Abingdon Press, 1976.
Jewett, *Chronology*	R. Jewett, *A Chronology of Paul's Life.* Philadelphia: Fortress Press, 1979.
Jonas, *Gnostic Religion*	H. Jonas, *The Gnostic Religion.* 2nd ed. Boston: Beacon Press, 1962.
Käsemann, *Essays*	E. Käsemann, *Essays on New Testament Themes.* Trans. W. Montague. London: SCM, 1964; Philadelphia: Fortress, 1982.
Koester, *Introduction*	H. Koester, *Introduction to the New Testament*, 2 vols. Philadelphia: Fortress Press, 1982.
Kümmel,	W. G. Kümmel, *Introduction to the New*

Introduction	*Testament*, rev. Eng. ed. trans. by H. C. Kee from 17th Ger. ed. New York/Nashville: Abingdon Press, 1975.
LCL	*The Loeb Classical Library*, founded by J. Loeb, 450 vols., eds. G. P. Goold, et al. Cambridge, Mass.: Harvard Univ. Press; London: William Heinemann.
Perrin, *Jesus*	N. Perrin, *Jesus and the Language of the Kingdom, Symbol and Metaphor in New Testament Interpretation* (Philadelphia: Fortress Press, 1976).
Robinson, *Nag Hammadi*	J. M. Robinson, gen. ed., *The Nag Hammadi Library in English*, trans. by members of the Coptic Gnostic Library Project of the Institute for Antiquity & Christianity. San Francisco: Harper & Row, 1977.
Rudolph, *Gnosis*	K. Rudolph, *Gnosis, The Nature and History of Gnosticism*. Trans. R. McL. Wilson, et al. San Francisco: Harper & Row, 1983.
Schürer, *History*	E. Schürer, *The History of the Jewish People In the Age of Jesus Christ (175* B.C.–A.D. *135)*, rev. & edited by G. Vermes, et al., 2 vols. Edinburgh: T. & T. Clark, 1973, 1979.
SLA	*Studies in Luke-Acts.* Edited by L. E. Keck and J. L. Martyn. Nashville: Abingdon, 1966.
Talbert, *Literary*	C. H. Talbert, *Literary Patterns, Theological Themes and the Genre of Luke-Acts.* Missoula, Mont.: Scholars Press, 1974.
TDNT	G. Kittel, ed. *Theological Dictionary of the New Testament*, 10 vols., trans. by G. W. Bromiley. Grand Rapids: Wm. B. Eerdmans, 1964–76.
ZPE	M. C. Tenney, gen. ed., *The Zondervan Pictorial Encyclopedia*, 5 vols. Grand Rapids: Zondervan Publishing House, 1975.

Introduction

The apostle Paul, spirited letter writer, preacher, and missionary to the Gentiles, has been a figure of controversy and misunderstanding from the beginning. Some of his contemporaries and those of later generations regarded him as a false apostle and a despiser of God's laws, but the heretic Marcion defended him as the only true apostle. In the modern period, Frederick Nietzsche called him the Jewish preacher of bad news and George Bernard Shaw accused him of making a monstrous imposition upon Jesus. Today, some are convinced that Paul grossly misunderstood the Jewish law.

Despite the controversy and misunderstanding, the apostle Paul has many admirers. The Acts of the Apostles presents him as a dynamic preacher and missionary who fulfills Israel's role as a light to the nations. The second century Acts of Paul portrays him as a model Christian ascetic. Many gnostic Christians revered his teaching. In the fourth century, Augustine of Hippo became a Christian after reading one of his letters. Martin Luther, the sixteenth century Reformer, believed that Paul was God's apostle of faith and the champion of Christian freedom. In the early twentieth century, Karl Barth challenged the theology of his day with bold expositions of the apostle's writings.[1]

[1]For a helpful resource of information on Paul's critics, interpreters, and admirers, see: Wayne E. Meeks, ed., *The Writings of St. Paul* (New York: W. W. Norton & Co., 1972) chaps. 3–6. For further discussion, see: D. R. MacDonald, *The Legend and the Apostle: The Battle for Paul in Story and Canon* (Philadelphia: Westminster Press, 1983); W. S. Babcock, ed., *Paul and the Legacies of Paul* (Dallas: SMU Press, 1990); E. H. Pagels, *The Gnostic Paul: Gnostic Exege-*

How we understand the apostle depends on our interpretation of his famous (or infamous) writings in the New Testament. Beginning with his Letter to the Romans, thirteen books are ascribed to Paul, with the Letter to the Hebrews having a close relationship to the collection.[2]

Paul's letters provide some data about his life and background. He refers to himself as a Hebrew of Hebrew origins and a Pharisee in his interpretation of Jewish law (Phil 3:5; Rom 11:1). He often quotes and alludes to the Hebrew Scriptures, but mostly in a widely-used Greek translation. He is immersed in hellenistic culture and thought, an ingenious debater, and seasoned traveler to cities of the Roman world. He calls himself an apostle of Jesus Christ and proclaims his "good news" with the passion of one who has experienced its liberating power. He quarrels with his critics, shows deep concern for the churches founded by or affiliated with him, and pleads for mutual understanding among Jews and Gentiles.

This book exposes the student to the life and thought of Paul with a letter-by-letter introduction to his writings. It acquaints her with some of the basic issues of who really wrote what, when it was written, social setting, audience, and literary characteristics as she begins to read the letters on her own. The book also includes an overview of the letter genre, a chronology of Paul, and the rhetorical arrangement of his writings.

The particular order of the book chapters is more the result of convenience and conviction than chronology. For example,

sis of the Pauline Letters (Philadelphia: Fortress Press, 1975; paperback ed., Philadelphia: TPI, 1992); M. Wiles, *The Interpretation of St. Paul's Letters in the Early Church* (London: Cambridge Univ. Press, 1967).

[2]In most of our earliest Greek manuscripts, Hebrews occurs in the Pauline collection. The anonymous author also betrays some acqaintance with Pauline Christianity. See H. Attridge, *Hebrews,* Hermeneia (Minneapolis: Fortress Press, 1989) 31–32.

References to Paul in the Acts of the Apostles will be addressed when discussion in the letters occasions it. See also my discussion on Acts and Paul's letters in "A Chronology of Paul's Life."

For books outside of the New Testament that attempt to narrate some of Paul's activities or claim to be written by him, see: E. Hennecke, *New Testament Apocrypha,* ed. W. Schneemelcher, trans. R. McL. Wilson et al., vol. 2 (Philadelphia: Westminster Press, 1965) 128–141, 322–389, 755–797; MacDonald, *The Legend and the Apostle.*

Paul's Letter to the Galatians is a good introduction to the apostle in action although it is probably not his first letter. Some letters are appropriately grouped together for internal reasons (e.g. 1 and 2 Thess, Col and Eph). Hebrews is located in the midst of Paul's letters, as in the earliest collections. Perhaps the placing of the chapter on the Pastoral Letters at the end conveys the most chronological arrangement.

This book is intended to be a helpful reference tool as well as textbook. Many introductions to Paul ignore or abbreviate discussions of authorship, sources, and literary integrity. Knowledge about these issues is important for understanding Paul, reading biblical commentaries, and doing research. The detailed rhetorical outlines are an attempt to lay bare the logic of the apostle. The organizing of Paul's thoughts with the use of hellenistic categories seems more appropriate than using those of modern western culture. Even the rabbinic arguments that Paul seems to employ, betray some hellenistic rhetorical influence.[3]

Because the focus of this book is on the content and origins of each Pauline writing as a unit, only those issues and texts will be examined that relate to the book as a whole and its history of composition. Further discussion and resources for understanding Paul's theology, apocalyptic perspectives, views on Jewish and Gentile relations, and his social and cultural contexts will be provided in the notes and bibliography.[4]

[3]See for example: D. Daube, "Rabbinic Methods of Interpretation and Hellenistic Rhetoric" *Hebrew Union College Annual Bulletin* 22 (1949) 239–64; G. M. Phillips, "The Practice of Rhetoric at the Talmudic Academies" *Speech Monographs* 26 (1959) 37–47; H. A. Fischel, *Rabbinic Literature and Greco-Roman Philosophy* (Leiden: E. J. Brill, 1973).

On Paul and hellenistic rhetoric, see: W. Wuellner, "Greek Rhetoric and Pauline Argumentation," *Early Christian Literature and the Classical Tradition,* eds., W. R. Schoedel and R. L. Wilken (Paris: Beauchesne, 1979) 177-88; C. C. Black II, "The Rhetorical Form of the Hellenistic Jewish and Early Christian Sermon: A Response to Lawrence Wills," *Harvard Theological Review* 81 (1, 1988) 1–18; G. A. Kennedy, *New Testament Interpretation Through Rhetorical Criticism* (Chapel Hill and London: The University of North Carolina Press, 1984); B. Mack, *Rhetoric and the New Testament* (Minneapolis: Fortress, 1990) 56–73.

[4]Secondary literature on the writings of Paul continues to multiply enormously. The reader is encouraged to consult the following academic journals which provide helpful studies and reviews of current research on the Pauline Epistles and other New Testament writings: e.g., *New Testament Abstracts* (Weston, Mass.),

The limits of this introduction and the great task before us might recall for some the limits of human understanding when confronted with something mysterious and overwhelming. The apostle Paul was profoundly aware of it:

> "O the depth of the riches and wisdom and knowledge of God! How unsearchable are his judgments and how unfathomable his ways!"
>
> (Romans 11:33)

Despite the challenge ahead, may we pursue it with the boldness and energy of the same apostle who wrote:

> "Do you not know that in a race all the runners compete, but only one receives the prize? So run that you may obtain it."
>
> (1 Corinthians 9:24)

Journal of Biblical Literature (Atlanta), *Catholic Biblical Quarterly* (Washington, D.C.), *New Testament Studies* (Cambridge), *Journal of New Testament Studies* (Sheffield), *Interpretation* (Richmond), and *Revue Biblique* (Jerusalem).

1

The Ancient Letter Genre

1. The Letter Genre: Its Importance

a. The NT

In the NT twenty-one of the twenty-seven books are labeled "letters" and both Acts and Revelation contain them (Acts 15:23-29; Rev 1:4–3:22). Despite its prevalence in the NT, all twenty-one books are not complete letters and the types we find are diverse. The letter to the Hebrews is actually a homily (or sermon), and both 2 Timothy and 2 Peter are farewell discourses with epistolary features. Ephesians and 1 Peter appear to be homilies in letter form; 1 Timothy and Titus are basically exhortations on worship and ethics. Even the undisputed letters of Paul show diversity: Philemon is a typical personal letter and Romans is a long letter essay. The forms of argumentation or rhetoric used by Paul in his letters are also varied.

b. Antiquity

Numerous examples of letters can be found in ancient Israelite-Jewish and Greco-Roman literature. The Hebrew Bible contains the letter form in Jeremiah 29; 2 Samuel 11; 1 Kings 21 and 2 Kings 10, and also in the Jewish historical book, 2 Maccabees. The Greco-Roman world records hundreds of letters by philosophers (e.g., Seneca, Plato, Epicurus), rulers (e.g., Alexander the Great, Augustus, Trajan), biographers (Plutarch), rhetoricians (Cicero), Roman officials (Pliny the Younger), and Christian leaders (Clement of Rome, Ignatius). Archaeologists in Egypt have discovered vast quantities of letters from the Hellenistic and Roman periods written by a variety of people: traders, merchants, rulers, soldiers, religious priests, friends, lovers, family members. The letter form was one of the most prominent literary categories in antiquity.

2. Basic Characteristics of Ancient Letters

The basic characteristics of the letter genre have changed little in history. Letters are a form of written communication between two parties when person-to-person contact is impossible or inappropriate. Letters presuppose a sender and addressee, everyone else is a third party outsider. The sender's side of the dialogue dominates the letter. The addressee's conversation can be inferred, but is not fully articulated until the addressee responds in written form as a sender. Letters are also occasional, written in response to some situation or set of circumstances. Something prompted the sender to write, even if it is merely the fact of physical distance. Letters are often spontaneous, written in reaction to an incident. The above observations apply to all letters, whether they are informal, personal, and private, or formal, official, and public.

a. Six Basic Types

From the hundreds of letters of antiquity, at least six letter types have been discovered. We will first state the letter type, next, the contents or parties concerned, then provide examples.[1]

[1]Material in this section has been derived from: W. Doty, *Letters in Primitive Christianity* 4–8, 55–63, © 1973 Fortress Press. Used by permission of Augsburg Fortress. See also N. A. Dahl, "Letter," *IDBSup* 538–41 (with helpful bibliography); Kümmel, *Introduction* 247–52; Roetzel, *Letters;* O. J. F. Seitz, "Letter," *IDB* 4:113-14; S. K. Stowers, *Letter Writing in Greco-Roman Antiquity* (Louisville: Westminster/John Knox, 1986).

1. *personal*—love letters, letters of friendship, private business, commendation or introduction between family or friends, (e.g., Philemon [commendation], papyri letters from Egypt).
2. *business*—dealing with trade taxes, wills, land (e.g., Egyptian papyri).
3. *official*—from political or military leaders to constituents, subservients or superiors (e.g., letters from Augustus, Pliny to Trajan).
4. *public letters*—literary, public pleas, and philosophical treatises (e.g., letters from Isocrates, Plato).
5. *fictitious letters*—purporting to come from heaven, an epistolary novel or pseudonymous (letters of Hippocrates, Letter of Aristeas, 2 Peter, 2 Clement).
6. *discursive or essay*—expostion of teaching, a monograph (e.g., 2 Maccabees 1; Martyrdom of Polycarp, Paul's letter to the Romans).

Some overlapping of the above categories does occur, since we have personal letters of Roman officials written to friends and family. Fictitious letters include fantastic letters purporting to come from heaven (Hippocrates) and pseudonymous documents written in the name of or attributed to some famous individual (letters of Jeremy, Aristeas, 2 Peter, 2 Clement). The contents of these subcategories vary greatly.

b. Fixed Patterns

Letters of antiquity followed a basic pattern as they do today. In modern personal letters we see the following fixed forms:

(1) Indication of place and date: St. Louis, Mo.; May 7, 1993
(2) Name of recipient: Dear John
(3) Apology for not writing sooner
(4) Statement of writer's good health and the hope that the recipient is in good health
(5) Body
(6) Salutation: "yours truly" with name of Sender.

In ancient letters we detect the following pattern:

(1) Opening (sender, addressee, greeting)
(2) Thanksgiving, wish for health

(3) Body (formal opening followed by the business which occasioned the letter)
(4) Closing (greetings, wishes for other people, final greeting, wish or prayer, sometimes a date)

Here is an example of an ancient letter using the above fixed form:

(1) Opening: Apion to Epimachus, his father and lord, heartiest greetings.
(2) Thanksgiving: First of all I pray that you are in health and continually prosper and fare well with my sister and her daughter and my brother.
(3) Body: I thank the lord Sarapis that when I was in danger at sea he saved me. Straightway upon entering Misenum I received traveling money from Caesar, three gold pieces. And I am well. I beg you therefore, honored father, write me a few lines, first regarding your health, secondly regarding that of my brother and sister, thirdly that I may welcome respectfully your hand[writing] . . .
(4) Closing: Greetings to Capito, to my brother and sister, to Sernilla and to my friends. I send you by Euctemon a little portrait of myself. My military name is Antonius Maximus. I pray for your good health. Athenonike Company[2]

Most early Christian letters, especially those of Paul, expand various portions and add new features to the above letter pattern. First, the thanksgiving section is usually expanded (e.g., 1 Thes 1:2–2:16; Phil 1:3-11). Second, many early Christian letters add new features such as: (a) an eschatological comment which concludes certain sections (1 Thes 3:11-13; 1 Cor 1:8-9; 4:6-13); (b) mention of travel plans (1 Thes 2:17–3:13; Phil 2:19-24), (c) a section of parenesis or ethical exhortations (1 Thes 4:1–5:22; Rom 12:1–15:13; Eph 4:1–6:20), and (d) a doxology or benediction is included (1 Thes 5:28; Rom 15:33; 16:20,25-27). With the above features in view, the following outline will be presented on the basic pattern of early Christian letters.

(1) Opening (sender, addressee, greeting)

[2]Letter derived from: Deissmann, *Light from the Ancient East* 179–83.

(2) Thanksgiving (often with a prayer of intercession and an eschatological ending)
(3) Body (formal opening; often having a note on travel plans and an eschatological ending)
(4) Parenesis (ethical exhortation)
(5) Closing (greetings, doxology, benediction)

3. The Use of the Letter Form by Early Christians

What type of letters were written by the apostle Paul? Using two examples from his undisputed letters we find a diversity of types. Paul's letter to Philemon is a personal letter of recommendation to a friend. It does not appear to be written for the official literary public but to a housechurch of several families. There are many parallels from the Egyptian papyri of this letter type. Paul's Letter to the Romans, on the other hand, appears to be a letter essay like those of Epicurus and Plutarch.[3] This lengthy exposition of religious teaching and ethics was probably intended to be circulated in Rome and elsewhere.

a. Four Official Features

Four common features of early Christian letters give them an official quality: 1) the frequent use of an amanuensis or executive secretary (1 Cor 16:21; Rom 16:22; Gal 6:11; 2 Thes 3:17; Col 4:18), (2) the use of co-workers as messengers who deliver the letters (e.g., Rom 16:1-2; Phlm 10-12; 1 Cor 16:10; 2 Cor 8:16-18; Eph 6:21; Col 4:7), (3) the apostolic authority of the sender making the letter an official pronouncement (Rom 1:1,11; 1 Cor 1:1; 2 Cor 1:1; Gal 1:1; Eph 1:1), and (4) the associates of the sender are often included in the opening (1 Cor 1:1; 2 Cor 1:1; Phil 1:1; Phlm l; Col 1:1). The use of secretaries (Lat. amanuenses) and messengers is typical in ancient letters. An amanuensis' role as the sender's co-worker combined with the sender's apostolic

[3]The letters attributed to the 3rd-cent. BC Greek philosopher, Epicurus, are found in Diogenes Laertius, *Lives of Eminent Philosophers* 10.35-38; 84-116, 122-35. Those of the 1st-cent. AD Greek biographer, Plutarch, are found in his *Moralia* 478A; 502B; 783A.

authority to give most early Christian letters an official quality not unlike that of a ruler's correspondence to his constituents.

b. Eight Literary Forms

In the letters of Paul and other early Christians we find numerous literary forms and stylistic features. We will first outline eight examples of the literary forms. And then we will discuss four types of stylistic features.

The following are the literary forms:

1. *Autobiography.* These are statements about the sender's experiences and situation. In the case of Paul they refer to the travels and experiences of his apostolic ministry (2 Cor 1:8-10; 7:5; 12:1-10; Phil 1:12-14; 1 Thes 2:1-12). Some accounts also seek to defend his apostolic authority (Gal 1:11–2:14; 1 Cor 9).
2. *Apocalyptic material.* These unveilings of the end time refer to the Lord's coming, apostolic afflictions and trials, and other more typical features of the apocalyptic (e.g., angels, demons, new Jerusalem, final judgment). They also employ symbolic language and include visions, blessings, and special revelations. Examples are found in 1 Thes 4:13–5:11; 2 Thes 1:5-10; 2:1-17; 1 Cor 15:12-28; Jude; 2 Pet 2–3; Heb 1–2; Revelation.
3. *Catalogues and lists.* These include the Hellenistic lists of vices and virtues (e.g., Gal 5:19-23; Col 3:5-15), household rules (e.g., Col 3:18–4:1; Eph 5:21–6:9; Ti 2:1-10) and rules for the community (e.g., 1 Tim 2; 5; 1 Pet 2:13–3:7). Some lists are merely descriptive and lead to threats of condemnation or a contrast with Christian behavior (Rom 1:18-32; 1 Cor 6:9-11). Other lists are parenetic and are utilized for teaching a moral code of behavior (Col 3:5-11; Gal 5:16-24).
4. *Catechesis.* Specific accounts of teaching on Christian holiness are found in 1 Thes 4:1-9 and 1 Pet 1:13-22. Other passages teach abstinence from evil and the pursuit of righteousness (Col 3:8–4:12; Eph 4:22-25).
5. *Confessional Statements.* These brief honorific titles confessing faith in Jesus as God's agent are found in Rom 10:9; 1 Cor 11:23 and 1 Tim 3:16.

6. *Hymns.* These traditional elements are probably fragments of songs originally used in worship. There are hymns about Christ (Phil 2:2-11; 1 Pet 2:21-24; Col 1:15-20) and baptism (Eph 2:19-22; Ti 3:4-7; Rom 6), to use two examples. Hymn-like passages usually distinguish themselves from their context by a conscious parallelism, unique vocabulary, and special grammatical features.
7. *Kerygma.* This pertains to specific preaching accounts about Christ. They often refer to prophetic fulfillment of Christ, his crucifixion, resurrection, exaltation, and the promise of his coming with a subsequent call to repentance (e.g. Rom 1:1-3; 1 Cor 15:1-7; Gal 1:3-4; see also Acts 2:14-29, 10:36-43).
8. *Prophetic denouncements.* Like the Hebrew prophetic writings, these include: (a) an introduction, (b) a statement of offense, (c) resulting punishment threatened, and (d) a hortatory conclusion (e.g., Gal 1:6-9; Rom 1:18-32; 1 Cor 5:1-13; 2 Thes 1:5-12).

c. *Four Stylistic Features*

It is no surprise that the early Christian letters are replete with the stylistic habits and thought patterns of late antiquity. This diversity of literary and stylistic features will be outlined in four areas: (1) principles of literary balance, (2) figures of speech, (3) rhetorical devices, and (4) grammatical and stylistic peculiarities.

Literary Balance. Two types of literary balance found in Hebrew poetry and Hellenistic literature are evident in early Christian letters: regular and inverted parallelism. Regular parallelism follows the A B: A' B' pattern where the elements of the second group are repeated in the same order as the first. This principle of balance was also discussed in the "Literary Features of Luke-Acts" (e.g., Peter-Paul, Jesus-Paul parallels, ch 11). In early Christian letters as in Hebrew poetry, regular parallelism is usually confined to smaller units and involves contrasting as well as synonymous correspondence. The following pattern from 1 Cor 9:20 is an example of synonymous parallelism:

(A) To the Jews
(B) I become as a Jew

(C) in order to win the Jews
(A′) To those under the law
(B′) I became as one under the law
(C′) that might win those under the law.

Here the thoughts of the first stanza (A B C) are repeated with different words in the second stanza (A′ B′ C′). Synonymous parallelism can also be detected in Rom 12:4-15 (and Lk 12:48). Examples of antithetical or contrasting parallelism are found in: 1 Cor 7:29-34; 10:6-10; Rom 4:25; 5:10; 2 Cor 5:13.

Inverted parallelism or chiasm is another principle of balance detected in early Christian letters. This introverted A B: B′ A′ pattern also occurs in Greco-Roman and other early Christian literature (e.g., Herodotus, *History;* Virgil's *Aeneid;* Luke-Acts). In Rom 2:6-11 we find the following chiastic pattern: [A] God judges all, v 6; [B] the righteous receive eternal life, v 7; [C] the wicked receive wrath, v 8; [C′] the wicked experience distress, v 9; [B′] the good experience glory, v 10; [A′] God is impartial, v 11. It has also been argued that 1 Cor 5:2-6 is a chiasm within a chiasm:[4]

A	B	C	B′	A′
puffed up v 2a	misconduct a	Lord Jesus a	Satan a	boasting v 6a
	presence b	you b	distortion b	
	presence b′	me b′	flesh c	
	misconduct a′	Lord Jesus a′	spirit c′	
			salvation b′	
			day of word a′	

The types of correspondence in a chiastic pattern vary. There can be, for example, contrasting or synonymous parallels, correspondences of exact words or similar thoughts. Other examples of chiasm are found in Rom 11:30-31; 1 Cor 7:3; 9:19-22; 22:8-12; Col 3:3-4.

The two principles of balance explained above are characteristic of the ancient world. They are evident in different literary

[4]R.N. Soulen, *Handbook of Biblical Criticism* 2nd ed. (Atlanta: John Knox, 1981) 41.

genres (e.g., Hebrew poetry, Hellenistic biography, early Christian letters). The chiastic pattern is also evident in Roman art and architecture. For example, the Jewish menorah (candelabra) on the arch of Titus at Rome consists of a centerpiece paralleled on either side by three pieces and thus exhibits the A B C D C′ B′ A′ pattern.[5]

Figures of Speech. The language of the early Christian letters, like that of human language in general, abounds with symbolic words and images.[6] Therefore only a few examples of this nonliteral use of language will be given. We will look at the figures of comparison and contradiction, as well as rhetorical questions and assertions.

Figures of comparison occur when familiar images are employed to clarify, highlight, or dramatize the speaker's ideas by means of analogy or illustration. Comparisons are drawn from family relations, the human body, sickness and death, nature, various trades, war, and athletic contests. Figures of comparison include simile, where the comparison is expressed, and metaphor, where it is implied. Paul's use of simile can be seen in 1 Thes 2:11-12, "*like* a father with his children, we exhorted each one of you." Other examples are found in Phil 2:15,22; Rom 9:27-29; 1 Cor 3:1; 4:13; 2 Cor 6:8-10; Gal 4:14; 1 Peter and James also contain many similes. In metaphors there is greater semantic power. In Gal 5:1, Paul states, "do not submit again to a yoke of slavery" and employs the imagery of slave constraints (cf. Sir 33:25-26) to describe the Galatians' futile lapse into Jewish legalism. Paul also uses slave imagery positively, to depict his obligatory relationship to Christ: Paul, a "slave (Gk. *doulos*) of Christ" (Gal 1:10; Rom 1:1). Other metaphors used by Paul are "sowing and reaping," "*fruit* of the Spirit," "*body* of Christ," and "stumbling

[5]For illustrations of this concentric symmetry in other works, see "Greek Art," in *Encyclopedia Britannica* (Chicago: Encyclopedia Britannica, Inc., 1971) 10:837–40; L. Richmond, "The Temples of Apollo and Divus Augustus on Roman Coins," in *Essays and Studies Presented to William Ridgeway,* ed., E. C. Quiggin (Cambridge: Cambridge Univ. Press, 1913) 198–212.

[6]For further study, see Bullinger, *Figures of Speech;* Caird, *Language and Imagery;* Soulen, *Handbook;* N. Turner, *Style,* vol. 4, in J. Moulton, *A Grammar of NT Greek* (Edinburgh: T. & T. Clark, 1976).

block.'' These familiar images of everyday life were effective vehicles for conveying Paul's teaching.

Figures of contradiction are irony and paradox. Irony, a statement which intends to convey its opposite meaning, occurs frequently in 2 Cor 10–13. In these chapters Paul's dialogue with the boastful charlatans of Corinth is full of irony and sarcasm in the Socratic tradition. (See also 1 Cor 4:8; 6:4; 2 Cor 5:3). Paradox, or an apparent contradiction that may reveal some profound truth, occurs often. For Paul, the crucifixion is a foundational paradox, 1 Cor 1:22-25. Paradoxical statements are also found in 1 Cor 7:22; 2 Cor 4:8-11; 5:17; 6:9-10; 12:10; Phil 3:7; Rom 7:15,19.

Rhetorical questions require no direct answer but are used by the speaker to attract the attention of the hearer. This provocative use of interrogation was widely employed by Hellenistic philosophers like Seneca and Epictetus. Paul in Rom 6:15 asks: ''What then? Are we to sin because we are not under law; but under grace? By no means!'' The answer, generally given, is self-evident but the rhetorical device itself is effective in evoking a response. Rhetorical questions occur frequently in Romans (2:3–4,21-23; 3:1-9,27-29; 4:1; 6:1; 9:19; 11:1) and James (2:4,6-7,20-21,25; 4:1,4,14).

Rhetorical assertions are numerous, so only a few examples will be given. Hyperbole, or exaggeration for the sake of emphasis, is found in Gal 1:8 ''But even if we or *an angel from heaven,* should preach to you a gospel contrary to that which we preached to you, let him be accursed!'' See also Gal 4:15; 5:12. Hyperbole is used often in prophetic denouncements or judicial indictments (e.g., Mt 23; Jas 5:1-6). Assertions of understatement, called ''meiosis'' are also found in Gal 5:23 ''against such there is no law'' and Rom 1:16 ''I am not ashamed of the gospel.'' Those understatements, the opposite of hyperbole, are used for emphasis or convey a certain effect. Another form of understatement is ''litotes,'' which affirms a fact by denying its opposite: ''they make much of you, *for no good purpose''* (Gal 4:17). Litotes is also used in Acts (Acts 12:18; 19-11; 21:39). This cautious use of language was effective in courtroom rhetoric (e.g., Lysias, Cicero).

Rhetorical Devices. Rhetorical devices coincide with the previous category, since ancient techniques of effective speaking and persuasion employed much figurative language. First we will examine those dialogical and rhetorical features that Paul shares with the Hellenistic diatribe, then briefly look at the types of Hellenistic oratory with which the letters of Paul coincide.

Some early Christian letters, e.g., Rom 2–11, Jas 2, seem to employ the dialogical features of the diatribe.[7] This form of discourse and discussion probably originated in philosophical schools, where a teacher would try to expose the errors of his students and lead them into truth. It was previously thought that the diatribe was a form of Cynic propaganda for the masses, but this viewpoint only finds some support in a few sources (e.g., Bion, Dio of Prusa). Most of the primary documents for the diatribe were written by teachers of philosophical schools: e.g., Teles *Bion* (3rd cent. BC); Epictetus *Discourses* (1st cent. AD); Musonius Rufus (1st cent. AD); Plutarch (1st cent. AD); Seneca, *Moral Epistles* (1st cent. AD). Since the diatribe presupposes a student-teacher setting, then it was probably not addressed to outsiders nor does it contain polemics against opponents, as some scholars have previously held.

The diatribe envisions two audiences: real and imagined. The real audience is comprised of disciples of the author who are in need of further enlightenment. The imagined audience includes a fictitious dialogue partner or objector who represents a false viewpoint. The dialogue opens with an address of indignation (*apostrophe*) to this imaginary "interlocutor" who is usually a caricature of a proud or pretentious person and represents the false views of the real audience. A dialogical exchange follows where the author resolves objections to his viewpoint or corrects false conclusions drawn from his line of reasoning. These objections and false conclusions are usually raised by the imaginary interlocutor. The purpose of the dialogue is to lead the real audience into truth by exposing false thinking or behavior.

[7]See especially: Stowers, *Diatribe;* idem, "Paul's Dialogue with A Fellow Jew in Romans 3:1-9," *CBQ* 46 (4, 1984) 707–22; A. J. Malherbe, *"Mē Genoito* in the Diatribe and Paul," *HTR* 73 (1/2, 1980) 231–40. See also Donfried, *Romans Debate* (1977) 132–41.

The above discussion of diatribe has significance for understanding the argumentation in Romans and James. Both contain many of its dialogical features. In Rom 1–11, for example, the dialogical style is central to the letter's message. Paul and the author of James probably used the diatribe to expose error and lead their readers into a deeper commitment to the Christian life. It is probable that the diatribe was one of the major teaching techniques of early Christianity.

Since the NT letters are primarily written dialogues and discourses, and many are sermons in letter form, they have close affinities with Hellenistic oratory. According to the influential works on persuasion and public speaking by Aristotle, Cicero, and Quintilian there were different types of speeches characterized by a certain arrangement.[8] Political speeches and funeral orations concerned with merits and honor were called epideictic or demonstrative. Their function to display common virtues and values is similar to the purpose of Paul's letter to the Romans (cf. Colossians, Ephesians, Jude, 2 Peter, 2 Timothy). Courtroom or judicial speeches concerned with justice (accusatory or defensive) coincide well with the apologetic functions of Galatians and 2 Cor 10–13. Speeches that provide advice for future decisions were labeled deliberative or symboleutic. First Corinthians 7–16, where Paul provides specific advice to his readers, seems to fit this category (cf. 2 Cor 8–9, Philemon, Hebrews, James, 1 Timothy, Titus).

The arrangement of these types of speeches falls into the basic pattern of: (a) introduction or exordium (e.g., Gal 1:6-10; Rom 1:1-15; Heb 1:1–4:16); (b) propositio or thesis to be demonstrated (Gal 1:11-12); (c) the facts of the case or narratio (Gal 1:11–2:14; Heb 5:1–6:20); (d) argumentation, called probatio (Gal 3:1–4:31) or confirmatio (Rom 1:18–15:13; Heb 7:1–10:18); and (e) closing summation or peroratio (Gal 6:11-18; Rom 15:14–16:23; Heb 10:19–13:21). Further comparisons of early Christian letters and Hellenistic rhetoric will be pursued in this book.

[8]On Hellenistic rhetoric and the NT, see Betz, *Galatians;* Kennedy, *NT Rhetoric;* W. Wuellner, "Paul's Rhetoric of Argumentation in Romans," *CBQ* 38 (1976) 330–51; idem, "Where Is Rhetorical Criticism Taking Us?" *CBQ* 49 (3, 1987) 448–63; B. Mack, *Rhetoric and the New Testament* GBS (Minneapolis: Fortress, 1990).

Stylstic Peculiarities. The following examples of stylistic peculiarities will be examined: (a) abrupt changes in syntax and thought, (b) unclear idioms, and (c) borrowings from the Septuagint (LXX).

Abrupt changes in syntax and thought occur frequently in Paul's letters. The technical term for such a sudden break is *anacoluthon* (Gk.), but some of the phenomenon could be interpreted as either a parenthesis (i.e., a clause inserted into a sentence without regard for its syntax) or an interpolation (i.e., a block of inserted material by the author or a later editor).

An example of *anacoluthon* is found in Rom 2:15-16, where Paul is talking about the conscience of the Gentiles serving them as a moral umpire *but* suddenly breaks in with "on that day when, according to my gospel, God judges the secrets of men by Christ Jesus." The change of thought, as well as sentence structure, is sudden and unexpected. It may be either intentional or unintentional; either a stylistic device to arouse the reader's attention or the author's losing his current train of thought as a new idea is suddenly pursued. Other examples of *anacolutha* are: Gal 2:4-6; 2 Cor 1:22-23; and a large digression in 2 Cor 5:14–6:2.

Parenthetical phrases are often noted in English translations: e.g., Rom 1:13 ("but thus far have been prevented"); 2 Cor 11:21 ("I am speaking as a fool"); 2 Pet 2:8 (entire verse). An interpolation (or gloss) is a larger insertion of material disrupting the original flow of thought. It is either the work of the author or a later editor. In 2 Corinthians it has been argued that 6:14–7:1 is an interpolation by a later editor, because (a) there is no direct connection of 6:14–7:1 to what precedes or follows, (b) 2 Cor 6:13 and 7:2 connect smoothly without the passage, and (c) the vocabulary and conceptions are never or rarely used by Paul elsewhere (leading to the hypothesis that it is non-Pauline). Examples of other possible interpolations are Phil 3:2–4:3 (a later polemical fragment by Paul?) and 1 Thes 2:13-16 (which appears to be a post-70 denouncement of the Jews).

Idiomatic expressions are unclear to modern readers for at least two reasons. First, they are cultural statements foreign to us. Second, the sender often assumes his intended readers are already familiar with their meanings. Remember that we are outsiders reading these ancient letters from a third party perspective. One random example is in Gal 3:20, translated literally: "now the mediator is not of one, but God is one." In v 19 Paul is speaking of the law being ordained by angels through a mediator, but commentators are unclear about what inference Paul is trying to establish in v 20. For other examples of unclear idioms, the meanings of which are important for understanding the overall arguments, see Rom 3:7; 8:22; 1 Cor 2:16c; 15:29 (the last ref. probably reflecting an ancient practice).

Borrowings from the LXX are numerous in early Christian letters. Over seventy direct quotations from the Jewish Scriptures (Gk. or Heb. texts) are made in Paul's letters. Sometimes explicit mention is made of the source (e.g., Rom 1:17; 9:29) and frequently the source is not stated (e.g., Rom 10:13; 1 Cor 2:16; 5:13; 10:26). There are places in the letters of Paul where his entire discussion is permeated with a wide variety of lengthy scriptural quotations: e.g., Rom 9–11 (citing Isaiah, Jeremiah, Hosea, Joel, Deuteronomy, Psalms, Leviticus, Exodus, Proverbs, and 1 Kings). Generally such passages are the most difficult to interpret because the modern reader is unfamiliar with Paul's methods of interpreting the Jewish Scriptures. Many of Paul's awkward sentence constructions are also due to his use of Septuagintal or Semitic phrasings (Rom 10:5-17). What has been mentioned here of Paul's letters also applies to the non-Pauline correspondence, since all make ample use of the LXX, although the selection of passages and their interpretations are generally different.

4. Summary

In the discussion of early Christian letters we first distinguished them from the Gospels and Acts because of their more conversational and personal style. We looked at the importance of the letter form in the NT, antiquity, and today. Twenty-one out of twenty-seven NT books are labeled "letters" although some like Heb and 1 Pet are closer to sermons. We saw the importance and wide variety of letters in antiquity, e.g., personal, official, business. We also noted our widespread exposure to the letter genre today.

The fixed patterns of writing followed by both ancient and modern letters was also discussed. We especially paid attention to the letter form of antiquity: opening, thanksgiving, body, and closing. Various expansions (thanksgiving) and new additions (eschatological comment, parenesis) found in early Christian letters were also noted.

The second section of the study was devoted to the literary forms and stylistic features of the early Christian letters. Under literary forms, we listed: e.g., autobiography, catalogues and lists, hymns, confessional statements, catechesis, kerygma. In the discussion of stylistic features we looked at: (1) principles of literary balance (regular parallelism and chiasm); (2) figures of speech (e.g., metaphor, paradox, rhetorical questions); (3) rhetorical devices (e.g., diatribe, features of Greek oratory); and (4) grammatical and stylistic peculiarities (e.g., abrupt changes in syntax, unclear idioms, and use of the LXX).

Most of the early Christian letters fit generally into the category of ancient letter. However, the distinctive literary forms and stylistic features detected in the NT letters qualify many of them as sermons and speeches in the context of early Christian community needs.

2

A Chronology of Paul's Life

The problems of Pauline chronology are similar to those in the study of Jesus. Evidence is sparse and scattered, and the sources are often dominated by literary and religious purposes. Factors that are distinctive for a chronology of Paul are: (a) we have the apostle's own words about certain events in his life; (b) references to Paul's life in Acts sometimes coincide with statements in Paul's letters; and (c) an ancient inscription confirms the Lukan account of Paul's appearance before Gallio (Acts 18:12-22).

The document of primary importance in determining a chronology of Paul is the Gallio Inscription found at Delphi, Greece (Achaia). Gallio's proconsulship of Achaia, mentioned in Acts 18:12-22, is independently attested by this document and can be dated within narrow limits. The inscription, with conjectural supplements [in square brackets] reads as follows:[1]

> Tiberius [Claudius] Caesar Augustus Germanicus [Pontifex Maximus, in his tribunician] power [year 12, acclaimed Emperor for] the 26th time, father of the country, [consul for the 5th time, censor, sends greetings to the city of Delphi.] I have long been zealous for the city of Delphi [and favorable to it from the] beginning, and I have always observed the cult of the [Pythian] Apollo, [but with regard to] the present stories, and those quarrels of the citizens of which [a report has been

[1]From: Barrett, *NTB* 48–49, and *BC* 5:461.

> made by Lucius] Junios Gallio my friend, and [pro] consul [of Achaea].

A knowledge of stereotyped titles in official inscriptions confirms that the addressor is Claudius who became emperor on January 25, AD 41. The acclamations were irregular but from other inscriptions, we learn that he was acclaimed emperor for the 22nd, 23rd, and 24th times in his 11th year of reign (AD 51) and that the 27th acclamation took place in the second half of his 12th year of reign (AD 52 before August).[2] The 26th acclamation must therefore have taken place at the close of the 11th year (AD 51) or probably the first half of the 12th year: between January 25 and August 1, AD 52. Achaia was a senatorial province, governed by a proconsul, who was customarily appointed by the senate for a one-year term. The one-year appointments were made in early summer (July 1 under Emperor Tiberius). Even though alternative dates have been suggested within the AD 50–53 limit, a convincing case has been made for the Gallio proconsulship of Achaia from July 1, 51 to July 1, 52.[3] Paul's appearance before Gallio (Acts 18:12-22) was probably soon after his accession to office (July AD 51). This would be an opportune occasion for Paul's opponents to gain a fresh hearing and possibly influence the decision of the new incoming proconsul.

Before examining key events in Paul's life, we must state at the outset that priority will be given to the data found in Paul's letters. There are a number of reasons for proceeding in this manner.[4] First, Paul's letters are the earliest data available, predating the Acts of the Apostles by decades. Second, the details in the letters are not motivated by chronological considerations or any assumption regarding the periodization of the church's history. Third, material from the letters is primary historical data and therefore has intrinsic priority over the secondary information we find in the Acts of the Apostles.

[2] K. Lake "The Chronology of Acts," in *BC* 5:462–63.

[3] Jewett, *Chronology* 38–40; G. Lüdemann, *Paul, Apostle to the Gentiles: Studies in Chronology*, trans. F. S. Jones (Philadelphia: Fortress Press, 1984) 163–64.

[4] Derived from Jewett, *Chronology* 22–24, see also J. Knox, *Chapters in the Life of Paul* (Nashville: Abingdon-Cokesbury, 1950) 13–29; Lüdemann, *Paul* 1–43.

These reasons do *not* imply that the data in Paul's letters is free from apologetic and theological influences. The information, however, is closer historically to the events, they are the apostle's own words about his own life, and thus they qualify as eyewitness material. Therefore a general outline of Paul's life must be first worked out from the data of the letters of Paul. Material from Acts is usable in our Pauline chronology only when it does not conflict with the evidence in the letters.[5]

Conversion and Call, AD 34

The primary data for Paul's conversion and call are found in Gal 1:15-16 and 1 Cor 15:8. Later evidence supporting this event in a more idealized and dramatic manner is Acts 9:1-9; 22:6-21; 26:12-18.[6] In Gal 1:15-16, this is identified as the initial event of Paul's missionary career. It includes a call from God (1:15) and a revealing of God's Son to Paul (1:16). This revelation is identified in 1 Cor 15:8 as a final appearance of the resurrected Christ to his followers. Even though the data from Acts do not include the appearance of Christ as the last of the post-Easter appearances and includes details (e.g., Ananias, blindness, charismata) that are not mentioned in Paul's letters, they agree in the following areas. First, Paul was previously a persecutor of the church (Gal 1:13; 1 Cor 15:9; Acts 26:9-11; 9:1-5). Second, the vision of Christ is connected with Paul's missionary call to the Gentiles (Gal 1:16; Acts 26:16). Third, the whole event is connected with the Syrian city of Damascus (Gal 1:17; Acts 9; 22; 26).

The Pauline connection of the appearance of Christ as the last post-Easter appearance (not found in Acts) has extrabiblical sup-

[5]See the following article for both possible and probable conflicts between Acts and Paul's letters: P. Vielhauer, "On the 'Paulinism' of Acts," in *Studies in Luke-Acts,* ed. L. E. Keck and J. L. Martyn (Nashville: Abingdon, 1966) 33–50. See also Lüdemann, *Paul* 23–29.

[6]For discussion of the similarities and discrepancies of Acts 9, 22, and 26, along with Paul's letters, see G. Lohfink, *The Conversion of St. Paul,* trans. of *Paulus vor Damaskus* (Chicago: Franciscan Herald, 1976) 20–26, C. W. Hedrick, "Paul's Conversion/Call: A Comparative Analysis of the Three Reports in Acts," *JBL* 100 (3, 1981) 415–32.

port. From gnostic and early Christian sources there is a tradition of the post-resurrection appearances of Christ extending eighteen months. The gnostic traditions found in Irenaeus' *Against Heresies* state that post-resurrection appearances lasted eighteen months.[7] The second-century Christian work, the Ascension of Isaiah, mentions post-Easter appearances lasting 545 days (9.16).[8] The second-century Christian gnostic Apocryphon of James refers to 550 days of resurrection appearances (2.20-21).[9] This eighteen-month period may be a historical recollection derived from Pauline tradition.[10]

Basing the dating of Paul's conversion/call on the argument for Jesus' crucifixion at AD 33,[11] we arrive at October of AD 34; eighteen months after the Passover (April). As we proceed in dating the other key events in Paul's life, the AD 34 conversion call will find further support.

First Jerusalem Visit, AD 37

Paul states in Gal 1:17-18 that after his conversion/call, he went into Arabia, returned to Damascus, then "after three years" went to Jerusalem for the first time. Second Corinthians 11:32-33 describes this departure from Damascus as an escape from the ethnarch of King Aretas who guarded the city to seize him. Acts 9:22-26 supports the Damascus-Jerusalem sequence of Galatians without referring to the Arabian trip, and also describes the Damascus escape without mentioning the ethnarch of King Aretas.

If Paul's conversion/call was AD 34, and he left Damascus for Jerusalem "after three years," the first Jerusalem visit would take place around AD 37. Is there any datum to substantiate the date for this trip? The historical allusion to the ethnarch of King Aretas

[7]This tradition is found among the gnostic Ophites (Irenaeus, *Against Heresies* 1.28.7) and the gnostic disciples of Ptolemaeus (1.3.2).

[8]Cited in Hennecke, *NTA* 2:657.

[9]Robinson, *Nag Hammadi* 30.

[10]Jewett, *Chronology* 29.

[11]Scholars defending an AD 33 crucifixion are B. Reicke, *The NT Era* (Philadelphia: Fortress, 1974) 183–84 and H. Hoehner, *Chronological Aspects of the Life of Christ* (Grand Rapids: Zondervan, 1977) 103–14.

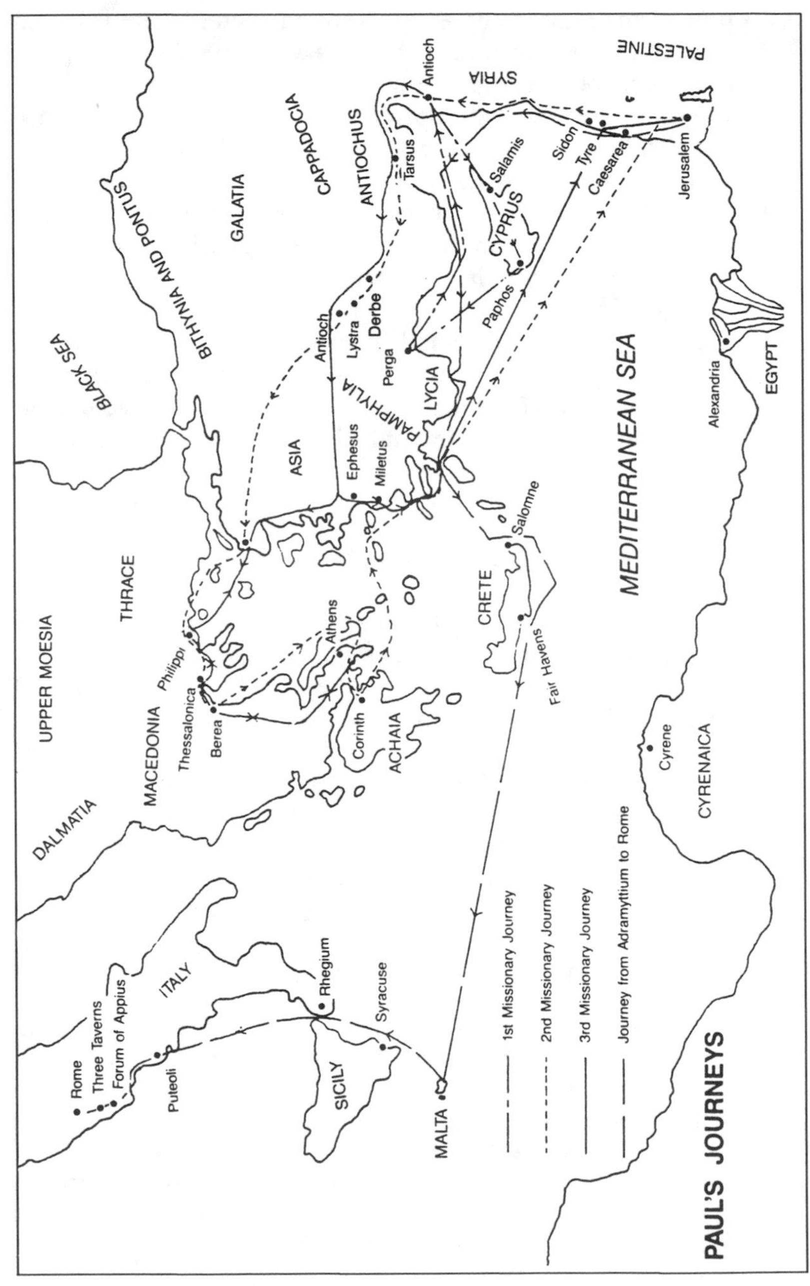
PAUL'S JOURNEYS
1st Missionary Journey
2nd Missionary Journey
3rd Missionary Journey
Journey from Adramyttium to Rome
MEDITERRANEAN SEA
BLACK SEA
BITHYNIA AND PONTUS
GALATIA
CAPPADOCIA
ANTIOCHUS
SYRIA
PALESTINE
CYPRUS
LYCIA
PAMPHYLIA
ASIA
THRACE
UPPER MOESIA
MACEDONIA
DALMATIA
ACHAIA
CRETE
CYRENAICA
EGYPT
ITALY
SICILY
MALTA
Antioch
Tarsus
Salamis
Sidon
Tyre
Caesarea
Jerusalem
Paphos
Perga
Derbe
Lystra
Antioch
Ephesus
Miletus
Salomne
Fair Havens
Alexandria
Cyrene
Philippi
Thessalonica
Berea
Athens
Corinth
Rome
Three Taverns
Forum of Appius
Puteoli
Rhegium
Syracuse

guarding Damascus to seize Paul (2 Cor 11:32) may provide this support. The crucial issue will concern the extent of Aretas' rule around AD 37.

Did the Nabatean King Aretas have jurisdiction over Damascus around AD 37? His rule over Nabatea and other regions was from 9 BC to his death in AD 39.[12] Aretas probably did not have control of Damascus until after the death of Tiberius Caesar (March AD 37). Tiberius discouraged native client kingdoms and favored Herod Antipas over Aretas in a border conflict between the two in AD 36. However, after the death of Tiberius in March of 37, there was a change in frontier policy under Emperor Gaius Caligula. This change of policy would provide a favorable setting for Nabatean control of Damascus. Gaius reestablished a system of client kings in the east, refrained from any punitive measures against Aretas for the AD 36 border dispute, and even adopted a friendly attitude towards the Nabatean king.[13] It was probably during this favorable change of policy after March AD 37 that Damascus would have been transferred to Nabatean control (2 Cor 11:32). Paul's escape therefore occurred sometime within the two-year span up to the death of King Aretas in AD 39.

Our discussion provides some support for dating Paul's first Jerusalem visit at AD 37 (or 38). It also helps to substantiate the AD 34 conversion/call date three years earlier (Gal 1:15-18). Further confirmation for these dates will be provided when interlocked with other events in Paul's life.

Missionary Activity, AD *37–51*

The time frame for this period is based on the fourteen-year span between the two Jerusalem trips, mentioned in Gal 1:21; 2:1. After the first Jerusalem trip, Paul goes into the regions of Syria and Cilicia (1:21) and "after fourteen years" returns to Jerusalem (2:1).[14] In Acts the references to Syria and Cilicia in Gal 1:21,

[12]Josephus, *Ant.* 10.131-185; 16.293-299, Jewett, *Chronology* 30–33, 121.

[13]The above arguments are substantiated in Jewett, *Chronology* 32–33.

[14]Discussion of the Jerusalem trips in Acts 11:27-30; 15 and Gal 2:1-10 will be discussed below.

find specific support in the allusions to Paul's trip to Tarsus of Cilicia (Acts 9:30) and his story in Antioch of Syria (11:25-26; 13:1-2). However, there is no indication that Paul is attempting to be exhaustive in Gal 1:21.[15] Therefore, most of the missionary activities graphically portrayed in Acts 13–14 and 15:36–18:22 probably occurred at this time.

The date of Paul's second visit to Jerusalem coincides with Paul's appearance before Gallio in Corinth (AD 51). According to Acts 18, after Paul is acquitted by Gallio, he sailed for Syria (v 18), stopping at Ephesus, Caesarea, and the church at Jerusalem (v 22). As we have argued at the beginning of this chapter, the summer of AD 51 would have been an opportune time for Paul's opponents to present the apostle before the newly appointed proconsul. The most that we can miscalculate on this point is one year (e.g., 50 or 52).

We have placed both missionary journeys of Paul (Acts 13–14, 15:36–18:22) into the fourteen-year framework for the following reasons. First, we have taken seriously the fourteen-year time span (Gal 1:21; 2:1) without resorting to fractions of years (e.g., 12 or 13) where part of a year may be reckoned as a whole year.[16] Second, it takes seriously Paul's busy itinerary in Acts 15:31–18:1. This "second missionary journey" of Paul includes over fifteen stops and covers over 2000 miles. Since Paul traveled on land by foot and by sea in ancient Roman boats, this journey would probably take three or four years.[17] This lengthy time of travel poses problems for anyone attempting to follow the order of Acts and reconcile it with the Gallio inscription.

The order of Acts places the first missionary journey (13–14) before the Jerusalem conference (15). The second journey follows

[15]In agreement with H. D. Betz, we regard Gal 1:13–2:14 as the narratio of Paul's apologetic letter. According to Quintilian's rhetorical handbook, details in the narratio may be omitted or key events treated later as the cause, the reason for the conflict. See Betz, "Literary Compositions," *NTS* 21 (1975) 362–67; Lüdemann, *Paul* 54–59.

[16]E.g., counting fractions of years as whole years, one might declare that he or she attended college for four years since classes were taken in 1990, 1991, 1992 and 1993. However, this may actually be only *three school years:* (1) fall 1990–spring 1991, (2) fall 1991–spring 1992, (3) fall 1992–spring 1993.

[17]Jewett, *Chronology* 59–62.

the Jerusalem conference and ends with Paul leaving Corinth (15:36–18:22). The Jerusalem conference and Paul's departure from Corinth limit the time span of the second journey to two or three years.[18] But the distance and time required in the second journey requires three to four years.[19] This is why we have included both the first and second journeys of Paul into the fourteen-year time frame and transposed the conference of Acts 15 to a later period.

Second Jerusalem Visit, AD *51*

It may be necessary at this point to further explain why: (a) the two Jerusalem trips of Acts 11:27-30 and 15 have been transposed to a later date (AD 51) and (b) why both missionary journeys depicted in Acts 13–14 and 15:30–18:22 are included within the fourteen years of Gal 1:21 and 2:1 (AD 37–51). By linking the Gal 2 conference (cf. Acts 15) with Paul's trip "up to" Jerusalem (Acts 18:22), we escape the necessity of positing seventeen empty years at the beginning of Paul's ministry and crowding virtually all that is known about his activity into the last few years.[20]

The Jerusalem offering (1 Cor 16:1-8; Rom 15:25-27), designed to bridge the gap between the Palestinian and Hellenistic churches, provided the motivation for the final trip to Jerusalem, although Luke omitted reference to it except for one detail (Acts 25:17). In order to account for the general knowledge in the early church that Paul had indeed brought an offering to Jerusalem, Luke placed the trip back in the early life of Paul in connection with a famine (Acts 11:27-30). Paul is careful to mention only an "ac-

[18]Most scholars date the Jerusalem conference of Acts 15 between 48 and 50, and Paul's departure from Corinth (Gallio inscription) between 51 and 52 (see Caird, "Chronology of New Testament," *IDB* 1:605-7). This time frame usually puts a limit of two to three years on Paul's second missionary journey (15:36–18:22).

[19]Jewett, *Chronology* 59–62.

[20]Jewett, *Chronology* 79; although he dates the Jerusalem conference earlier (47, possibly 50), Lüdemann finds indications that a Pauline mission (Gal 2:7-8) and even Paul's conflict at Antioch (2:11-14) occurred before the conference, Lüdemann, *Paul* 64–75.

quaintance" trip and a "conference" journey, and this is sufficient to overrule Luke's chronology at this point.[21]

The following is a chart of the Jerusalem trips in both Paul's letters and Acts, reflecting our interpretation:

Jerusalem Visits	*Paul*	*Acts*
First trip, AD 37 (acquaintance visit)	Gal 1:18-20	9:26-27
Second trip, AD 51 (apostolic conference)	Gal 2:1-10	Acts 15
Final trip, AD 57 (collection and arrest)	Rom 15:25-27	Acts 21:17-36 [11:27-30]

The dating of the Jerusalem conference will be determined by the relationships of the following texts: Gal 2:1-10; Acts 11:27-30; and Acts 15:1-35. Is Galatians 2 Paul's version of either the Jerusalem conference in Acts 15 or the famine relief visit of Acts 11:27-30? Note the chart of similarities and differences:

	Galatians 2	*Acts 11*	*Acts 15*
(1) Paul and associates present	Paul, Barnabas and Titus (v 1)	Barnabas and Paul (v 30)	Barnabas, Paul, and others (v 2)
(2) nature of appointment	by revelation (v 2)	sent by church (v 30)	appointed by church (v 2)
(3) occasion	circumcision of Gentiles by false brethren (vv 3-4)	famine relief (vv 28-29)	circumcision of Gentiles by men from Judea (v 1)
(4) Jerusalem officials present	James, Cephas, John (v 9)	――――――	Peter, James, apostles, and elders (v 4)
(5) type of meeting	private (v 2)	――――――	public assembly (4,12-14)
(6) mention of poor	remember the poor (v 10)	relief for famine victims (v 29)	

[21]Ibid.

The similarities between Gal 2 and Acts 15 are the most significant (#1,3,4). The differences (#2,5,6) between Gal 2 and Acts 15 can be explained as two different versions of the same event (#2,6) or as two different meetings on the same occasion (#5). Paul's omission of the apostolic decrees (Acts 15:19-20; 21:25) may have been due to: Paul's own difficulties with such "legalistic" stipulations (Gal 2:6) or the possibility that they were introduced after the conference when Paul made his final trip to Jerusalem (Acts 21:25).

It seems unlikely that Gal 2:10 ("remember the poor") is an allusion to the famine relief visit (Acts 11:27-30). We regard the relief visit as a displaced reference to the collection which Paul brought on his final visit to Jerusalem (Acts 24:17; Rom 15:25-27).[22] In his letters, Paul's only concern for a famine relief is the collection for "the poor among the saints at Jerusalem" (Rom 15:26). The reference to "remember the poor" in Gal 2:10 may even be an indication that the collection for the Jerusalem saints had already begun.[23]

We link the Gal 2 and Acts 15 conference with Paul's trip "up to" Jerusalem after his second missionary journey (Acts 18:22; AD 51) for the following reasons. First, it best conforms to the fourteen-year gap between the two Jerusalem visits (Gal 1:18; 2:1). Second, it allows enough time for Paul to undertake his extensive missionary travels described in Acts 13-14; 15:35–18:22. Third, it takes seriously the priority of Paul's letters over Acts for a Pauline chronology. Because of these reasons, we date the Jerusalem conference at AD 51 (Gal 2 = Acts 15 = Acts 18:22) instead of between 48 and 50 as many scholars have argued.

[22]Knox, chs 53–57; Jewett, *Chronology* 79. Lüdemann, however, views Acts 11:27ff. as part of a tripling of Paul's second visit to Jerusalem (cf. Acts 15:1ff.; 18:22), Lüdemann, *Paul* 149–57. Nevertheless, in all of the above cases, Acts 11:27-30 is viewed as a Lukan insertion which is chronologically out of place in the narrative.

[23]Nickle, *Collection* 59–62; Lüdemann, *Paul* 77–80.

Further Missionary Activity, AD 52–57

This period includes Paul's twenty-seven month stay in Ephesus (Acts 19:8-10; Phil 1; 4; Phlm; 2 Cor 1:8) with brief visits to Corinth (2 Cor 2:1; 12:14; 13:1), Troas (2 Cor 2:12), Macedonia (2:13; Acts 20:1), Illyricum (Rom 15:19), and Achaia (Rom 15:25; 16:1; Acts 20:2f.), before Paul's final trip to Jerusalem (Acts 20:16; Rom 15:25). During these years, Paul's "collection for the saints" was begun (spring of 55; 1 Cor 16:1-8), continued among the churches of Macedonia and Achaia (2 Cor 8–9), and was completed for delivery to Jerusalem (AD 57, Rom 15:25-27). All of Paul's undisputed letters were also written at this time, with the exception of 1 Thessalonians (AD 50 from Corinth).

Final Jerusalem Visit, AD 57

This last journey to Jerusalem is anticipated in Rom 15:25-27 and described in Acts 20:16; 21:1-18. According to Acts, the following events take place in Jerusalem.

(1) Conference with church and participation in a Jewish ritual at the temple (21:17-26)
(2) Seized by a mob in the temple and taken into Roman custody (21:27-36)
(3) Address to multitude and hearing before Sanhedrin (21:39–23:10)
(4) Conspiracy discovered and Paul is transferred to Caesarea (23:11-31)
(5) Paul stays in Caesarea for two years (24:27) where he appears on trial before the procurators Felix and Festus (24–25) and the Herodian King Agrippa 11 (26).
(6) Paul appeals to Caesar (25:10-12) and is sent to Rome (27:1–28:16)

Some verification for Paul's arrival in Jerusalem at AD 57 can be attained by dating the procuratorships of Felix and Festus (Acts 24–25). If one favors the reports of Josephus over that of Tacitus (as most scholars do), the arrival of Felix as procurator of

Judea can be established around AD 52–53.[24] If one follows the progression of Roman procurators in the years prior to the Jewish war (AD 66–70), a date of 59 or 60 can be maintained for the arrival of Festus as the successor of Felix.[25]

Acts 24:27 states that when two years had elapsed (since Paul's transfer to Caesarea as a prisoner), the Roman procurator was succeeded by Porcius Festus. Based on our dating of these procuratorships, Paul's arrival in Caesarea would have been around AD 57. According to Acts, Paul's transfer from Jerusalem to Caesarea took place about two weeks after his arrival in Jerusalem around Pentecost, the summer of 57 (Acts 20:16; 21:17,26-27,22:30; 23:11-12,31-33).

As a result of our discussion we can outline the chronology of this phase as follows:

(1) Arrival in Jerusalem (Acts 21:17), summer of 57
(2) Hearing before Felix in Caesarea (24:10-22), summer of 57
(3) Hearing before Festus and Agrippa (25–26) after two years (24:27), summer of 59
(4) Departure from Caesarea for Rome (27:1-8), late summer or early fall of 59

Journey to Rome, AD 59–60

After his appeal to Caesar had been granted (Acts 25:10-12; 26:32), Paul and other prisoners set sail for Italy under Roman custody (27:1). The sea voyage was probably undertaken before

[24]Emperor Claudius appointed Felix as Cumanus' successor around the 12th year of his reign (ca. 53), Josephus, *Ant.* 20.134-140.; see also *War 2.245–249.* In Tacitus, *Annals* 12.54 Felix and Cumanus were procurators at the same time over a divided Palestine.

[25]Because there are dating problems connected with Josephus' own report on the circumstances immediately following the dismissal of Felix (*Ant.* 20.182–184), we prefer to work back from Josephus' reports on the procurators of Judea from the Jewish War (66–70) back to the years of rule shared by Felix and his successor Festus (ca. 52–62). Festus served for a brief period until his death in AD 61 or 62 (*Ant.* 20.197-203).

the dangerous season for sailing (before mid-September). Paul and the others boarded a sailing vessel to Myra of Lycia (southern Asia Minor) where they transferred to a larger grain ship en route to Italy (27:7-8). As the summer months came to an end, sailing became difficult on the eastern Mediterranean.[26]

Paul and company stayed at Fair Havens after the day of the Atonement "fast" (Acts 27:9). According to the solar calendar, in AD 59, the day of Atonement (Tishri 10) took place on October 5.[27]

Since the dangerous sailing season had begun, the pilot and shipowner attempted to winter at a seaport in Crete (27:9-12). The ship, however, was caught in a gale and driven westward (vv 13-20). Following the chronological notations of Acts (27:20,27,33, 39), the boat shipwrecked at Malta in early November of 59 (27:39–28:1). After staying at Malta for three months and three days (28:7,11), they sailed for Rome in early February of 60 and arrived there within two weeks (28:11-16).

According to Acts 28:30, Paul stayed in Rome for "two whole years." He awaited his appeal to Caesar with some degree of freedom. The apostle was also under house arrest and able to receive visitors (28:16-17,23,31).[28]

Execution, AD 62

The evidence concerning the end of Paul's life is related to the question of the authorship of the Pastoral Letters. References to

[26] J. Smith, *The Voyage and Shipwreck of St. Paul,* reprint of 1880 ed. (Grand Rapids: Baker, 1978) 74–81. For recent discussion see C. J. Hemer, "Euraquilo and Melito," *JTS* (26, 1975) 100–111.

[27] Bruce, *Book of Acts* (1952) 506.

[28] If the variant reading of Acts 28:16 in the Western text (5th cent.) is correct (Paul and the prisoners were handed over to the "stratodeparch") and it refers to the emperor's pretorian guard, the last *single* office holder was Afranius Burrus who died in AD 62. This variant would establish a latest possible date for Paul's arrival in Rome (Jewett, *Chronology* 44). For a detailed discussion of Acts 28, see C. B. Puskas, "The Conclusion of Luke-Acts: An Investigation of the Literary Function and Theological Significance of Acts 28:16-31," Unpublished Ph.D. dissertation, Saint Louis University (Ann Arbor, Mich.: University Microfilms, 1980).

the "first defense" in 2 Tim 4:16 and his "rescue" in 4:17 have led some scholars to conclude that Paul was released after the two-year imprisonment in Acts 28:30. Since we contend that the Pastorals were not written by Paul, this evidence should be excluded.[29] The references to Paul's journey to Spain in the Muratorian Fragment and 1 Clem 5 are probably derived from Rom 15:24, although the allusion in 1 Clem 5.7 does not require a mission to Spain interpretation.[30]

The decisive evidence for the death of Paul is in Acts 28:30-31 and 20:24,38. The author of Acts appears to bring his work to a positive conclusion (28:30-31), but seems aware of Paul's death (20:24,38). In all probability the execution of Paul took place immediately after his two-year stay in Rome, under Nero.[31]

The reign of Nero in AD 62 was marked by growing suspicion and the restoration of treason trials. Early in AD 62, the efficient administrator S. A. Burrus had died and the wise advisor Seneca was dismissed. In the summer of AD 62 Octavia, Nero's former wife, was executed. Because Nero's government had changed from one of judicial fairness to treachery and suspicion in early 62, it is unnecessary to link Paul's death with the later persecution of Christians in connection with the great fire of Rome (AD 64).[32]

A Chronology of Paul's Life[33]

Conversion/Call	AD 34 (see Gal 1:15-16; 1 Cor 15:8; Acts 9:1-9)

[29]See Kümmel, *Introduction* 370–84, on the authorship and date or the Pastorals.

[30]1 Clem 5.7 states that Paul "reached the limits of the west" before his death. This phrase could refer to Rome, Illyricum or Spain. The death of Peter is also mentioned as contemporary with that of Paul (5.2-5), which cannot be verified.

[31]Although influenced by the Pastorals in asserting that Paul was released and retried, Eusebius does state that Paul "suffered martyrdom under Nero" in Rome (Eusebius, *Eccl Hist* 2.22).

[32]On Nero, the fire in Rome, and the local persecution of Christians, see Tacitus, *Annals* 15.44 and Sulpicius Severus, *Chronicle* 2.29.

[33]Derived from the following work and used with permission by the publisher: Robert Jewett, *A Chronology of Paul's Life* 98–103, Copyright © 1979 by Fortress Press. Used by permission of Augsburg Fortress.

For further study on Paul see: K. Stendahl, *Paul among Jews and Gentiles* (Philadelphia: Fortress Press, 1976); E. Käsemann, *Perspectives on Paul* (Philadel-

First Jerusalem visit	AD 37 (Gal 1:18-19; Acts 9:26-28)
Missionary activity	AD 37–51 (Gal 1:21; Acts 13–14; 16:1–18:22)
Second Jerusalem visit	AD 51 (Gal 2:1-20; Acts 15) apostolic conference
Further missionary work e.g., collection for the saints	(Acts 19–20; 1 Cor 16:1-8; 2 Cor 8–9; Rom 15:25-27)
Final visit to Jerusalem: arrest and imprisonment	AD 57 (Acts 21:17-18, 27–33)
Arrival in Rome	AD 60 (Acts 28:16, 30f.)
Execution of Paul	AD 62 (1 Clem 5; Eusebius, *Eccl Hist* 2.22)

phia: Fortress Press, 1971); J. P. Sampley, *Pauline Partnership in Christ* (Philadelphia: Fortress Press, 1980); L. E. Keck, *Paul and His Letters* (Philadelphia: Fortress, 1979); J. C. Beker, *The Triumph of God: The Essence of Paul's Thought*, trans. L. Stuckenbruck (Minneapolis: Fortress Press, 1990). J. Jervell, *The Unknown Paul* (Minneapolis: Augsburg, 1984); H. J. Schoeps, *Paul. The Theology of the Apostle in the Light of Jewish Religious History* (Philadelphia: Westminster, 1961); H. N. Ridderbos, *Paul. An Outline of His Theology* (Grand Rapids: Eerdmans, 1975); W. D. Davies, *Paul and Rabbinic Judaism*, 3rd ed. (Philadelphia: Fortress Press, 1980); idem, *Jewish and Pauline Studies* (Philadelphia: Fortress Press, 1984); A. F. Segal, *Paul the Convert: The Apostolate and Apostasy of Saul the Pharisee* (New Haven: Yale University Press, 1990). G. Bornkamm, *Paul* (New York: Harper & Row, 1971); E. P. Sanders, *Paul and Palestinian Judaism* (Philadelphia: Fortress Press, 1977); W. Meeks, *The First Urban Christians* (Philadelphia: Fortress Press, 1983); F. F. Bruce, *Paul, Apostle of the Heart Set Free* (Grand Rapids: Eerdmans, 1977); J. Munck, *Paul and the Salvation of Mankind* (Richmond: John Knox, 1959); N. T. Wright, *The Climax of the Covenant: Christ and the Law in Pauline Theology* (Minneapolis: Fortress Press, 1991).

3

Galatians

1. Introduction

Paul's letter to the Galatians was both a product and producer of controversy. Its writing was occasioned by the debate over whether Jewish circumcision should be a prerequisite for Christian salvation. Its controversial reception helped precipitate the eventual separation of Christianity from Judaism. Galatians won the admiration of the anti-Jewish heretic Marcion and aroused disdain among the Jewish Christian Ebionites. Martin Luther's *Commentary on Galatians* was the manifesto of the revolt against the medieval Church of his day, making Paul's salvation by grace the cornerstone of the Protestant Reformation. Galatians also became an important document in the reconstruction of Paul as the libertine opponent of the legalistic Peter according to the nineteenth-century Tübingen scholar, F. C. Baur. This controversial reconstruction still yields great influence in contemporary NT studies. One cannot escape the argumentative tone and defensive posture of the letter when it is read today.

2. The Occasion

To understand better the occasion of Galatians let us imagine ourselves in different roles at a different place and time. We are a group of Gentiles living in Asia Minor in the mid-first century

AD. We belong to several house churches founded by the apostle Paul. For many months we rejoiced in our new spiritual experience of faith in Christ as God's agent of salvation, but some problems have now occurred.[1]

Some of our people are struggling with problems of the flesh (e.g., lust, immorality), and we do not know how to deal with it. Many of us feel that perhaps our spiritual experiences and the basic teaching about "the gospel" from Paul are not enough to cope with the problem.

About this time some Jewish Christians appear with a complete system of legal requirements, whose demands appeal to many of us. This system is an assortment of various moral and ceremonial observances that are supposed to be essential for our identity as a people of God. One external observance prominent in this legal system is the circumcision of all males as a sign of one's covenant relationship with God. This Jewish-Christian group is also highly skeptical of Paul's teaching, believing it to be popular libertine propaganda.

We seriously consider the offer to submit to this set of legal requirements and many from our group embrace them wholeheartedly; many males are circumcised and try to observe all the ceremonial laws. In the process, much of the original teaching on salvation by grace from Paul has been set aside.

The apostle Paul has received news that many of us have gone over to the teachings of this other group. He regards this adherence to the teaching of the Jewish Christians as a serious error and threat to his entire work among us. This scenario may illustrate the situation to which Paul addressed his letter to the Galatians.

3. The Structure

We have briefly looked at the occasion of the letter, now we will examine its form and function. How did Paul deal with this situation? How does he address the problem as he sees it?

[1]Derived from: H. Betz, "In Defense of the Spirit: Paul's Letter to the Galatians as a Document of Christian Apologetics," in *Aspects of Religious Propaganda in Judaism and Early Christianity*, ed. E. Fiorenza (Notre Dame: University Press, 1976) 99–114.

Unable to visit his readers immediately, Paul writes a letter to the Galatians. What type of letter is it? It is certainly not a personal letter of recommendation like Philemon; the tone is defensive like Plato's letter of self-defense to the friends of Dion of Sicily (Epistle 7). Although Galatians contains the basic components of an early Christian letter (opening: Gal 1:1-2; body: 1:6–4:31; parenesis: 5:1–6:17; closing: 6:18), it lacks a thanksgiving section (e.g., 1 Thes 1:2-10; 1 Cor 1:4-9; Phil 1:3-11) and is dominated with argumentation defending Paul's authority and reasserting his own teaching.

a. Basic Features

What type of argumentation did Paul employ in addressing this crisis situation? It appears from the tone of the letter and the literary devices employed that Paul was using the language of the Greco-Roman courtroom, judicial rhetoric.[2] This effective form of forensic persuasion was concerned with the justice of a wrongdoing committed in the past.

Rules for this courtroom argumentation were well-known in Paul's time. Both Jews and Gentiles of the Hellenistic period were taught in grammar school using the textbooks of Aristotle and Cicero on persuasion (rhetoric) and public speaking (oratory). Works by Aristotle in the fourth century and Cicero in the first century BC were established classics by the time of Paul's writing.

b. Examples from the Greco-Roman World

A few examples of judicial rhetoric will be given. One is the famous *Apology of Socrates* narrated by Plato. In the courtroom setting, Socrates is accused by certain officials of corrupting the youth and mocking the gods of Athens. In response to the charges, Socrates makes an impressive defense, but he is eventually sentenced to die by the council of Athens. Another example is the work of the fourth-century BC orator, Isocrates, called *Antido-*

[2]See also from the 4th cent. BC: Isocrates, *Antidosis* (his own *apologia pro vita sua*). But some view Galatians as deliberative rhetoric, e.g. G. A. Kennedy, *New Testament Interpretation Through Rhetorical Criticism* (Chapel Hill): Univ. of N. Carolina Press, 1984); J. Smit, "The Letter of Paul to the Galatians: A Deliberative Speech," *NTS* 35 (1989) 1–26.

sis. It is basically a defense of his own conduct and life. A third example of judicial rhetoric is Cicero's *Brutus*. In this work, the great Roman orator defends his own style of oratory before his critics using both historical and autobiographical arguments.

A close parallel to Galatians as an apologetic letter is Plato's letter of self-defense to the friends of Dion (Letter 7) which we mentioned earlier. Dion was a former student of Plato and a leader in Sicily. He was killed in a revolt against a former friend, Dionysius, who had become a tyrannical ruler of Sicily. Plato had served as tutor and advisor to both Dion and Dionysius. The artificial courtroom setting consists of the following situation. The friends of the deceased Dion have questioned Plato's competence and effectiveness as a result of this civil unrest. Plato defends himself by giving an autobiography of his life and experiences in Sicily with both Dion and Dionysius. In this autobiographical argument, Plato seeks to defend his position and the credibility of his teaching with well-formulated arguments. In Galatians, Paul also employs an autobiographical argument, establishing the credibility of his ministry among the Galatians (1:11–2:14).

c. *An Outline of Galatians*

Now let us look at the judicial setting and rhetorical arrangement of Galatians. As in Cicero's *Brutus* and Plato's letter to friends of Dion, the "courtroom setting" of Galatians is artificial. Who is the defender in the case? Paul. Who are the accusers? The Judaizers. Who is the jury? The Galatians. Before whom is the forum? Christians, both Gentiles and Jews. What is Paul's defense? That the experience of the Spirit through faith in Christ is sufficient for the Galatians. Let us now look at the rhetorical arrangement of Galatians to see how Paul unfolds his argument.[3] This arrangement coincides closely with the categories outlined by Aristotle, Quintilian, and Cicero.

[3]The outline of Galatians is adapted from the following work and used with permission from the publisher: H. D. Betz, *Galatians*, Hermeneia, 14–23, Copyright (c) 1979 by Fortress. Used by permission of Augsburg Fortress. Minor changes in 1:11–2:14 are derived from: J. D. Hester, "The Rhetorical Structure of Galatians 1:11–2:14," *JBL* 103 (2, 1984) 223–33.

The Rhetorical Structure of Galatians

I. Epistolary prescript	1:1-5
A. Senders and addressees	1:1-2
B. Salutation	1:3-4
C. Doxology	1:5
II. Introduction to the case (or exordium)	1:6-10
A. Statement of the cause of letter	1:6-7
B. Issuing of a double curse	1:8-9
C. Transition	1:10
III. Statement of facts (or narratio)	1:11–2:14
A. Thesis to be demonstrated	1:11-12
B. Transition	1:13-14
C. Part One: Paul's call/conversion, visit to Jerusalem and ministry in Asia Minor	1:15-24
D. Part Two: Paul's second visit to Jerusalem	2:1-10
E. Digression: conflict at Antioch	2:11-14
IV. Summary of situation (or propositio)	2:15-21
A. Point of Agreement: justification by faith	2:15-16
B. Point of disagreement: its consequence for Gentile Christians	2:17-18
C. The exposition of thesis	2:19-20
D. The refutation of an accusation	2:21
V. Argumentation (or probatio)	3:1–4:31
A. Indisputable evidence (apostrophe)	3:1-5
B. Argument from Scripture	3:6-14
C. Argument from human practice	3:15-18
D. Digression: the true function of the Law	3:19-25
E. Argument from Christian tradition	3:26–4:11
F. Appeal to friendship (*pathos*)	4:12–4:20
G. Allegorical argument from Scripture	4:21-31
VI. Ethical exhortations (or *parenesis*)	5:1–6:10
A. A warning against acceptance of the Jewish Torah	5:1-12
B. A warning against corruption by the flesh	5:13-24
C. Recommendations in the form of maxims (or sententiae) concerning ethical praxis	5:25–6:10
VII. Epistolary postscript (or conclusio)	6:11-18
A. A formula of epistolary authentication	6:11
B. The recapitulation (or peroratio)	6:12-17
recapitulation of argument vv 12-14	
emotional appeal (or conquestio)	6:17
C. Final benediction	6:18

The Epistolary Prescript (1:1-5). Galatians contains epistolary features in both 1:1-5 and 6:11-18. It also includes the rhetorical devices of restating Paul's argument (6:12-14) and achieving *pathos* or emotional appeal (6:17).

The Exordium (1:6-10). The body of the letter coincides with most of the components of judicial rhetoric. Paul's opening statements about the problem at Galatia (1:6-10) constitute the exordium or introduction to the case. Mention of one's adversaries and the seriousness of the case (including threats) was typical. A smooth transition often occurs from the exordium to the narratio and this provides some rationale for a division between v 10 and v 11.

The Narratio (1:11–2:14). In the narratio, Paul states his thesis that his gospel came not from someone, but through a revelation of Jesus Christ (vv 11-12). Since Paul's life in Judaism and his activity as persecutor of the church (vv 13-14) are not under question, they serve as a transition to the actual facts of the case (1:15–2:10). The account of Paul's birth, conversion/call, and apostolic ministry (1:15–2:10) serves a number of functions: (a) it provides a preceding history that led to the present situation, and (b) substantiates the thesis statement in 1:11-12. Gal 2:11-14 concludes the narratio and prepares for the propositio.

The Propositio (2:15-21). Paul's statements in Gal 2:15-21 function adequately as the propositio, which generally occurs between the narratio (1:11–2:14) and the probatio (3:1–4:31). Along with summarized expositions that are to be elaborated later (2:19-21), the propositio contains points of argument (2:15-16) and disagreement (17-18) shared between the defendant and accusers.

The Probatio (3:1–4:31). The central section, which contains most of Paul's doctrinal or theological teaching (3:1–4:31), corresponds to the probatio or proofs of the case. In forensic speeches, the probatio is the most decisive section because in it the main arguments of the case are presented. Six arguments are detected: (1) an appeal to "the reception of the Spirit," an experience undisputed by both Paul and the Galatians (3:1-5);[4] (2)

[4]Paul's appeal is reinforced by his use of *apostrophe* or expression of indignation; see *Rhetorica Ad Herrenium* 4.15.22 and Cicero, *On Invention* 1.53 (indignatio).

argumentation from Scripture, citing passages from Genesis, Leviticus, Deuteronomy, and Habakkuk (Gal 3:6-14); (3) an example from human practice (3:15-18; with 3:19-25, a short digression on the law's function); (4) reminders of their favored status as Christians (3:26–4:11); (5) a personal appeal to friendship (4:12-20); and (6) an allegorical argument from Scripture (4:21-31).

The Exhortatio (5:1–6:10). The ethical exhortation or *parenesis* (5:1–6:10) is a distinctive element of Paul's argumentation although it has a similar function as deliberative persuasion in rhetorical handbooks. *Parenesis*, as we know, was used a great deal in philosophical dialogues and it forms part of Paul's argument in Galatians. It can be argued that Gal 5:1,13,25 repeat the conclusion of Paul's probatio in 4:31 (which alludes to arguments 3:9,14,24,29; 4:7) and contain warnings against adherence to the Jewish Torah (5:1-12) and corruption by the flesh (5:13-24). All of the above are effective arguments for the sufficiency of the Galatians' spiritual experience without legalism.

The Conclusio (6:11-18). A final defensive weapon envelopes the letter and dramatically intensifies Paul's argument. In the exordium (1:8-9) Paul invokes a curse for those who follow legalism and in the conclusio (6:16) invokes a blessing on those who follow the "rule" of freedom (cf. 3:9; 4:7; 5:1,13). This conditional curse and blessing gives Galatians a magical potency over the reader. Parallels to the binding force of the curse or blessing can be found in both the Jewish writings of Qumran (1 QS 2.5-17) and the Greek Hippocratic oath.

Applied to the situation of the Galatians the curse/blessing probably had the following effect. The Galatians are confronted with a choice. After reading the letter they will make a choice between the curse or the blessing. The letter itself serves as the carrier of the curse or the blessing. Reading the letter will automatically produce the "judgment." The readers who are both the judge and the jury will either be acquitted and freed or will be sent to the cosmic prison (cf. 4:1-10). By conveying this imagery, Paul repeats the initial confrontation with the gospel. Having read the letter, they see themselves transferred back into the moment when they first encountered gospel. As a result Paul's defense of the Spirit coincides with the proclamation of Jesus Christ.

4. The Historical Situation

Let us summarize the situation at Galatia and how Paul sought to address it.[5] First, the Galatians as recipients of Paul's gospel without legalism became a people of the Spirit liberated from the evil world (4:3-6). They became recipients of God's Spirit and salvation merely by trusting in Christ as God's agent of salvation. Second, the Galatians experienced some transgression in their midst (6:1) related to problems with the "flesh" (5:13,15,26; 6:9) probably concerning some misconduct or immorality. These problems constitute an abuse or exploitation of their Christian freedom. Deficiencies in the Christian experience of the Galatians soon became evident to many.

Third, the position of Paul's opponents, the Jewish-Christian missionaries (Judaizers), becomes influential. From the perspective of the Judaizers, people who live apart from the Jewish law and customs are lawless sinners. For these zealous Jewish Christians, immorality is a natural consequence of not observing the law. As they saw it, Paul's gospel is lawless and has made Christ a "servant of sin" (2:17,21). The Galatians must therefore accept the Jewish law and observe the rite of circumcision in order to be partakers of the Sinai covenant and all the securities that would come with it.

Fourth, Paul's apologetic response can be outlined in the following three arguments: (1) The Galatians' experience of the Spirit through faith in Christ is sufficient. By responding to Paul's gospel they have become recipients of God's salvation and its benefits without conforming to Jewish laws. (2) The opponents of Paul lack the evidence of the Spirit which the Galatians have experienced. They also are historically inconsistent with the way God has dealt with his people. Finally their undertakings are contrary to the Jewish Scriptures which reveal God's will. (3) The Galatians are reminded, before Paul gives his proofs, that he was appointed by Christ himself to preach this gospel without legalism and to bring salvation to the Gentiles.

[5]Betz, "In Defense of the Spirit," 105–14.

5. Destination and Date

Before concluding this discussion, the related problems of the book's destination and date need to be examined. Although it is clear that the addressees of the letter are "Galatians" (1:2; 3:1), their specific identity is uncertain. The question of date is also related to this first problem.

Two theories on the destination and date of Galatians prevail. (1) It was written to the inhabitants of North Galatia (the geographical region since 3rd cent. BC) during Paul's twenty-seven month stay in Ephesus (Acts 19:8,10) about AD 53–54. (2) It was written to those from South Galatia (the Roman province since the late-1st cent. BC) soon after Paul's so-called first missionary journey through that area (Acts 13–14) from the city of Antioch (14:26-28) around AD 48–49.[6]

Let us look at some of the key issues involved in these two theories. First is the question of whether Paul was employing the older ethnic name of "Galatia"[7] (where the cities of Ancyra and Gordium are located) or the newer Roman provincial designation which included the southern regions of Lycaonia and Phyrigia where Paul traveled on his first journey (Acts 13–14). Second is the question of whether Gal 2 refers to the Jerusalem Conference of Acts 15 or the earlier famine relief visit according to Acts (11:30; 12:25).

Although arguments can be presented for both theories, we favor the North Galatia destination and the early 50s date for the following five reasons. First, since both the author of Acts and Paul employ the geographical designations (e.g., Pamphylia, Acts

[6]An early argument for the South Galatian theory is found in W. M. Ramsay, *A Historical Commentary on St. Paul's Epistle to the Galatians* (New York: G. P. Putnam's Sons, 1900). For the classic statement of the North Galatian theory, see J. B. Lightfoot, *The Epistle of St. Paul to the Galatians* 10th ed. (London: Macmillan, 1890). Some have combined the South Galatian theory with the later date AD 53–54 favored by North Galatian advocates, see, e.g., R. Fuller, *Critical Introduction to the New Testament* (London, 1966) 23-26.

[7]The ethnic region of Galatia is named after the *Galatai*, migrating tribes from Gaul who eventually settled in northern Phrygia, see W. Tarn and G. Griffith, *Hellenistic Civilization* (London: Arnold Press, 1952) 14, and M. Austin, *The Hellenistic World from Alexander to the Roman Conquest* (Cambridge: Cambridge Univ. Press, 1981) 239–40.

13:13; Pisidia, 13:14; Lycaonia, 14:6; Syria and Cilicia, Gal 1:21), it is safe to assume that both refer to the geographical region of Galatia in the north (Acts 16:6; 18:23; Gal 1:2; 3:1).[8] Second, the book of Acts does not attempt to give an exhaustive treatment of Paul's missionary activity (e.g., Paul in Arabia, Gal 1:17), and this may explain why little is given about Paul's activity in the northern region of Galatia (Acts 16:16; 18:23).[9]

Third, Gal 2 can be interpreted as Paul's account of a private meeting connected with the larger church conference of Jerusalem (Acts 15).[10] Paul's omission in Galatians of the apostolic decrees (Acts 15:19-20; 21:25) may have been due to either his own difficulties with these stipulations, or the possibility that they were introduced after the conference when Paul made his final trip to Jerusalem (Acts 21:25). It has also been argued (convincingly by some) that the famine relief visit of Acts 11:27-30; 12:25 (which did not occur between Paul's acquaintance visit and the Jerusalem meeting according to Gal 1–2) is a displaced account that occurred on Paul's final Jerusalem visit (Acts 24:17).[11] Fourth, the theory that Paul wrote Galatians shortly after his *second* visit to North Galatia (Acts 18:23) finds some support in the letter itself. The Greek word in Gal 4:13, *to proteron* could be understood as the former of *two* visits. The exclamation about

[8]It must be qualified that Paul, on certain occasions, does employ Roman provincial designations such as Macedonia for the ethnic region of Thrace and also the ethnic names of Achaia and Asia (1 Cor 16:5,15,19). But these few instances appear to be "exceptions to the rule" in the Pauline corpus.

[9]We also cannot be certain about the complete accuracy of Paul's so-called first missionary journey (Acts 13–14). Most of the locations are not mentioned by Paul in his letters (although it is unlikely that he is presenting an exhaustive account!). It is also written like a model missionary journey for late-1st-cent. Christians with a model sermon on natural theology (14:15-17) and the example of appointing presbyters (14:23), see E. Haenchen, *The Acts of the Apostles, A Commentary,* trans. B. Noble et al. (Philadelphia: Westminster, 1971) 429-34.

[10]In Gal 2 and Acts 15 both Barnabas and Paul are present. The occasion of both meetings is because of the circumcision of the Gentiles by certain judaizing Christians. Mention is also made in both accounts to remember the poor. Finally James and Peter are mentioned in both accounts. The differences between Gal 2 and Acts 15 concern more specific points. In Gal 2, Paul was prompted to go to Jerusalem by a special revelation and a private meeting is described. In Acts 15 Paul and Barnabas are sent by the Antioch church and the meeting appears to be open to church leaders and delegates.

[11]For further discussion on Gal 1-2 and Acts see "A Chronology of Paul's Life" in ch. 2.

how "quickly they have deserted" him could be best understood if Paul wrote from Ephesus shortly after visiting them (Acts 18:23; 19:1).

The fifth reason supports the later dating. If Galatians were written in AD 53–54 it would be chronologically closer to 2 Corinthians and Romans, which would help explain their theological similarities.[12] Galatians is closer theologically to Romans than 1 Thessalonians with its imminent eschatology. Advocates for the early date would have to place Galatians chronologically before 1 Thessalonians and must therefore explain the divergencies in these two letters.

6. Summary

In this chapter we saw that Paul probably wrote his letter from Ephesus to Christians of North Galatia around AD 53–54. It was written in response to a crisis in the Galatian churches founded by the apostle. Many in these churches, struggling with problems of the flesh, assumed a complete system of legal requirements as advocated by Paul's opponents, the Judaizing Christians. In his attempt to defend his ministry and the spiritual experiences of the Galatians, Paul writes his letter arranging the arguments in a manner similar to the judicial or courtroom rhetoric of Cicero and Quintilian.[13]

[12]In Galatians and Rom, we have (for example) similar teaching on justification, the promise to Abraham, sonship, union with Christ and walk in the Spirit. In 2 Corinthians, Paul defends himself against similar attacks as in Galatians (Gal 1:6,10; 2:4 with 2 Cor 11:4; 5:11; 11:26).

[13]For further research, see the following commentaries and studies: H. D. Betz, "The Literary Composition and Function of Paul's Letter to the Galatians," *NTS* 21 (1975) 353–79; B. H. Brinsmead, *Galatians—Dialogical Response to Opponents* SBLDS 65 (Chico, Calif.: Scholars Press, 1982); F. F. Bruce, *Commentary on Galatians*, NIGTC (Grand Rapids: Eerdmans, 1982) and "Galatian Problems: II. North or South Galatians?" *BJRL* 52 (1969/70) 243–46; E. D. Burton, *A Critical and Exegetical Commentary on the Epistle of Paul to the Galatians*, ICC (Edinburgh: T. & T. Clark, 1921); C. H. Cosgrove, *The Cross and the Spirit: A Study in the Argument and Theology of Galatians.* Macon, GA: Mercer University Press, 1989); G. S. Duncan, *The Epistle of Paul to the Galatians* (New York: Harper & Row, 1934); D. Guthrie, *Galatians* NCB (London: Thomas Nelson and Sons, 1969); G. Howard, *Paul: Crisis in Galatia. A Study in Early Christian Theology.*

SNTSMS 35. 2nd ed. (Cambridge and New York: Cambridge Univ. Press, 1990). R. Jewett, "The Agitators and the Galatian Congregation," *NTS* 17 (1971) 198–212; D. J. Lull, *The Spirit in Galatia. Paul's Interpretation of Pneuma as Divine Power*, SBLDS 49 (Chico, Calif.: Scholars Press, 1980); J. Munck, *Paul and the Salvation of Mankind*, trans. F. Clarke (Atlanta: John Knox, 1977, orig, ed., 1959) 87–134; W. Schmithals, *Paul and the Gnostics*, trans. J. Steely (Nashville: Abingdon, 1972).

4

Paul's Corinthian Correspondence

1. Introduction

The importance of Paul's first and second letters to the Corinthians cannot be underestimated. They are the most extensive, ongoing record of the development of an early Christian community that we possess.[1] They also provide special insights into the everyday problems experienced by an early church and its founding leader. Finally, as written conversations between an apostle and his church, they are important primary sources which are close to the events under discussion.

Our survey of 1 and 2 Corinthians involves: a brief description of the city, the church, the visits and letters to Corinth, and discussions on the genre and structure. Investigations of settings and dates will also be undertaken.

2. The City of Corinth

In Paul's day Corinth was a bustling young city even though it had a long influential history dating back to classical Greece.[2] Why? Because the city was destroyed by the Romans in 146 BC and rebuilt as a Roman colony under Julius Caesar (44 BC). By

[1]D. Georgi, "Corinthians, First Letter to the," *IDBSup* 181.

[2]O. Broneer, "Corinth: Center of Paul's Missionary Work in Greece," *BA* 14 (1951) 78–96; idem, "The Apostle Paul and the Isthmian Games," *BA* 25 (1962) 2–31; idem, "Corinth, A Brief History of the City and A Guide to the Excava-

the first century AD, Corinth enjoyed good trade and commerce. It also experienced a great influx of different peoples and customs.

Located on a narrow isthmus connecting the Aegean and Adriatic seas, Corinth benefited from both sea and land trade. Corinth's isthmus was the only land bridge connecting the mainland with the southern peninsula (Peloponnesus). Sea merchants preferred to stop there at one of the seaports (Lechaeum and Cenchreae) rather than risk the hazardous voyage around the rocky southern tip of Greece. Because of its strategic location, Corinth attracted many travelers, merchants, and sailors from all regions of the Mediterranean world.

Archaeological excavations of first-century Corinth have revealed a bustling marketplace with many shops, an impressive heating and cooling water system, temples of Apollo, Poseidon, Demeter, and Asclepius, a theater, a gymnasium, and a *bēma* or tribunal rostrum. Nearby, to the east, the popular Isthmian games were held every other year. Excavations at the temple sites have revealed diverse religious practices involving cultic meals and sacrificial offerings. The discovery of the inscription "synagogue of the Hebrews" (2nd–3rd cent. AD?) confirms the presence of Jews in Roman Corinth (cf. Acts 18).

3. The Church at Corinth

a. Origin and Nature

The story of the founding of the Corinthian church is derived from 1 Corinthians and Acts. Upon Paul's arrival in the city he worked with Priscilla and Aquila (Acts 18:1-3; 1 Cor 16:19) as a tentmaker or leatherworker.[3] After debating in the synagogue

tions," American School of Classical Studies, Athens, revised 1972; J. Finegan, "Corinth," *IDB* 1:683–84; J. Murphy-O'Connor, *St. Paul's Corinth, Texts and Archaeology* (Wilmington, Del.: Michael Glazier, 1983); idem, "The Corinth that Saint Paul Saw," *BA* 47 (3, 1984) 147–59; idem, "Corinth," *ABD* 1:1134–39; V. P. Furnish, *II Corinthians*, AB 32A (Garden City, N.Y.: Doubleday, 1984) 4–22; J. R. Wiseman, "Ancient Corinth: The Gymnasium Area," *Arch* 22 (1969) 216–25.

[3]R. Hock, *The Social Context of Paul's Ministry: Tentmaking and Apostleship* (Philadelphia: Fortress, 1980).

(Acts 18:4), Paul worked among the Gentiles, staying with Titius Justus (Acts 18:7). About this time Paul baptized Crispus the synagogue ruler (Acts 18:8; 1 Cor 1:14). Sosthenes, Paul's co-worker (1 Cor 1:1), also may have been the synagogue ruler who was seized by a mob for befriending Paul (Acts 18:17). Erastus, the city treasurer mentioned in Rom 16:23, might also be the one who "laid (road pavement) at his own expense" (1st cent. Corinth inscription).[4]

The households of Stephanus (1 Cor 1:16; 16:15) and Chloe (1:11) were also Paul's converts and thus original members of the church. Other persons belonging to the Corinthian church are listed in 1 Corinthians 16 (Achaicus, Fortunatus) and Romans 16 (Jason, Lucius, Phoebe, Tertius, Quartus, Sosipater). Most of these persons have Roman names and represent the upper urban classes (e.g., lifestyles in 1 Cor 10:27; 11:17-34), even though many of the Corinthians were from the lower social stratum (1 Cor 1:26-29). Some lower-class trades of Corinth, however, were highly respected in the Mediterranean world, e.g., bronze metalsmiths.

The Christians at Corinth, like most early believers, worshipped in house churches (Rom 16:23; 1 Cor 16:29). These were probably the larger homes of wealthier church members (e.g., Gaius, Aquila). Four houses of the Roman period have been discovered at Corinth. The public rooms, i.e., the courtyard and dining room, were about 50 square meters each (approx. 538 sq. ft.). If homes like these became house churches, about 20 to 30 people of several families could meet there.[5]

The close, informal settings of these house churches and the diversity of its members would have occasioned numerous conflicts. In 1 Corinthians we learn of tension between upper and lower classes, weak and strong members, and Jews and Gentiles, on issues like the *agapē* feasts held before the Lord's Supper (11:17-34), eating meat sacrificed to idols (8; 10:14–11:1), and the use of spiritual gifts (chs 12–14). The tendency to cluster around favorite teachers, (e.g., "I am of Paul, I am of Apollos") could

[4]Murphy-O'Connor, *St. Paul's Corinth* 37.

[5]Ibid., 153–161 (with helpful diagrams of Roman villas). See also "Houses, Greek," "Houses, Italian," in *Oxford Class Dict* (Oxford: Oxford Univ. Press, 1970) 531–33.

have been reinforced by these social, religious, and ethnic distinctions.

b. Problems in the Church

Under this category we will discuss the factions at Corinth and the misunderstanding of Paul's gospel which resembles an early form of Gnosticism. We will conclude with a discussion of Paul's opponents in 2 Corinthians.

Factions. The nature of the factions or parties at Corinth (1:10-13; 3:5-9, 21-23) is difficult to determine. It seems uncertain whether there were four distinct parties at Corinth, those of Paul, Apollos, Cephas, and Christ (1:12). Cephas or Peter is briefly alluded to in several passages (1:12; 3:22; 9:5; 15:5). Even though Paul ranks him with the apostles (1 Cor 9:5; 15:5; Gal 2:9), he opposed Peter in Antioch for inconsistent behavior toward the Gentiles (Gal 2:11ff.). Possibly the concerns of the "weaker" brother that seem judaistic (1 Cor 8; 10; cf. Rom 14) mirror those of the Cephas group. It is unclear what is meant by "I am of Christ" (1:12; 2 Cor 10:7). It may signify renouncement of all human leadership, direct access to Christ as in Gnosticism, or direct succession to the historical Jesus as an original apostle.

There seem to be sufficient clues in the NT to postulate an Apollos school. From Acts 18:24-28, we learn that Apollos was an eloquent Jewish Christian from Alexandria, a center for Greek learning and Near Eastern wisdom. Some of Paul's discussion on human and divine wisdom (1 Cor 1:18–3:4) could be interpreted as corrective teaching for those Corinthians who were attracted to Apollos, because of his eloquence, Hellenistic learning, and possible acquaintance with ancient wisdom. It is apparent from 1 Corinthians, that Paul had respect for the ministry of Apollos (3:5-9,21-23; 16:21).

Data for a Pauline school also can be detected.[6] The household of Stephanus (1:16; 16:15), for example, was among Paul's first converts in Achaia. It will be argued later, that they were probably the bearers of the Corinthian letter of questions (1 Cor

[6]R. Jewett, "The Redaction of 1 Corinthians and the Trajectory of the Pauline School," *JAARS* 44 (1978) 389–444.

7:1), and may have caused a division in Corinth by insisting that Paul alone (not Apollos) respond to it. Crispus and Gaius were also baptized by Paul (1:14) and probably attached great importance to this rite being performed by the apostle. The image of Paul as founder of a new religious group is disparaged enough times by him to presuppose the existence of such a group who revered him in this manner (e.g., 1:13-17; 3:5-15,21-23).

Gnosticism. Although the identities of the factions are uncertain, the nature of the Corinthian misunderstanding has a distinct gnostic tendency. They regard themselves as both mature and spiritual, and are proud of their knowledge (1 Cor 8:1-3). For them, all things are permitted (10:23-31). As possessors of the Spirit they already have attained the resurrection spiritually (1 Cor 15:29-32). The heavenly Christ has precedence over the early Jesus (1 Cor 12:3). The preaching of the cross is foolishness to them (1:18-32). They also attach great importance to spiritual manifestations, such as speaking in other tongues (14:1-40). In this way they assert their superiority over those who are not possessed by the Spirit. Such characteristics have similarities with Gnosticism.[7]

Paul's Opponents. From 1 Corinthians with its factions and errors, we move to 2 Corinthians with specific opponents from outside the church (2 Cor 11:4).[8] They were probably itinerant Jewish-Christian preachers. In 2 Cor 10-13, we learn the following points. First, they attack Paul for his lack of eloquent speech (10:1,10), visionary experiences (12:1), and miraculous powers (12:12). These opponents also accuse him of foolishness (11:16-

[7]Schmithals, *Gnosticism in Corinth*; R. McL. Wilson, "How Gnostic Were the Corinthians?" *NTS* (1972–73) 65–74. Gnostics advocated spiritual liberation and identity with the divine through revealed knowledge (*gnōsis*). This process of salvation is revealed in elaborate myths of heavenly beings emanating from a transcendent deity that often included a story of separation from and restoration to the divine realm. Christian gnostic systems utilized material from the Four Gospels and Paul. The Nag Hammadi documents from Egypt contain many diverse gnostic writings, dating from the 3rd cent AD.

[8]See: C. K. Barrett, "Paul's Opponents in II Corinthians," *NTS* 17 (1971) 233–54; D. Kee, "Who Were the 'Super-Apostles' of 2 Corinthians 10–13?" *RestQ* 23 (1980) 65–76; M. E. Thrall, "Super-Apostles, Servants of Christ, and Servants of Satan," *JSNT* 6 (1980) 42–57.

19) and dishonesty (12:16-19). Second, they boast of worldly things (11:16,18), their advantage as Hebrews (11:22), and their status as apostles (11:5,12-15; 12:11-12). Third, although Jewish Christians with letters of recommendation (from Palestine ?), they do not appear to be Judaizers. Paul makes no attempt to refute the practice of circumcision in 2 Corinthians as he had done in Galatians. These opponents may have viewed themselves as Hellenistic divine men.[9] They boasted of their privileged status and probably believed that ecstatic speech, miracles, and visions were manifestations of a divine nature. Fourth, in response to these attacks and errors, Paul boasts in the Lord who alone commends his ministry (10:17f.). If he must boast of himself it will be of his sufferings for Christ so that God's power is perfected in him (12:9f.). His authority is given from the Lord for the upbuilding of the churches (10:8; 13:10). He is devoted to the truth and prays for the restoration of the Corinthians (13:8f.).

4. The Visits and the Letters

There are many theories about the number of visits to Corinth and letters sent there. A basic outline will be provided and some of the theories considered.

a. Paul's First Visit (Acts 18:1-18; 1 Cor 1:14-16; 2:1; 16:15)

According to Acts 18, Paul visited Corinth after leaving Athens. He spent eighteen months in the city, first preaching at the synagogue and then at the house of Titius Justus. The mention of Crispus as Paul's convert (v 8) is supported by 1 Cor 1:14.

The dating of Paul's appearance before Gallio, which ended his eighteen-month stay, finds some confirmation in the Gallio inscription at Delphi. A convincing case has been made for the Corinthian proconsulship of Gallio to be from July 51 to July 52, with Paul's appearance near the beginning (summer of 51).[10]

[9]D. Georgi, *The Opponents of Paul in 2 Corinthians.* Philadelphia: Fortress, 1985.

[10]Murphy-O'Connor, *St. Paul's Corinth* 141–52 (Gallio inscription); Jewett, *Chronology* 38–40 (summer of 51).

This would make Paul's departure from Corinth in the summer of 51 and his arrival eighteen months before this date in the winter of 49.

b. Paul's First Letter (1 Cor 5:9-11)

The contents of this letter are only alluded to in 1 Cor 5:9-11. It seems that Paul's injunctions "not to associate with sexually immoral people" pertained only to those who professed to be Christians (v 11). It was misinterpreted by the Corinthians, however, to perhaps mean withdrawal from all immoral people (v 10). Some have argued that 2 Cor 6:14–7:1 was originally this letter. When 2 Corinthians was written it was inserted into the text. However, this theory is unlikely, since the vocabulary of this interpolation is non-Pauline and its contents seem to support the Corinthian interpretation and not Paul's viewpoint (1 Cor 5:9-11).

Arguments that 2 Cor 6:14–7:1 is a non-Pauline interpolation are convincing, although it is probably not the letter referred to in 1 Cor 5:9. First, the text interrupts the logical flow of the passage. The topic of 6:11-13 (appeal for openness) abruptly changes at v 14 and is not resumed until 7:2. The vocabulary and style of 6:14–7:1 are also different from the rest of 2 Corinthians and Paul's letters. Its contents are similar to the ethical dualism found in both the Dead Sea Scrolls and gnostic writings.[11] Third, this stark interruption of thought and style is unlike Paul's typical digressions and *anacolutha* (e.g., Rom 2:15-16; Gal 2:4-6; 2 Cor 1:22-23; 5:14–6:2).

c. Report from Corinth (1 Cor 1:11)

The nature of the oral report is as follows:

> For it has been reported to me by Chloe's people that there is quarreling among you, my brethren. What I mean is that each one of you says, "I belong to Paul," or "I belong to Apollos,"

[11]H. D. Betz, "2 Cor 6:14–7:1: An Anti-Pauline Fragment?" *JBL* 92 (1973) 88–108; G. D. Fee, "II Corinthians vi.14–vii.1 and Food Offered to Idols," *NTS* 23 (1977) 140–61; M. E. Thrall, "The Problem of II Cor vi.14–vii.1 in Some Recent Discussion," *NTS* 24 (1977) 132–48.

> or "I belong to Cephas," or "I belong to Christ" (1 Cor 1:11-12).

These factions probably involved the allegiance of certain members to a particular leader, like the philosophical schools of Stoicism: e.g., "I belong to the school of Chrysippus," "I belong to the school of Cleanthes." In addition to factions, it is possible that Chloe's household reported other problems to Paul: e.g., misbehavior in connection with the Lord's Supper (11:17-34), the case of the man living with his father's wife (5:1-2), and the issue of lawsuits among church members (6:1-8).

d. The Letter from Corinth (1 Cor 7:1)

The issues in the church letter, probably concerned the following questions:[12] (1) Should not our married couples forego sexual relations (7:1-5) and our unmarrieds remain single (vv 25,36) so that they may become better Christians? (2) Should Christians eat meat, part of which had been previously sacrificed to a pagan idol (8:1)? (3) Should women be veiled during worship (11:5)? (4) Is speaking in tongues the foremost gift of the Spirit (12:1; 14:6)? (5) Is it necessary to believe in the future resurrection of the body (15:12,35)? (6) What plans have been made concerning the collection for the Jerusalem church (16:1)?

It might be assumed from these questions and his responses to them, that Paul did not give his congregations blueprints for faith and practice. He probably explored with them the possibilities and ranges of a living message and faith. Paul's early preaching at Corinth probably focused on the nearness of the Lord's return and a gospel free from Jewish legalism. Such emphases would have evoked from the Corinthians a variety of questions about ethics, doctrine, and worship.

e. Paul's Second Letter (1 Corinthians)

Paul is writing from Ephesus just before the Feast of Pente-

[12] Adapted from: J. C. Hurd, *The Origin of First Corinthians* (London: SPCK, 1965) 168, 181, Table 7.

cost (1 Cor 16:8,19; cf. Acts 19), probably in the spring of AD 55. Because of the way Paul recommends them to the congregation (1 Cor 16:15-18), Stephanus, Fortunatus, and Achaicus probably brought the letter to Corinth. Even though the letter contains some discrepancies in content and style,[13] most scholars do not regard them as sufficient to argue that 1 Corinthians is a composite of two or more letter fragments. First Corinthians was no doubt written in the midst of a busy apostolic ministry. It may have been laid aside from time to time and taken up again after an interval. Therefore it lacks both the uniform arrangement of a church manual and the specific directives of a bishop's encyclical. It provides only general advice on a variety of issues by an apostle who wanted to secure church harmony and maintain credibility with his readers.

f. The Visits of Timothy (1 Cor 4:17; 16:10-11; Acts 19:21-22)

In 1 Corinthians it appears that Timothy has already made one visit ("I sent to you Timothy," 4:17) and a second one is proposed ("And if Timothy should come," 16:10). The Corinthians probably received 1 Corinthians between these two visits. In the first visit, Timothy reminded the Corinthians of Paul's "ways in Christ" as the apostle taught them "everywhere in the church" (4:17). The arrival of 1 Corinthians seems to have followed this first visit. In 16:10, Paul seems to anticipate Timothy's second visit *after* they read his letter. Therefore Timothy is probably not the carrier of the letter. It is plausible that Acts 19:21-22 refers to this second visit of Timothy. Paul may have sent him and Erastus to Achaia (Corinth) via Macedonia, since the apostle planned to visit both regions before going to Jerusalem.

[13]Some alleged discrepancies in 1 Corinthians are: (a) In 4:19, Paul says he will come to Corinth but in 16:5-9 says that his coming will be delayed. (b) In 10:1-22, Paul takes a rigorous attitude against food sacrificed to idols but in 8:1-13 and 10:23–11:1 abstinence in these matters is simply an act of charity on behalf of the weaker brother. (c) The abrupt renewal of Paul's apostolic defense in ch 9 after completing it in 1 Cor 1–4. Paul's rhetorical techniques can account for most of these discrepancies in thought. See discussion in C. K. Barrett, *The First Epistle to the Corinthians*, HNTC (New York: Harper & Row, 1968) 12–17.

g. Paul's Second Visit (2 Cor 2:1; 12:14; 13:1)

The following circumstances prompted this "painful visit." A crisis in Corinth breaks out; probably when Timothy was there. It was caused by certain Jewish-Christian missionaries who oppose Paul's authority (2 Cor 10:10; 11:23; 12:6f.). Timothy, evidently at a loss to deal with it, returns to Ephesus with news of the problem. On receiving Timothy's report, Paul makes his second visit to Corinth to handle personally the situation. This he later refers to as the "painful visit" (2 Cor 2:1). It can be deduced from chs 1–2 and 7 that Paul's trip was a failure and he was forced to return to Ephesus in great distress.

h. Paul's Third Letter (2 Cor 2:3-4; 7:8)

After the failure of his "painful visit," Paul writes his third letter "out of much affliction and anguish of heart and with many tears" (2 Cor 2:4). We are not certain about the contents of this letter, although some have postulated that it is partially preserved in 2 Cor 10–13.

The theory that 2 Cor 10–13 is a separate letter is convincing.[14] First, the tone of these chapters is very different from that of 2 Cor 1–9. They are more polemical and sarcastic than the earlier chapters. Second, a different attitude towards self-commendation occurs in chs 10–13. In 2 Cor 1–9, the apostle appears to deplore self-commendation (3:1; 5:12), whereas in 2 Corinthians 10, Paul takes great effort to commend himself. Third, 2 Cor 1–9 may even presuppose 10–13. In 13:2,10, Paul speaks of the possibility of making another painful visit, whereas in 1:23–2:1, the severe letter has already served as a substitute for this visit. In 13:10, Paul appears to be writing the "severe letter," whereas in 2:3-4, it has already been written. Fourth, the geographical situation of 2 Cor 10-13 appears to be Ephesus (10:16; 11:9-10) instead of Macedonia where he probably wrote chs 1–9 (e.g., 2:13; 7:5; 8:1; 9:2). It seems plausible, therefore, that 2 Cor 10–13 was a separate let-

[14]C. K. Barrett, *The Second Epistle to the Corinthians*, HNTC (New York: Harper & Row, 1973) 11-14; Furnish, *II Corinthians* 30–48; R. P. Martin, *2 Corinthians*, WBC (Dallas: Word, 1986) xxxviii–lii.

ter. Later, it was combined with chs 1–9 either by Paul or one of his disciples.

i. The Visit of Titus (2 Cor 2:13; 7:6-7; cf. Acts 20:1)

After Paul had left Ephesus he went to Troas (2 Cor 2:12) but when he did not find Titus there he went on to Macedonia (2:13) with great consternation (7:5). Titus finally arrives and comforts Paul with a report that the church crisis is over (7:6-16).

j. Paul's Fourth Letter (2 Cor 1–9)

Paul responds to the comforting news of Titus with 2 Cor 1–9. It contains words of comfort, self-authentication, and commendation. This letter is sent from Macedonia around AD 56. The carriers are probably Titus and "two other brothers" (2 Cor 8:16-18,22).

At least two problems have surfaced concerning the integrity of 2 Cor 1–9. First, chs 2:14–7:4 (excluding 6:14–7:1) interrupt a narrative discourse which opens in 2:1-13 and closes at 7:5-16. Second Corinthians 2:14–7:4 is apologetic in tone, whereas 1:1–2:13 and 7:5-16 are informative and conciliatory. This break in narration, however, can be explained by Paul's rhetorical structure of a narration of facts (1:8–2:13) before his defense, and a peroration (7:2-16) which recapitulates the arguments of the narration.[15]

The second argument against the integrity of 2 Cor 1–9 is weightier because it concerns chs 8 and 9 as separate letters.[16] They are not only different in tone and contents from 1–7, but also appear to be independent of each other. Chapter 8 does not continue the conciliatory theme of ch 7. Also in 2 Cor 7 Titus has just returned from Corinth, whereas in ch 8 he is ready to depart for Corinth (vv 6,16-24). Next, ch 9 takes up the issue of the collection as if it had not been previously discussed (8). It also ap-

[15]See our outline of 2 Corinthians for details on how the peroration (7) functions as a summary of key points in the narration (1:8–2:13).

[16]See: H. D. Betz, *2 Corinthians 8 and 9*, Hermeneia (Philadelphia: Fortress, 1985).

pears to be addressed to all Achaia. Finally, the delegation in ch 8 seems to have already departed (8:16-24), whereas in ch 9, they are about to be sent (9:3-5).

Although these points argue impressively for chs 8 and 9 as independent units, Paul could have hastily incorporated them into one letter during his stay in Macedonia. Our outline supports 8 and 9 as combined letters added to 1–7. Rhetorically, ch 9 functions as the peroration of ch 8, recapitulating several points that seek a contribution for the relief of the Jerusalem church. Some of the chronological discrepancies might be explained by suggesting that Paul composed 8 and 9 on two separate occasions. Together, chs 8–9 also serve as an effective conclusion to 2 Corinthians in a manner similar to the structure of 1 Corinthians which also ends with discussion on the collection (16:1-4).

Even though sections of 2 Cor 8 and 9 could have been composed earlier in Ephesus, chs 1–9 seem to reflect the same Pauline setting in Macedonia (1:16; 2:13; 7:5; 8:1; 9:2,4). This observation may indicate the location of their final compilation. The theories of sending chs 8 and 9 later on two separate occasions is possible. But how does one account for the length of time involved to send them as separate correspondences? We find less difficulty in maintaining that Paul combined these letter fragments (1–7; 8; 9) within a short period of time and sent them to the Corinthians as a composite letter (AD 56).

k. Paul's Third Visit (2 Cor 12:14; 13:1; 15:25-27; Acts 20:2-3)

According to 2 Cor 12:14; 13:1, Paul plans to make a third visit to Corinth. Romans 15:25-27 indicates a visit was made to pick up the collection for the saints in Jerusalem. Acts 20:2-3 probably refers to this same trip just before Paul takes his final voyage to Jerusalem. This third visit to Corinth probably occurred in the winter of AD 56–57, when Paul wrote his letter to the Romans from nearby Cenchreae (16:1-2).[17]

[17]See our discussion of the dating of Romans, ch 5. See also Jewett, *Chronology* 40–44, 100–102.

5. The Genre and the Structure of 1 Corinthians

Because Paul is unable to be present at Corinth, he writes a letter. First Corinthians contains all the features of an early Christian letter: opening 1:1-2; thanksgiving, 1:4-9; body, 1:10–4:21; exhortations and instructions 5:1–16:18, and closing, 16:19-24.

What type of letter is 1 Corinthians? It is much longer than the typical letters of antiquity, and the identities of its author and recipients (i.e., the apostle Paul [and his associate] to the church in Corinth) give the letter a public and official character. Because of these features, 1 Corinthians seems to be a letter-essay, not unlike Romans in this respect. Letter-essays were written by authoritative persons such as philosophers (Plato, Epicurus), biographers (e.g., Plutarch), and statesmen (Isocrates, Cicero); they also envisioned a wide audience (e.g., I-you-they).

It is not enough to identify 1 Corinthians as a letter-essay. In order to grasp better the form and content, we must ask: what type of discourse did Paul use to accomplish his purpose? Therefore, as in Galatians, we will analyze 1 Corinthians rhetorically.

First Corinthians contains both apologetic and advisory features. Like Galatians, it shares some apologetic features, such as a defense of Paul's apostolic ministry. This classes it with judicial rhetoric (e.g., 1 Cor 1:10–4:41; 9).[18] However, 1 Corinthians also seeks to give advice to its readers on various questions and problems in their communities (e.g., 1 Cor 5:1-2; 6:1-5; 7:1-7; 8:1-3; 11:17-22; 12:1-3; 15:12,35; 16:1-4).[19] This advisory form of persuasion is called symboleutic or deliberative rhetoric.

Deliberative persuasion is different from judicial, because it is concerned with decision making in a political (or public assembly), not judgments in a courtroom. It is also to be distinguished from demonstrative or epideictic rhetoric, because it emphasizes what is practical or expedient over what is praiseworthy or honorable. Judicial rhetoric is concerned with just actions of the past

[18]J. B. Chance "Paul's Apology to the Corinthians," *PerRelSt* 9 (1, 1982) 146–55.

[19]Galatians also contains both apologetic (chs 1–2) and deliberative rhetoric (chs 5–6) since these last chapters are NT ethical exhortations (*pareneses*) which seek to persuade or dissuade the addressees in their decision making on various ethical issues.

and demonstrative focuses on virtues in the present, but deliberative persuasion concentrates on what is expedient for the future.

The following works are examples of deliberative rhetoric. In Demosthenes, *Third Philippic* (341 BC), the famous statesman advises the Athenian assembly to unite with other Greek city-states in opposition to Philip of Macedon. Isocrates, in his *On Peace* (355 BC), proposes, before the political assembly of Athens, a policy of lasting peace between Athens and her neighbors. The speech of John Milton to the English Parliament on the liberty of unlicensed printing, *Areopagitica* (London, 1644), also employs most of the techniques of deliberative rhetoric (e.g., Is it possible? Is it honorable? Is it expedient?). Finally, it will be shown in later chapters that the ethical exhortations of Ephesians and Hebrews reflect similar rhetorical concerns.

Guidelines for composing deliberative (judicial and demonstrative) speeches are found in the rhetorical handbooks of Aristotle, Cicero, and Quintilian.[20] The structure and arrangement of 1 Corinthians coincides with some of these rules in the rhetorical handbooks.

There are specific parallels to the rhetorical arrangement of 1 Corinthians. The Letters 7 and 8 of Plato to friends of Dion in Sicily are the first example. The seventh letter has already been discussed as an autobiographical defense of Plato among the Silicians comparable to Gal 1–2. It will also be shown that 1 Cor 1:10–4:21 and ch 9 function in a similar apologetic manner. In Letter 8, however, Plato gives specific advice to his readers on certain problems and issues. This "deliberative" function is similar to that which we find in 1 Cor 5–16 (excluding ch. 9). Second, in Isocrates' *Address to Philip of Macedon* (346 BC), the Athenian statesman first justifies his own actions (1–23) before advising King Philip on what noble and honorable policies to pursue (24–153). Third, reminiscent of 1 Cor 7:1, the following letters are responses by teachers to questions asked by their students. See for example: Epicurus, Letter II, *To Pythocles* and Plutarch,

[20]Most of the editions of classical rhetoricians are found in the LCL or Loeb Classical Library (Cambridge, Mass.: Harvard Univ. Press). For full bibliographical information on major handbooks, see Kennedy, *NT Rhetoric* 161 and B. Mack, *Rhetoric and the NT, GBS* (Minneapolis: Fortress, 1990) 103.

Letter III, *On the Tranquility of the Mind* (in Moralia 1012B–1030C).[21]

The Rhetorical Structure[22] of 1 Corinthians

Part One: A Defense of Paul's Authority

I.	Epistolary prescript	1:1-3
	Senders and addressees	1:1-2
	Salutation	1:3
II.	Proem (Thanksgiving)	1:4-9
III.	Proposition: Divisions at Corinth (probably relating to *who* has the authority to answer their letter of questions; cf. 7:1)	1:10
IV.	Narration of facts	1:11-13
V.	Refutation of charges: Paul is not responsible for these divisions	1:14-17

[21]The letters of Epicurus are found in Diogenes Laertius, *Lives of Eminent Philosophers*, Book 10 (vol. 2 of LCL). Plutarch's letter is found in *Moralia* (vol. 6 of LCL).

[22]This outline presupposes the following studies: Barrett, *First Corinthians* 28–29; N. A. Dahl, "Paul and the Church at Corinth," *Studies in Paul* (Minneapolis: Augsburg, 1977) 49–55; Kennedy, *NT Rhetoric*. For other commentaries and studies, see D. L. Balch, "Backgrounds of 1 Cor VII: Sayings of the Lord in Q; Moses as an Ascetic *Theios Anēr* in 2 Cor 3," *NTS* 18 (1972) 351–64; S. S. Bartchy, *Mallon Chrēsai: First Century Slavery and the Interpretation of 1 Corinthians 7:21* (Missoula, Mont.: Scholars Press, 1973); H. D. Betz and M. M. Mitchell, "Corinthians, First Epistle to the," *ABD* 1:1139–1148. T. Callan, "Prophecy and Ecstasy in Greco-Roman Religion and 1 Corinthians," *NovT* 27 (2, 1985) 125–40; H. Conzelmann, *1 Corinthians* (Philadelphia: Fortress, 1975); E. E. Ellis, "Paul and His Co-workers," *NTS* 17 (1971) 437–53; G. D. Fee, *The First Epistle to the Corinthians*, NIC (Grand Rapids: Eerdmans, 1987); E. S. Fiorenza, "Rhetorical Situation and Historical Reconstruction in 1 Corinthians," *NTS* 33 (1987) 386–403. R. H. Gundry, *Sōma in Biblical Theology, with Emphasis on Pauline Anthropology*, SNTSMS 29 (Cambridge: Cambridge Univ. Press, 1976); A. E. Hill, "The Temple of Asclepius: An Alternative Source for Paul's Body Theology?" *JBL* 99 (3, 1980) 437–39; E. Käsemann, "The Pauline Doctrine of the Lord's Supper," in idem, *Essays* 108–35; J. J. Klijne, "We, Us and Our in I and II Corinthians," *NovT* 8 (1966) 171–79; K. A. Plank, "Resurrection Theology: The Corinthian Controversy Reexamined," *PerRelSt* 8 (1, 1981) 41–54; G. Theissen, *The Social Setting of Pauline Christianity. Essays on Corinth*, trans. J. Shutz (Philadelphia: Fortress, 1982); W. Willis, *Idol Meat in Corinth: Pauline Argument in 1 Corinthians 8 and 10*, SBLDS 68 (Chico, Calif.: Scholars Press, 1985). A. C. Wire, *The Corinthian Women Prophets: A Reconstruction Through Paul's Rhetoric* (Minneapolis: Fortress, 1990).

VI.	Various topics to be developed	1:18–2:5
	A. The power and wisdom of God versus human wisdom	1:18-30
	B. Paul's relations with the Corinthians	2:1-5
VII.	Argumentation and development of topics (in 1:18–2:5)	2:6–4:21
	A. The spiritual wisdom that Paul imparts	2:6–3:4
	B. The functions of Paul and other servants of Christ	3:5-23
	C. Paul's relations with the Corinthian churches (vv 1-2 transitional)	4:1-13
VIII.	Peroration (recapitulation of argument) (includes *pathos* or emotional appeal, v 21)	4:14-21

Part Two: Paul Addresses Issues at Corinth

IX.	Issues concerning immorality and lawsuits	5-6
	A. A specific case of sexual immorality	5:1-8
	B. Note on previous letter: "Do not associate with immoral people"	5:9-13
	C. Lawsuits among the brothers	6:1-4
	D. General comment on licentious behavior	6:12-20
X.	Reply to Corinthian letter of questions	7:1–16:4
	A. Concerning celibacy and marriage in this passing world	7:1-40
	B. Concerning food offered to idols	8:1–11:1
	1. The topics of idols and self-restraint	8
	2. Paul's life as an example (amplification of apostolic defense topics in 1:14-17; 2:1-5; 3:5-23)	9
	3. Amplification of topic on idols: the warning example of the wilderness generation	10:1–11:1
	C. Issues concerning the veiling of woman in public worship	11:2-16
	D. Issues connected with the Lord's Supper	11:17-34
	E. Concerning spiritual gifts in the community	12:1–14:40
	1. An encomium on love as the rule of behavior in the church	13
	2. Specific advice on the gifts of tongues and prophecy	14:1-40
	F. Questions about the bodily resurrection of the dead	15

G. Concerning the collection of the saints	16:1-4
XI. Epistolary postscript (conclusion)	16:5-24
A. Travelogue of Paul's duties and plans	16:5-9
B. Peroration (summary of argument)	16:10-18
1. Paul commends Timothy and Apollos as his fellow servants of Christ (cf. 1:11-17; 3:3–4:6)	16:10-12
2. Paul exhorts the Corinthians in their decision making (cf. 1:10; 4:16; 5:1-2; 7:1; 8:1; 12:1)	vv 13-14
3. Paul commends the household of Stephanus (1:16), converts of the apostle who brought him the Corinthian letter, an action probably contributing to the division (cf. "I am of Paul," 1:11-17; 3:3–4:6).	vv 15-18
C. Other personal appeals	vv 19-24
Final greetings	vv 19-20
Formula of epistolary authentication	v 21
Emotional appeal	v 22
Benediction	vv 23-24

Our rhetorical outline presupposes a close connection between Paul's judicial argument (1:10–4:21; 9) and the deliberative sections of his letter (chs 5–16, excluding 9). The first reason for making this assumption is rhetorical: Paul wishes to first reestablish his authority and qualifications before advising the Corinthians on their problems. The second reason is historical. It has been suggested that the household of Stephanus, who were converts of Paul, may have caused a division at Corinth by insisting that "the letter of questions" be sent to Paul, not Apollos or Cephas (e.g., "I am of Paul").[23]

The practical topics of immorality (ch 5), marriage (ch 7), freedom (ch 8), and the speculative questions on immortality (ch 15; Is there a resurrection? What about the resurrected bodies?) were often used in rhetorical exercises (*progymnasmata*) at Hellenistic schools. Throughout his letter, Paul also employs the rhetorical *devices* of deliberative rhetoric: e.g., appeals to the common good, or what is beneficial, or expedient, leaving certain matters for the

[23]Dahl, "Paul and Church at Corinth," *Studies in Paul* 49–55.

audience to decide, and warnings about the seriousness of a decision on some issue. Finally, in accordance with the rhetorical handbooks, Paul makes use of: *enthymemes* (logical inferences including a premise and conclusion), amplification of a topic, examples from the past, proofs (e.g., scriptural proofs), proverbs or maxims, hortatory addresses, three types of appeals to the speaker's character (*ethos*), or emotions of the audience (*pathos*), or reason (*logos*), comparisons and contrasts, rhetorical questions, and peroration (i.e., an epilogue, recapitulating key points).

First Corinthians provides valuable insight into the everyday problems of one of Paul's churches. It also discloses early traditions of the primitive church, such as the kerygmatic formula (15:3-7), the Lord's Supper (11:23-25), and apocalyptic material (7:29-31; 15:24-28). In 1 Cor 16 we are introduced to the ecumenical effort of the collection for the saints in Jerusalem, which is discussed further in 2 Cor 8–9 and Rom 16.

6. The Genre and Structure of 2 Corinthians

In its final form, Paul's Second Letter to the Corinthians, like 1 Corinthians, contains the following features. First, it has most of the characteristics of an ancient letter. Second, the authority of the sender and its public character also constitute it a letter-essay. Third, it contains a combination of judicial and deliberative types of rhetoric.

In its final form, 2 Corinthians reads like an ancient letter. It contains a letter opening 1:1-2 with a sender, addressee, and greetings. It also has a thanksgiving section, 1:3-7, a letter body (chs 1–9; 10–13) and brief *parenesis* (13:11). Finally, it contains a letter closing, with greetings (13:12-13) and a Pauline benediction (v 14).

The length of this composite letter, sent by an "apostle of Christ Jesus" to members of "the church of God which is at Corinth," gives the letter a public and official character. As a letter-essay, 2 Corinthians can be classed with Paul's other major letters, Romans and 1 Corinthians.[24]

[24]For further information on the characteristics of the letter essay, see M. L. Stirewalt, "Form and Function of the Greek Letter Essay," *Romans Debate* (1977) 175–206.

Like 1 Corinthians, 2 Corinthians contains both types of judicial and deliberative rhetoric. These forms of persuasion are so distinct, that most scholars maintain that 2 Corinthians is a composite letter, containing two to four separate letter fragments.[25] In 2 Cor 1:1–7:16, Paul employs judicial rhetoric in defending his ministry as sincere, from God, and proclaiming Christ. In 2 Cor 8–9, deliberative rhetoric is used to urge the Corinthians to complete the collection for the Jerusalem church that they had begun a year ago. Finally, in 2 Cor 10–13, Paul again employs judicial rhetoric to refute the charges of his opponents that his letters are strong but his bodily presence and speech are weak. The order in which these three types of rhetoric are organized is not necessarily chronological. It has been argued that 2 Cor 10–13 may have been the harsh or "tearful" letter that is mentioned in 2 Cor 2:4, "For I wrote you out of much affliction and anguish of heart and with many tears." If these three types of rhetoric represent three different letters, both the letter openings of 2 Cor 8–9 and 10–13 and the letter closings of 2 Cor 1–7 and 8–9 are now lost!

Rhetorical Structure[26] of 2 Corinthians

The Rhetorical Structure of 2 Cor 1:1–7:16

I. Epistolary prescript	1:1-2
II. Proem: The God of mercy and comfort, who comforts Paul in his affliction, and shares this comfort with the Corinthians	1:3-7
III. Narration of facts to refute the charges against Paul	1:8–2:13
A. Paul's situation in Asia: God delivered him from affliction and death	1:8-11
B. Paul's relations with the Corinthians	1:12–2:13
1. His overall actions are characterized by simplicity and sincerity	1:12-14

[25]For discussion, see Barrett, *Second Corinthians*, 11–14; W. H. Bates, "The Integrity of 2 Corinthians," *NTS* 12 (1965) 56–59; Furnish, *II Corinthians* 30–48; Martin, *2 Corinthians* xxxviii-lii. We have also discussed in this chapter the composite nature of 2 Corinthians under "The Visits and the Letters."

[26]Suggestions for this outline have been derived from: Kennedy, *NT Rhetoric* 86–96. The commentaries on 2 Corinthians by Barrett, Betz, Furnish, and Martin have also been consulted.

2. Paul explains his canceled visit and justifies his "tearful" letter	1:15–2:11
C. Paul's current setting in Macedonia	2:12-13
IV. Proposition: Paul's ministry as sincere, from God, and proclaiming Christ	2:14-17
A. Illustrated by the metaphors of military triumph and royal or religious incense	vv 14-16
B. Stated in both negative and positive propositions	v 17
V. Character witnesses: The Corinthians as Paul's letters of recommendation	3:1-3
VI. Argumentation of proposition	3:4–6:13
A. Our competence is *from God* who made us competent ministers of a new covenant in the Spirit	3:4–4:1
B. Paul's sincerity in practice and preaching	4:2-6
C. A ministry reflecting God's power despite the afflictions	4:7-12
D. Paul's sincerity of belief gives him confidence	4:13–5:10
E. Paul's apostolic witness to Christ	5:11–6:10
His motivation (vv 11-15); the work of Christ and Paul's ministry (vv 16-21); personal appeals (6:1-2); tribulation lists legitimizing Paul's ministry (6:3-9)	
Interpolation: Do not be coupled together with unbelievers 6:14–7:1	
VII. Peroration of Paul's defense (excluding 6:14–7:1)	6:11–7:16
A. Personal appeals for an open heart (*pathos*)	6:11–7:4
B. The narrative of Paul's experience since arriving in Macedonia (cf. 2:13)	7:5-16
1. God comforts Paul in his affliction with the arrival of Titus (cf. 1:3-4)	7:5-7
2. Paul amplifies his rationale for the "tearful" letter (cf. 2:3-4)	7:8-13a
3. Closing exultation over the good news from Titus	7:13b-16

The Rhetorical Structure of 2 Cor 8–9[27]

[27]This outline is adapted from: Kennedy, *NT Rhetoric* 91–92. For an alternative rhetorical analysis, see Betz, *2 Corinthians 8 and 9* 38–41, 88–90. On the Pauline collection, see K. Nickle, *The Collection, A Study in Paul's Strategy*, SBT 48 (Naperville, Ill.: Alec R. Allenson, 1966).

Address ("Brethren," 8:1), Salutation (Lost)

I. Narrative of Macedonian generosity: An example for the Corinthians 8:1-9
   - A. Example of Macedonian generosity 8:1-5
   - B. Application to Corinthians 8:6-7
   - C. Transition preparing for proposition 8:8-9

II. Proposition: "Complete what you began a year ago (and desire to do it)" 8:10-11

III. Argumentation of proposition vv 12-15
   - A. Reasons on readiness to share with those in need vv 12-14
   - B. Proof from Scripture (Ex 16:18) v 15

IV. Recommendation of Titus who will act as Paul's agent in the collection 8:16-24

V. Paul's reason for writing: So that he may boast in the collection from (Corinth) Achaia 9:1-5

VI. Peroration (epilogue) 9:6-15
   - A. Recapitulation of request to give bountifully 9:6
   - B. Reasons supporting the request to give (vv 7-8, 10-12) and proof from Scripture (v 9) 9:7-12
   - C. Emotional appeals: You will glorify God and bless others vv 13-14

VII. Conclusion: "Thanks be to God!" v 15

Letter closing (Lost)

The Rhetorical Structure of 2 Cor 10–13

Address, salutation (Lost)

I. Introduction to case 10:1-6
   - A. Statement on cause of letter: "I who am humble when face to face with you but bold to you when I am away" v 1
   - B. Paul's appeal for Corinthians to understand the nature of the opposition vv 2-6

II. Proposition: To refute the charge that "his letters are weighty and strong but his bodily presence is weak and speech is of no account" (v 10) vv 7-11

III. Argumentation: answering fools according to their folly[28] 10:12–12:13

[28]Barrett, *Second Corinthians* 52, 288–318. See also A. B. Spencer, "The Wise Fool (and the Foolish Wise): A Study of Irony in Paul," *NovT* 23 (1981) 349–60; E. A. Judge, "St. Paul and Socrates," *Interchange* 14 (1980) 106–16.

- A. Introduction: Paul and "the Fools" 10:12–11:15
  - 1. In contrast to his rivals, Paul's boasting will be limited by the Lord 10:12-18
  - 2. Paul compares himself with the rival apostles 11:1-15
- B. Argument one, Paul boasts of his apostolic qualifications: A ministry of suffering 11:16-33
- C. Argument two: Paul boasts of his divine revelations 12:1-10
- D. Conclusion of argumentation: "I was not at all inferior to these superlative apostles." 12:11-13

IV. Peroration 12:14–13:10

- A. A Third visit is proposed (cf. 10:1-2) and Paul reminds his readers that he did not and will not burden them (cf. 11:7-11) 12:14-18
- B. Reiteration of defense with further response to the charge of Paul's weak physical presence among them (cf. 10:7-11) 12:19-21
- C. Sharp apostolic warnings 13:1-10
  - 1. Ground rules for future indictments v 1
  - 2. The threat of another "painful visit" (cf. 2:1-2) for future offenders v 2-4
  - 3. Concluding appeals (*pathos* and *logos*) vv 5-9
  - 4. Concluding reason for writing v 10

V. Epistolary postscript 13:11-14

- A. Greetings topoi vv 11-12
- B. Benediction v 14

Second Corinthians pulsates with the life of the apostle. Even though penetrating in his attack of opponents, he is eager to forgive the penitent. Devoted to his churches, he willingly suffers for their benefit. Although discouraged by failure, his faith in God and mystical identity with Christ empower him with inner strength. Of chief importance in its teachings is Paul's concept of apostleship. For him, apostleship and gospel are inseparable. As an apostle Paul is called to proclaim the gospel of Christ. His self-sacrifice in ministry establishes high standards for all who would follow his work. In his person, the apostle seems to embody the gospel of the cross.[29]

[29]For further study on the teachings of 2 Cor, see W. R. Baird, "Letters of Recommendation: A Study of 2 Cor 3:1-3," *JBL* 80 (1961) 166–72; H. D. Betz

7. Summary

In this chapter we sought to acquaint you with Paul's Corinthian correspondence. First, we looked at the city of Corinth and information relevant for an understanding of the letters. Second, we examined the Corinthian church, comprised of rich and poor, Jew and Gentile with factions within and (later) opponents of Paul from outside. Third, we outlined Paul's three visits and four letters to Corinth, briefly explaining each. Fourth, we noted that the genre of 1 Corinthians is an open church letter by an apostle and outlined 1 Cor 1–4 as a defense of Paul's authority (judicial rhetoric) and 1 Cor 5–16 as advice from the apostle on various church issues (deliberative rhetoric).

Fifth, we noted that the genre of the final form of 2 Corinthians is that of an open letter written by an apostle. We also outlined 2 Cor 1:1–7:16 and 10–13 as refutations of charges against Paul (judicial rhetoric). Second Corinthians 6:14–7:1 is a non-Pauline interpolation. Chapters 8-9 are a complete unit of deliberative rhetoric encouraging the project of the Jerusalem collection.

The letters of Paul to the church of Corinth are important as the most extensive, continuous record of an early Christian community. They also provide us with special insights into the everyday dealings of the apostle with one of his churches. The Corinthian correspondences are excellent examples of written conversations in context.

and M. M. Mitchell, "Corinthians, Second Epistle to the," *ABD* 1:1148–54. G. R. Beasley-Murray, *Baptism in the NT* (London: Macmillan, 1962); J. D. G. Dunn, "2 Cor III.17- 'The Lord is Spirit,' " *JTS* 21 (1970) 309–20; E. E. Ellis, "II Cor v 1-10 in Pauline Eschatology," *NTS* 62 (1960) 211–24; J. T. Fitzgerald, "Paul, the Ancient Epistolary Theorists, and 2 Cor 10–13," in *Greek, Romans, and Christians,* ed. D. L. Balch (Minneapolis: Fortress, 1990) 190–200. V. P. Furnish, "The Ministry of Reconciliation," *CurTM* 4 (1977) 204–18, and *Theology and Ethics in Paul* (Nashville: Abingdon, 1968); R. Hodgson, "Paul the Apostle and First Century Tribulation Lists," *ZNW* 74 (1/2, 1983) 59–80; B. Holmberg, *Paul and Power: The Structure of Authority in the Primitive Church as Reflected in the Pauline Epistles* (Philadelphia: Fortress, 1978); R. Jewett, *Paul's Anthropological Terms. A Study of Their Use in Conflict Settings* (Leiden: Brill, 1971); E. A. Judge, "St. Paul and Classical Society," *JAC* 15 (1972) 19–36; T. Y. Mullins, "Paul's Thorn in the Flesh," *JBL* 76 (1957) 299–303; G. Mussies, *Dio Chrysostom and the New Testament* (Leiden: Brill, 1972): G. G. Collins, "Power Made Perfect in Weakness: 2 Cor 12:9-10," *CBQ* 33 (1971) 528–37; W. Schmithals, *The Office of the Apostle in the Early Church*, trans. J. Steely (Nashville: Abingdon, 1969); R. C. Tannehill, *Dying and Rising with Christ: A Study in Pauline Theology*, BZNW 32 (Berlin: Töpelmann, 1967); N. H. Taylor, "The Composition and Chronology of Second Corinthians," *JNTS* 44 (1991) 67–87. S. H. Travis, "Paul's Boasting in 2 Cor 10–12," *Studia Evangelica*, ed. E. A. Lingston (Berlin: Akademie-Verlag, 1973) 6:527–32.

5

Romans

1. Introduction

One of Paul's most influential works is his letter to the Romans, which summarizes and develops much of the teaching mentioned in his earlier writings. Romans draws heavily on the themes of justification by faith, the promise to Abraham, the failure of the works of the law, sonship, life in the Spirit, and union with Christ that are found in his letter to the Galatians. Furthermore, the apostle's discussions on Christ the second Adam, spiritual gifts and ministries, and the relations between the strong and weak appear in 1 Corinthians.

The subsequent influence of Romans can be seen in both the NT and the history of Christianity. In the NT, we find common themes that may indicate some acquaintance with Romans. First Peter includes the following topics mentioned earlier in Paul's letter: Jesus as the stone that causes some to stumble (Isa 28:16), spiritual sacrifices acceptable to God, obedience to the state, and the exercise of gifts and duties in the church. The letter to the Hebrews, as in Romans, portrays Abraham as a model of faith and has a quotation from Deut 32. Finally, the letter of James mentions the following motifs occurring in Romans: those who pass judgment on others, the emphasis on doing rather than hearing, the question of Abraham's justification by works, and sufferings or trials that produce character and faith. All of the above books contain themes found earlier in Paul's great letter.[1]

In early church history Romans had a definite influence on Western Christendom. Clement of Rome (AD 95) and Ignatius of Antioch (117) cited it frequently. The heretic Marcion included it in his own list of apostolic writings (140). The influential doctrines of inherited sin and imputed righteousness in the teaching of Augustine of Hippo (389–427) were mostly derived from Paul's letter to the Romans. The insightful commentaries on Romans by Martin Luther (1523) and John Calvin (1539) became major treatises of the Protestant Reformation. John Wesley, founder of the Methodist Church, was profoundly moved as he listened to a reading of the preface to Luther's commentary on Romans. In the twentieth century, the commentary on Romans by the Swiss pastor, Karl Barth (1919), sounded the death knell of nineteenth-century liberalism and inaugurated a new era of "neo-orthodoxy" which reasserted the doctrines of God's sovereignty and human sinfulness.

In attempts to discover its occasion and purpose, modern scholars have identified Romans as: a manifesto of Paul's deepest convictions, his position paper on vital Christian issues, the apostle's last will and testament, and Paul's letter of self-introduction. To clarify our own understanding of the book, we will examine its background, occasion and purpose, genre, and structure.

2. *The Occasion*

The letter was probably written in Corinth or Cenchrea, the port city of Corinth (Rom 16:1-2), shortly before Paul's trip to Jerusalem with a collection for the poor (Rom 15:25,31; cf. 1 Cor 16:1-3). This period corresponds with his three-month stay in Achaia according to Acts 20:2-3. The date is months before Pentecost (June) of AD 57, Paul's arrival in Jerusalem. It is probably

[1]Further discussion of these parallels is found in our treatments of James, 1 Peter, and Hebrews. See also W. Sanday and A. C. Headlam, *The Epistle to the Romans*, ICC (Edinburgh: T. & T. Clark, 1905) liv–lxii, lxxiv–lxxxv.

the winter of late 56 or early 57, since he left Achaia for Philippi by the Passover (April) according to Acts 20:6.[2]

3. The Church at Rome

The origin and development of the Roman church are obscure. We know that its existence was well known to Paul (Rom 1:8), although at the writing of the letter he had not been there. On a number of occasions (1:13) and for a number of years (15:23) he had sought to visit them, perhaps on his way to Spain (Rom 1:13; 15:22-25,28).

A vague allusion in Suetonius *Lives of Twelve Caesars* ("Claudius" 25) states that "since the Jews constantly made disturbances at the instigation of Chrestos, he (Claudius) expelled them from Rome." If the "the instigation of Chrestos" refers to preaching about Christ, and not some Jewish agitator named "Chrestos," it may indicate that there was a Roman church before AD 49 when the expulsion took place. Support for this Christian interpretation is found in Acts 18:2 where Aquila and Priscilla left Italy for Corinth "because Claudius had ordered all Jews to leave Rome." After the death of Claudius (AD 54) the ban was lifted and Jews, like Aquila and Priscilla, were able to return home (Rom 16:3; see also Dio Cassius *Roman History* 60.66).

Plausible support for a Roman church comprised of both Jews and Gentiles can be gleaned from Paul's letter. If Rom 16 was addressed to Rome (which we maintain), some of the Christians there had distinctly Jewish names (e.g., Aquila, Andronicus and Junia, "fellow countrymen," and Herodian). Also, several of Paul's arguments seem to presuppose a Jewish Christian audience (e.g., 4:1; 15:7-8). In addition to Jewish believers, Paul explicitly addresses Gentile Christians in 11:13-32 and probably 15:10-11. Unfortunately, only general clues can be derived from the above examples since it is difficult to distinguish the real from the im-

[2]For further discussion see Jewett, *Chronology* 49–50,100–3; G. Lüdemann, *Paul, Apostle to the Gentiles: Studies in Chronology*, trans. F. S. Jones (Philadelphia: Fortress, 1984); W. M. Ramsay, *St. Paul The Traveller and Roman Citizen*, 1897 ed. (Grand Rapids: Baker, 1962 reprint) 286–89.

agined addressees in Paul's style of argumentation (e.g., 2:1,17; 3:1,3; 9:19).

4. The Purpose of the Letter

Based on our discussion of the background situation, it appears that Paul sought the support of the Roman Christians for his immediate mission to Jerusalem and a future mission to Spain. Concerning his trip to Jerusalem Paul asks for the prayer support of the Roman Christians, since he expects opposition in the Jewish city (15:30-31). Regarding his anticipated trip to Spain, Paul hoped that Rome would serve as a base of operation for a western mission (15:22-25,28). He, therefore, anticipates the hospitality of the Roman Christians when he eventually visits them (15:22-25,28-29,32; also 16:1-2,23). It is with this background data that we can understand Paul's interest in writing to Rome, his constant mention of the Roman Christians in his prayers (1:9), and his desire to visit them soon (1:10-11,13).

Even though there has been much debate on the intended purpose of Romans,[3] our study has led us to some specific conclusions. The following themes, therefore, surface as major reasons for writing the letter: to promote solidarity, to secure support, and to encourage hospitality. These points will be explained in our discussion of the book's rhetorical structure.

5. The Integrity of Chapter 16

Because of its unusual contents (e.g., greetings to 26 people) and the displacement of the closing doxology in certain Greek manuscripts (i.e., 16:25-27, after chs 14 [mss A, P, L] or after

[3]The difficulty of acquainting the content of Romans with its purpose is underscored in: W. S. Campbell, "Why Did Paul Write Romans?" *ExpT* 85 (1974) 264–69; G. Bornkamm, "The Letter to Romans as Paul's Last Will and Testament," 17–31 and G. Klein, "Paul's Purpose in Writing the Epistle to the Romans," in *Romans Debate* (1977) 32–49, and G. Klein, "Romans, Letter to" in *IDBSup* 753–54; A. J. M. Wedderburn, *The Reasons for Romans* (Minneapolis: Fortress, 1991).

15 [p[46]]), it has been argued that Rom 16 was not originally part of the letter. Some have even argued that it was a letter fragment addressed to the Ephesians.[4] However, for the following reasons, Rom 1–16 has been viewed as a complete work. First, the textual evidence is too diverse to support the Rom 1–15 position, since, for example, Marcion's text and other manuscripts (A, P, L) end at ch 14! Second, the familiar names of ch 16 have ties with Rome and even the unknown names were common there (e.g., Latin inscriptions). Third, it can be shown that the numerous greetings of ch 16 serve as effective appeals for what Paul is trying to accomplish in the letter.[5]

6. The Genre of Romans

Because Paul is unable to be present in Rome he communicates with the Christians there by means of a letter. Romans contains all the features of an early Christian letter: opening, 1:1-7; thanksgiving, 1:8-17; body, 1:18–11:36; parenesis, 12:1–15:13; a travelogue, 15:14-32; and a lengthy closing 15:33–16:27 (including ch 16).

What type of letter is Romans? It is much longer than the typical letters of antiquity, has a didactic emphasis, and reads like a public or official document. Because of these features, it has been suggested that Romans is a letter-essay comparable to the

[4]See the textual problems outlined in: Metzger, *Textual Commentary* 533–41. For Romans 16 as a letter fragment addressed to Ephesus, see T. W. Manson, "St. Paul's Letter to the Romans—and Others," *BJRL* 31 (1948) 224–40; J. I. H. MacDonald, "Was Romans xvi a Separate Letter?" *NTS* 16 (1969–70) 369–72; N. R. Peterson, "On the Ending(s) to Paul's Letter to Rome," in *The Future of Early Christianity,* B. Pearson, ed. (Minneapolis: Fortress, 1991) 337–347.

[5]For arguments supporting Rom 1–16 as a complete letter, see K. Donfried, "A Short Note on Romans 16," *JBL* 89 (1970) 441–49; H. Gamble, *The Textual History of the Letter to the Romans* (Grand Rapids: Eerdmans, 1977) 36–55; C. K. Barrett, *The Epistle to the Romans*, HNTC (New York: Harper & Row, 1957) 9–13; C. E. B. Cranfield, *The Epistle to the Romans*, 2 vols., ICC (Edinburgh: T. & T. Clark, 1975) 1:5-11; J. B. Lightfoot, *St. Paul's Letter to the Philippians* (London: Macmillan, 1913) 171–77; Sandy and Headlam, *Romans* 418–28; T. Zahn, *Introduction to the New Testament*, 3 vols., trans. J. M. Trout et al., 3rd. ed., 1909 (Grand Rapids: Kregel, 1953) 1:389–94, 419–21.

letters of the philosopher Epicurus (Laertius *Lives* 10) and the biographer Plutarch (*Moralia* 1012B–1030C). All of these letters have an instructive (didactic) function, a public character (e.g., "I-you-they"), and are written by authoritative figures. Identifying Romans as a letter-essay, however, does not fully explain Paul's specific appeals and objectives in writing it. Therefore, it is also necessary to discern and outline the rhetorical structure, as we have done with the Galatian and Corinthian correspondences.

7. The Rhetorical Structure

Because of Paul's concern for Christian solidarity and his didactic emphasis in Romans, the letter corresponds impressively with epideictic or demonstrative rhetoric.[6] In comparison with the judicial persuasion of Galatians, Romans is not as defensive in tone, nor is it concerned with the issue of wrongdoing. Unlike the deliberative rhetoric in 1 Corinthians, Romans does not focus on issues of expediency and practical necessity. What seems to be Paul's effort here is to affirm common beliefs and values with the intention of gaining support from his readers.

a. Basic Features

Epideictic rhetoric is concerned with the display of common values and virtues held by both the addressor and addressees. "Epideictic" comes from the Greek word *epideixis*, meaning "a display" or "demonstration." This type of persuasion is characteristic of funeral orations, political speeches, and addresses at festivals or games. They seek to secure public sentiment by extolling the common virtues of the audiences addressed. Epideictic rhetoric has its roots in *encomia*, which attempts to honor certain individuals because of their outstanding characters or accomplishments.

[6]Discussions and outline of Romans as epideictic rhetoric have been adapted from: W. Wuellner, "Paul's Rhetoric of Argumentation in Romans," in *Romans Debate* (1977) 152–74.

b. Examples from the Greco-Roman World

Examples of epideictic oratory are: the speech of Pericles praising the virtues of Athens, in Thucydides, *The Peloponnesian Wars* 2.34-46 (5th cent. BC); the funeral oration of Aspasia to the Athenians, in Plato, *Menexenus* 236E–249C (4th cent. BC); and most of the speeches found in Isocrates *Panegyrics*, *Plataicus* (4th cent. BC), and Lysias *Olympicas* (late 4th cent. BC). In American history examples of epideictic rhetoric are: Lincoln's Gettysburg address, political campaign speeches, and most presidential addresses. All of these attempt to secure public sentiment and support by affirming common values (or denouncing common vices).

c. A Structural Outline of Romans

The structure of demonstrative speeches is discussed in the rhetorical handbooks of Aristotle, Cicero, and Quintilian. Paul's letter coincides well with the arrangement recommended by the rhetoricians.

The Rhetorical Structure of Romans

I. Introduction (exordium)	1:1-15
Letter opening	1:1,7
Thanksgiving	1:8-10
Occasion and thesis (v. 12 common faith)	1:8-15
II. Transition (transitio)	1:16-17
III. Exposition of argument (confirmatio)	1:18–15:13
A. Theological argument (probatio): God's righteousness in Christ	1:18–11:36
1. Negative argument: the human predicament without Christ (common vices)	1:18–3:20
2. Positive argument: righteousness by faith in Christ (common beliefs and values)	3:21–5:21
3. Fundamental assumptions: union with and participation in Christ	6:1–8:39
4. Israel and God's righteousness in Christ: Israel's present unbelief and God's sovereignty, God's future dealings with Israel	9:1–11:36
B. Practical exhortations (exhortatio): Christian solidarity	12:1–15:13

1. In worship and church relations	12
2. Concerning state and public relations	13
3. On issues concerning weak and strong	14:1–15:13
IV. Closing (conclusio)	15:14–16:23
A. Recapitulation of thesis (peroratio)	15:14-15
B. Travelogue: Paul's duties and plans	15:16-29
C. Personal appeals (*pathos*)	15:30–16:24
Greetings topoi	16:3-16,23
Doxology	16:25-27
Benediction	15:33; 16:20

In the exordium (1:1-15) Paul seeks to win the confidence of his audience and to affirm the common values which he and the Romans share. He appeals to *ethos* in order to establish himself as an agent of the gospel for the nations (1:1,5,14). His sense of identity and mission seems to correspond to that of the Roman Christians (1:8); this shared understanding becomes the basis for his ministry among them (1:5-6,13-15). As a result, Paul establishes his apostolic relations in the Roman churches and affirms those values which he and the Romans share as mutual agents of faith throughout the world (1:11-12).

Paul's concerns expressed in the exordium are restated in the closing (15:14–16:23). The peroratio (15:14-15) reiterates his thesis: he is convinced of their complete knowledge of Christianity but is writing to intensify adherence to their common faith. In the travelogue (15:16-29), Paul again conveys the *ethos* of his apostolic identity and mission. It is followed by an emotional appeal (*pathos*) for Roman support in prayer, because of the opposition awaiting him in Judea (15:30-32).

Paul's desire that he and the Romans be mutually encouraged by his visit, in the exordium (1:12), is reiterated in the conclusio by his hope to be spiritually refreshed by their company (15:30). The apostle's recommendation of Phoebe (16:1-2) and his list of greetings topoi (16:3-24) underscore his concern to encourage hospitality among the Romans. In direct opposition to the common values of Paul and his readers are "those who cause dissension and scandal" (15:17-20). This rhetorical arrangement lends additional support to the disputed view that ch 16 is an integral part of the letter.

Since it has been shown in the exordium and conclusio that Paul's major concern is to affirm common values, Rom 1:18–15:13 displays the evidence (confirmatio). Romans 1:16-17 serves as a transition from Paul's final comments in the exordium (1:13-15) to the exposition of his theological argument in the probatio (1:18–11:36).

The confirmatio consists of a probatio (1:18–11:36) and exhortatio (12:1–15:13). The probatio is concerned with Paul's doctrinal discussions on sin, divine judgment, justification/righteousness, faith, divine grace, union/identity with Christ, spiritual inheritance, Israel's unbelief, and God's sovereignty. These are the basic vices and virtues of the common faith that Paul shared with his readers.

8. Content

How common was this faith that Paul assumed on the part of his readers? Let us compare some of the central beliefs of Paul with the Judaism and Hellenism of his day. Paul's teaching on salvation by grace would have found some agreement with the Jews he encountered in debate. Israel's obedience to the law was also viewed as a covenant response to God's gracious election of Israel.[7] The verb, "be made righteous" (or "be justified"), however, is distinctly Pauline, denoting salvation by Christ.

What also distinguished Paul from his contemporary Jews were his views of both the death of Christ and participation in his death and resurrection. The death of Christ, for Paul, inaugurates the dawn of a new age and the birth of a new humanity. Participation in his death and resurrection frees one from the old covenant which required obedience to the law and places one in the realm of faith.[8] Possession of the Spirit is a guarantee of this new

[7]Note, e.g., the following passages on divine election as a basis for Torah obedience: Ex 19:3-6; Dt 4:35-40; Mekilta Bachodesh 1, 5-6, 10; Sifra Shemini pereq 12.4; Jub 1:17-18, 25; 2:19-20; Pss Sol 9.9-11.

[8]For further discussion on Paul and the Judaism of his day, see the excellent study: E. P. Sanders, *Paul and Palestinian Judaism: A Comparison of Patterns of Religions* (Philadelphia: Fortress, 1977). See also W. D. Davies, *Paul and Rabbinic Judaism: Some Rabbinic Elements in Pauline Theology* (London, 1948; 4th

vital relationship. Paul's discussions of human sinfulness and the frustration of keeping the law are therefore examples of the human condition without Christ. Even Paul's universalism, eliminating distinctions between Jew and Greek, has significance only for those who are "in Christ." Although his "in Christ" teaching has some Greco-Roman influences (e.g., communion with deity in the mystery cults, "one humanity" in Stoicism and Gnosticism), this vision of new self-awareness was not determined by private mystical experiences or mythological speculations. Concerning good works, they do not merit salvation for Paul (as in Judaism), but are a characteristic of one who "walks in newness of life," and an expression of service to Christ as the Lord (e.g., Rom 12–15). It is plausible that the Roman Christians affirmed most of these beliefs with Paul, especially if they were acquainted with some of his co-workers.

9. Style of Argumentation

In his argumentation, Paul employs the dialogical style of the diatribe.[9] This Socratic form of discussion was used by teachers in philosophical schools to censure the false views of students and lead them into truth (e.g., Epictetus, Plutarch, Seneca). These errors of students were exposed in the objections and false conclusions of an imaginary dialogue partner, i.e., interlocutor. By exposing these errors, the teacher was able to lead his students into a more correct understanding of philosophy and life.

ed., Philadelphia: Fortress, 1980); J. A. Sanders, "Torah and Christ," *Int* 29 (4, 1975) 372–90; S. Sandmel, *The Genius of Paul* (New York: Farrar, Strauss and Cudahy, 1958); H. Raisanen, *Paul and the Law* (Philadelphia: Fortress, 1986); H. J. Schoeps, *Paul, The Theology of Paul in the Light of Jewish Religious History*, trans. H. Knight (Philadelphia: Westminster, 1961).

[9]Discussion of the diatribe is found in ch 1, "The Ancient Letter Genre." For further discussion, see S. K. Stowers, *The Diatribe and Paul's Letter to the Romans* (Scholars Press, 1981); idem, "Paul's Dialogue with A Fellow Jew in Romans 3:1-9," *CBQ* 46 (4, 1984); A. J. Malherbe, "*Mē Genoito* in the Diatribe and Paul," *HTR* 73 (1/2, 1980) 231–40; idem, *Moral Exhortations, A Greco-Roman Sourcebook* (Philadelphia: Westminster, 1986) 129–34; Donfried, *Romans Debate* (1977) 133–41.

Since Paul's claims were controversial because of their implications for Christian behavior, he could effectively employ the diatribe form to indict false viewpoints and to lead his readers to a more correct understanding of his teachings. The dialogical forms in Rom 2–4; 6; 9–11; 14, therefore, do not contain polemics against opponents, but are didactic devices to lead his Christian readers into truth by exposing error.

Basic features of the diatribe include the following points. (1) It begins with an *apostrophe* or indicting address to an imaginary interlocutor (e.g., Rom 2:1,2,17,21; 9:19f.). Usually the interlocutor is a caricature of a proud or pretentious person who is censured by exposing his moral contradictions or rejecting his behavior. (2) Objections to the author's claims (e.g., Rom 3:1,2,7f.; 9:19; 11:19) or false conclusions drawn from the author's argumentation (3:9; 6:1,15-16; 9:14; 11:1,11) are raised either by the imaginary objector or the author himself. The author's reactions to them are diverse: abrupt rejection (e.g., *mē genoito*), counter question, example, analogy, wise saying, or indicting address. (3) A dialogical exchange follows where the author or the interlocutor leads the question but the author/teacher is in control and guides the discussion to its resolution (e.g., Rom 2:17-29; 3:27–4:12; 9:19-21). All of the above characteristics are found in the diatribes of Teles, Epictetus, Musonius Rufus, Plutarch, and Seneca (3rd cent. BC–1st cent. AD).

The diatribe form plays an important role in the teachings of Rom 1–11. By using it, Paul was able to expose erroneous views and lead his readers into a more correct understanding of the Christian faith. The didactic function of the diatribe complements the epideictic rhetoric of Romans and assists Paul's central purpose in writing the letter (cf. 1:8-15; 15:14-15). In Romans Paul was not concerned with polemics against opponents or with addressing specific church problems, but with promoting the Christian faith through dialogue and persuasion.

10. The Issue of Context

Even though many of the parenetic statements in the exhortatio seem to reflect situations in the church at Rome, this is unlikely.[10] The "expedient advice" rendered here is typical of that given to Paul's other churches. The exhortatio even contains stereotyped phrases and rhetorical devices found in other letters. For example, the discussion of the "weak" and "strong" reads like a generalized adaptation of Paul's more specific advice in 1 Corinthians (e.g., Rom 14:1-2/1 Cor 10:25,27; Rom 14:13/1 Cor 8:9; Rom 14:15/1 Cor 8:11; Rom 14:17/1 Cor 8:8; Rom 14:21/1 Cor 8:13). Furthermore, it is difficult to discern which specific groups or positions are addressed, since there are many general principles that are readily applicable to both (e.g., Rom 14:3,5c,13a,17-19,22-23; 15:2-12).

Since Paul had never been to Rome when he wrote his letter, it would be inappropriate to maintain that a precise correspondence exists between his arguments in Romans and actual situations in Rome. Even if Paul had received information on the Roman church from co-workers, like Phoebe or Aquila and Priscilla, it would still be secondhand data. If Paul did address actual problems in Rome, he did not prepare new teaching for a new situation. As we have shown, much of the content in Romans is typical of earlier "occasional" letters. Furthermore, our external sources for understanding the setting of the Roman church are both rare and obscure, providing little confirmation for theories on the Roman situation from Paul's letter.

Throughout the lengthy body of Romans, it becomes apparent that the apostle is attempting to encourage doctrinal harmony and Christian solidarity. This general concern to secure support by affirming common values is announced in the exordium, developed in the confirmatio through exposition and dialogue, and reiterated in the conclusio.[11]

[10]For example, in P. S. Minear, *The Obedience of the Faith*, SBT 19 (London: SCM, 1971), it is argued that Romans was written to deal with five specific factions of "weak" and "strong" Christians residing in Rome. This position has been refuted in R. J. Karris, "Rom. 14:1–15:13 and the Occasion of Romans," in *Romans Debate* (1977) 75–99. Some of these refutations have been used in our discussion of Rom 14–15, above. In our treatment of Rom, as in Gal, the deliberative functions of the ethical exhortations (Rom 12–15; cf., Gal 5–6) is influenced by, and therefore subordinate to, a broader rhetorical concern (i.e., epideictic in Romans; cf., judicial in Galatians).

[11]For further study of Romans, see Barrett, *The Epistle to Romans*; Cranfield, *The Epistle to the Romans*; C. H. Dodd, *The Epistle of Paul to the Romans*,

11. Summary

Paul's letter to the Romans, which drew upon his earlier teachings, became his most influential writing in both the NT and church history. The apostle probably wrote his letter from Corinth around AD 56–57 before his trip to Jerusalem with a collection for the poor. His reasons for writing include: (1) a request for their prayer support as he journeys to Jerusalem, (2) the encouraging of Christian hospitality when he fulfills his plan to visit Rome on his way to Spain, (3) a concern to secure their support as fellow agents of the gospel to the nations, and (4) an implied motive to establish a Roman base of operation for his westward mission to Spain (which he never undertook).

Paul's purposes for writing Romans coincide well with epideictic rhetoric, a form of persuasion that attempts to secure audience sentiment by extolling common virtues. The arrangement of Romans seems to follow what is recommended by the rhetorical handbooks. This approach also appropriately focuses on the rhetorical situation of the author instead of the hypothetical situation of the readers. In Romans, Paul's theological arguments and practical exhortations are concerned with reinforcing the common values shared by both him and the Romans. The letter promotes doctrinal harmony, ecclesiastical solidarity, and Christian hospitality. In writing Romans, the apostle hopes to secure support for his ministry by intensifying adherence to the beliefs and virtues that he held in common with the Roman Christians.

MNTC (New York: Harper & Row, 1932); K. Donfried, "False Presuppositions in the Study of Romans," in *Romans Debate* (1977) 120–48 (and other significant articles in that volume); J. D. Dunn, *Romans 1–8* and *Romans 9–16* (Dallas: Word, 1988). N. Elliott, *The Rhetoric of Romans* (Sheffield: JSOT, 1990). A. J. Guerra, "Romans: Paul's Purpose and Audience with Special Attention to Rom 9–11," *RevBib* 97 (1990) 219–37. A. J. Hultgren, *Paul's Gospel and Mission, The Outlook from His Letter to the Romans* (Philadelphia: Fortress, 1985); E. Käsemann, *Perspectives on Paul*, trans. M. Kohl (Philadelphia: Fortress, 1971); idem, *New Testament Questions of Today*, trans. W. Montague (Philadelphia: Fortress, 1969) 168–216; idem, *Commentary on Romans*, trans. G. Bromiley (Grand Rapids: Eerdmans, 1980); L. E. Keck, *Paul and His Letters*, 2nd ed PrC (Philadelphia: Fortress, 1988); J. Munck, *Paul and the Salvation of Mankind*, trans. F. Clarke (Atlanta: John Knox, 1977, orig. ed. 1959) 196–206; Sanders, *Paul and Palestinian Judaism*; Schoeps, *Paul*; K. Stendahl, *Paul Among Jews and Gentiles* (Philadelphia: Fortress, 1976).

6

Philippians and Philemon

1. Introduction

Philippians and Philemon, together with Colossians and Ephesians, are often labeled the Prison Epistles of Paul. There are several reasons for this identification. First, all purport to be written by the Apostle Paul (Phil 1:1; Phlm 1; Col 1:1; 4:18; Eph 1:1; 4:1). Second, all refer to Paul as a prisoner (Phil 1:7,13,14; Phlm 1,9; Col 4:18; Eph 3:1; 4:1; 6:20). Third, many of the same co-workers are mentioned. Both Philemon and Colossians mention Onesimus and Archippus (e.g., Phlm 1,12,17; Col 4:9-10,17). Both Colossians and Ephesians refer to Tychicus in a very similar manner (Col 4:7; Eph 6:21). Philippians, Philemon, and Colossians all refer to Timothy as Paul's co-sender (Phil 1:1; Phlm 1; Col 1:1).

Nevertheless, there are some difficulties with the classification of "Paul's Prison Epistles." First, the Pauline authorship of Colossians and Ephesians is suspect by many. Second, Ephesians reads more like a baptismal liturgy or homily than an early Christian letter. Third, Philippians stands apart from the other so-called Prison Epistles. The personal names in this letter are different: Epaphroditus (2:25; 4:18), Euodia and Syntyche (4:2). The travel plans are distinctive (2:19,23-29) and Paul's situation in prison was more uncertain than in the other letters (1:20-26; 2:17,24). Fourth, from what location did the imprisoned apostle write? In this chapter, we will discuss some of these questions as they relate to Philippians and Philemon.

2. Philippians

This letter opens a door into Paul's personal and pastoral character. It also provides helpful information about one early congregation with whom the apostle had fond and enduring relationships.[1]

a. The City of Philippi

Paul addressed his letter to the Christians who resided in Philippi (1:1). At the time he wrote, Philippi was already an old city. It was founded in 357 BC by Philip II of Macedon, the father of Alexander the Great, who named it after himself. It was located eight miles from the Aegean Sea in a fertile region enriched by an abundance of springs. Gold was also mined nearby.

After the Roman victory over the Persians in 168 BC, Philippi became part of the Roman Empire and belonged to the first four regions of Macedonia. It was also a major station along the *Via Egnatia*, a Roman road stretching from Adriatic coast to Byzantium. During the reign of Augustus (27 BC–AD 14), Philippi became a Roman colony and military outpost. As a colony it enjoyed the benefits of *ius Italicum* which gave the inhabits the same economic and legal privileges as the Italians.[2]

b. The Church at Philippi

The book of Acts and Paul's letters provide some information on the apostle's initial and continuing relationship with the church. Acts 16:6-40 provides a dramatic account of Paul's first visit to

[1]Commentaries and other works on Philippians are: F. W. Beare, *A Commentary on The Epistle to the Philippians*, 2nd ed. (London, 1969); F. F. Bruce, *Philippians,* NIBC (Peabody: Hendrickson, 1989); J. T. Fitzgerald, "Philippians, epistle to the," *ABD* 5:318–26; G. F. Hawthorne, *Philippians,* WBC (Dallas: Word Books, 1983); R. P. Martin, *Philippians* (Grand Rapids: Eerdmans, 1976); idem, *Carmen Christi, Philippians 2:5-11*, rev. ed. (Grand Rapids: Eerdmans, 1983); P. T. O'Brien, *Epistle to the Philippians* NIGTC (Grand Rapids: Eerdmans, 1991); Schmithals, *Paul and the Gnostics.*

[2]Acts 16:12; A. N. Sherwin-White, *Roman Society and Roman Law in the NT* (Oxford, 1963) 92–95; Cadbury in *BC* 4:190.

Philippi. The following five features find support in Philippians. First, a Roman presence is evident in the city (Acts 16:12,21,37-38; Phil 1:13,22). Second, prominence is given to women at the establishing of the church (e.g., Acts 16:14,40; Phil 4:2). Third, there are also the mention of hostile outsiders (Acts 16:19-24; cf. Phil 2:14) and the presence of Gentiles within the community (Acts 16:14-15,27-34; Phil 2:19,25; 4:2). Fourth, Paul stayed in contact with the Macedonian churches through Timothy (Acts 19:21-23; Phil 2:19,20) and probably visited them again at least twice (Acts 20:1-3; 2 Cor 7:5-6). Fifth, the apostle mentioned gifts sent to him from Philippi (Phil 4:15-16; 2 Cor 8:1-5; Acts 26:17) and maintained a positive attitude towards the community throughout his ministry.

c. *The Opponents*

Philippians 3:2–4:3 begins with some sharp warnings against false teachers and contains many statements that seem to denounce them. A variety of opinions have surfaced concerning the identities of the opponents presupposed in this passage.[3]

Judaizing Opponents. The following data in Phil 3:2–4:3 suggest a Judaizing threat. In describing his opponents as "dogs" (3:2), Paul could be denouncing the Judaizers with the same term of reproach they applied to immoral people or Gentiles (e.g., Isa 56:10-11; Mt 7:6; 15:26-27; Pseudo-Clementine *Homilies* 2.19). In Phil 3:2, a subtle Greek word change is employed to underscore the derogatory tone: the opponents are called "mutilators" (*katatomē*) instead of the more positive "circumcisers" (*peritomē*). Such defamation is reminiscent of Paul in Gal 5:12, "I wish they. . . would castrate themselves!" The mention of true circumcision (Phil 3:3) represents a stance in contrast to Judaism or Judaizing Christianity (e.g., Rom 15:8; Gal 2:7-9; Eph 2:11). The warning, "put no confidence in the flesh" (Phil 3:3), appears to be an implicit rebuttal of the Judaizers who did the opposite (e.g., Gal 6:13).

[3]Eighteen different types of opponents have been postulated by J. Gunther, *St. Paul's Opponents and Their Background* (Leiden: E. J. Brill, 1973) 2.

One apparent point of Paul's biographical sketch (Phil 3:4-11) is to respond to Jewish or Jewish-Christian claims of righteousness by works (cf. Rom 9:31; 10:5; Gal 2:21). Elsewhere Paul has referred to Jews "boasting" in their spiritual privileges (Rom 2:19-20). Paul's statements about not yet attaining perfection (Phil 3:12,14) may be a dialogue with the Jewish practice of attaining righteousness through the law (Rom 9:30-32). The reference to the opponents as "enemies of the cross" (Phil 3:18) could either denote the Jews to whom the cross was a scandal (1 Cor 1:23) or Judaizing Christians who might have evaded Jewish ridicule of the cross by promoting circumcision (Gal 6:12). The severe hyperbolic language in Phil 3:19 may be abusive rhetoric expressing Paul's anger and not necessarily characterizing a particular group (cf. Rom 16:18). Perhaps the group preaching Christ out of envy and selfish ambition (Phil 1:15,17) is also comprised of Judaizing Christians. It is plausible that just as Judaizers infiltrated the Pauline church of Galatia, so also a similar occurrence took place at Philippi; this would explain the harsh language of Phil 3:2,18-19 (esp. if it is a later letter fragment).

Gnostic Opponents. There is also persuasive evidence for gnostic opposition from within the Philippian congregation. When Paul speaks of those who put confidence in the flesh (3:3-4), he may be referring to Gnostics who boast of their exalted spiritual state (e.g., *Book of Thomas the Contender* 138.8-13; *Treatise of the Great Seth* 60.4-13). Paul's priority of obtaining the "excellency of the knowledge (*gnōseōs*) of Christ Jesus" (3:8) appears to be gnostic language used against the Gnostics. Paul's goal "to know" Christ and "the power of his resurrection" (3:10) and to "attain the resurrection of the dead" (v 11) is a present experience already claimed by the Gnostics (*Exegesis on the Soul* 134.7-16; *Gospel of Philip* 73.1-5). That is why Paul is quick to assert that he has not attained this state of perfection (Phil 3:12) in contrast to gnostic claims (e.g., *Gospel of Truth* 42.26-34). The apostle appears to address Gnostics as perfect ones (*teleioi*, Phil 3:15) in stressing Christian perfection as a future goal to attain rather than a present reality already experienced. His address to the perfect ones that "God shall *reveal* even this to you" (v 15) almost sounds like a sarcastic parody of gnostic revealed knowledge (e.g., *Seth* 50. 22-25; *On the Origin of the World* 127.6-17).

Paul's denouncement of his opponents as "enemies of the cross" (Phil 3:18) is applicable to Gnostics who despised the doctrine of the cross (e.g., *Apoc Pet* 74. 14-15) and denied that Jesus actually died on the cross (*Apoc Pet* 81,17-24). The harangues about those "whose god is their belly and whose glory is in their shame, who mind earthly things" (Phil 3:19) may refer to the immoral lifestyle of libertine Gnostics (Irenaeus, *Against Heresies* 1.6.2-3; Epiphanius, *Panarion* 25-26). The reference to awaiting the parousia of the Lord Jesus (Phil 3:20) appears to counter the realized eschatology of Gnosticism (*Gospel of Thomas,* sayings 51,113). Paul's hope for the transformation of our humble bodies into ones glorified like Christ's (Phil 3:21) seems anti-gnostic. The human body and the material world had no place in the redemptive scheme of Gnosticism (e.g., *Exegesis on the Soul* 134.7-30; *Gospel of Philip* 59,29-34).

Summary. Who were the opponents in Phil 3:2–4:3? From the above data, there are a number of possibilities: Judaizers and/or Gnostics, Jews and/or libertines, Jewish-Gnostics, perfectionist Christians, or pneumatics. From the evidence in Philippians it appears to us that Paul was addressing two different types of opponents: Judaizers from outside who are infiltrating the church and Gnostics influencing the church from within.[4] First, we find no convincing reason why Jews would pose a doctrinal and ethical threat to the Gentile congregation at Philippi. We have evidence, however, of a real threat that Judaizing Christians could bring to the Gentile congregations of Galatia. As in Philippi, these opponents were Jewish-Christian legalists who practiced circumcision. Second, the libertine and perfectionist problems that are evident in Philippians probably indicate gnostic opponents. There are sufficient parallels from gnostic writings to lend support to this claim.

d. The Christ Hymn of Philippians 2

Although Paul opposed certain Jewish and gnostic groups, the Christ Hymn of Phil 2 may serve as an example of the common

[4]Our position is similar to that found in R. Jewett, "Conflicting Movements in the Early Church as Reflected in Philippians," *NovT* 12 (1970) 367–90.

thought milieu that he shared with them. Even though Paul was anti-Gnostic, his hymn of Phil 2:6-11 (probably pre-Pauline) has contacts with the gnostic redeemer myth. First, the mention of Christ's preexistence has parallels in Gnosticism (*Odes of Solomon* 41.15; *First Apocalypse of James* 24.21-25; *Treatise on the Resurrection* 44,23-37; *also*: Wis 6:22; Sir 24:9).[5] Second, his existence "in the form of God" is also found in gnostic thought (*1 Apoc Jas* 25,1-5; 33,21-24; *also*: Philo).

Third, the descent of the Savior to the world has parallels (Mandean Liturgies 196-197; Seth 59,17-29; *Apoc Adam* 77.27-82,19; *Ascension of Isaiah* 10.17-30; *also*: Sir 24:8; Wis 9:10,16-17). Fourth, the Savior appeared in human *form* (*Gospel of Thomas* 28; *Gospel of Truth* 31.4-8; *Ascension of Isa* 11.1-18; *Treatise on Resurrection* 44,14-20). Fifth, the Redeemer suffered and died (*Gospel of Truth* 20,10-14; 20,23-21,2; *Ascension of Isa* 11.19-20; *also*: Jewish martyrology). Sixth, his return to the Father and exaltation also has parallels (*Treatise on Resurrection* 45.15-39; *Odes of Solomon* 41.12; *Ascension of Isa* 11.22-32; *Apocryphon of James* 14.20-41). Seventh, worship of the exalted Redeemer is enjoined (e.g., *Ascension of Isa* 11.32,36; *Apocryphon of James* 15.15-24) and innumerable titles are ascribed to him (e.g., Illuminator, the True Man, the Logos, the Soter, the Shepherd—all found in the Nag Hammadi codices).

As shown above, the vision of Christ in the Ascension of Isa 9.27-32; 10.17-11.32, which probably derives from the gnostic scheme of the Ophites (2nd cent. AD; in Irenaeus, *Against Heresies* 1.30.12-14), provides the most complete parallel to the Christ hymn of Phil 2:6-11. It does not, however, reveal any direct dependence on the Phil 2 hymn or any other NT hymn. The Phil 2 hymn, in the comparison, reads like a summary of the more extensive Christ myth in the *Ascension of Isaiah.* Although the latter work is later than Philippians (2nd cent.), it does contain earlier traditions (e.g., the Jewish martyrdom of Isa).

The above contacts of the Christ hymn of Phil 2:6-11 and Gnosticism seem to indicate that it originated in an oriental environment similar to that of Gnosticism. The obvious parallels with Jewish wisdom motifs reinforce the view of a common en-

[5]Reference will also be made to Hellenistic Jewish parallels which are not *explicitly* gnostic but contain features of oriental "gnosis."

vironment permeated by oriental gnosis.[6] Thus the Apostle Paul, who was anti-Gnostic, shared certain conceptions and perceptions with those whom he identified as opponents.

e. A Composite Letter

The suggestion that Philippians is a composite letter was first made in the seventeenth century[7] and this view has gained an increasing number of supporters through the years.[8] If 2 Corinthians is comprised of two to four letters, then it is not incredible to conceive of Phil as a composite of several letter fragments. Polycarp in his *Letter to the Philippians* even suggests it when he mentions that to the Philippians Paul "wrote letters" (*egrapsen epistolas*, Pol *Phil* 3.2).

There are at least three internal reasons for viewing Philippians as a composite letter. (1) There is an abrupt change from 3:1 and 3:2 which introduces a polemical section (3:2–4:3) whose tone is notably different from the rest of the letter. (2) Verses 3:1 and 4:4 fit together so well that it seems they were editorially separated. (3) Why would Paul wait until the very end of the letter (4:10-20) to thank the Philippians for their gift of support? Those who attempt to address these problems in defense of the letter's original unity usually resort to questionable psychological explanations (e.g., sudden despondency in prison, forgetfulness) or indefensible suggestions (e.g., belated stimulus from Timothy, the arrival of new reports). We have no parallels like the above in any single letter of Paul's.[9] We therefore maintain that Philip-

[6]Jonas, *Gnostic Religion* 13–27. See also the supporting view that the Jewish Wisdom myth is only a variant on the Revealer-myth developed in Hellenistic and gnostic literature, in R. Bultmann, *The Gospel of John, A Commentary*, trans. G. R. Beasley-Murray, et al. (Philadelphia: Westminster, 1971) 23.

[7]Stephan le Moyne, *Varia Sacra* (1685) 2:332–34 in Schmithals, *Paul and the Gnostics* 68 n. 14.

[8]Bornkamm, Koester, Schmithals, Beare, Gnilka. For survey of discussion, see G. Hawthorne, *Philippians* xxix–xxx.

[9]Even our argument for the unity of 2 Cor 1–9 presupposes that it is composite of three letter fragments (1–7; 8; 9) hastily combined by the apostle in Macedonia around AD 56 (see ch 4, Corinthian Correspondence). For two different positions on the question, see Hawthorne, *Philippians* xxxi–xxxii (favors unity) and Schmithals, *Paul and Gnostics* 67–81 (defends composite nature).

pians was originally comprised of three separate letters, which will be outlined below with annotations.[10]

Philippians as a Composite Letter

Occasion 1	*Letter A*	*Structure*
Paul (in prison in Ephesus? 4:14) receives a gift from the Philippian community via their "apostle" (2:25), Epaphroditus (ca. AD 54)[11]	Paul thanks Philippians for their gift	Prescript (lost) Body (4:10-20) Closing (4:21-23)
Occasion 2	*Letter B*	*Structure*
Epaphroditus ill (2:25-30); Paul, a prisoner in Ephesus, hears of divisions and adversaries in Philippi (1:27-30; ca. AD 55)	Paul's second letter, shortly before Corinthian correspondence	Prescript (1:1-2) Thanksgiving (1:3-11) Body (1:12–3:1;4:4-7) Closing (4:8-9)
Occasion 3	*Letter C*	*Structure*
Occasion 2 escalates; Epaphroditus returns to Philippi; Paul plans to send Timothy and to visit himself (1:26; 2:19-30; ca. AD 55)	Paul repeats admonition, this time more urgent	Prescript (lost) Body (3:2–4:3) Closing (4:8-9?)

f. The Date and Place of Composition

The questions of dates and location of composition are related issues for both Philippians and Philemon.[12] The dates are depen-

[10]Derived from: Schmithals, *Paul and Gnostics* 79–80.

[11]Theories on date and place will be explained in the next section.

[12]The dates and locations of Colossians and Ephesians will be discussed in a separate chapter.

dent on the following locations for the writing of Paul's prison letter: Caesarea (AD 57–58), Rome (AD 60–61), or Ephesus (AD 54–55).[13]

We will first examine the evidence from Philippians and Philemon before comparing it with the data on the three locations. (1) Paul was in prison when he wrote (Phil 1:7,13,17; Phlm 1,9-10,13). (2) He faced a trial that could end in his death (Phil 1:19-20; 2:17) or acquittal (1:25; 2:24; Phlm 22). (3) Wherever the location was there was a Roman praetorium guard (1:13) and "those who belonged to Caesar's household" (4:22). (4) Timothy was with Paul (Phil 1:1; 2:19-23; Phlm 1). (5) Evangelistic efforts were going on around Paul at that time (1:14-17). (6) The apostle planned to visit Philippi if he was acquitted (2:24). (7) Numerous trips were made to Philippi from where he wrote: (a) news came to them concerning Paul's arrest, (b) they sent Epaphroditus to Paul with a gift, (c) news about Epaphroditus came back to Philippi, (d) word reached Paul that they were greatly concerned about Epaphroditus, and (e) the apostle hoped to send Timothy back to them and receive encouragement from him before Paul himself set off for Philippi (2:19,24).[14]

A comparison of the above data with the three localities provides the following observations. (1) There is explicit mention in a secondary source of Paul's imprisonments in Caesarea (Acts 24:23,27) and Rome (Acts 28:16, 30-31; cf. 1 Clem 5.7; Eusebius, *Eccl Hist* 2.22). From two of Paul's own letters there are probable allusions to an Ephesian imprisonment (1 Cor 15:32; cf. Ign Rom 5.1; esp. 2 Cor 1:8-10) and the possibility of more than two imprisonments (2 Cor 11:23-25; cf. 1 Clem 5.6). (2) The prospect of a trial which would result in death or acquittal might be deduced from Acts concerning the Caesarean and Roman detentions. However, 2 Cor 11 and 1 Clem 5 imply more than two life-threatening trials and 2 Cor 1:8-10 seems to indicate a life-threatening detention specifically in Asia. (3) The praetorium more frequently denotes the imperial guards stationed throughout the provinces and

[13]Dates are based on the conclusions in ch 2: A Chronology of Paul's Life.

[14]Seven points derived from: Hawthorne, *Philippians* xxxvii. The data from Col and Eph will be discussed in a separate chapter.

is not necessarily restricted to Rome.[15] "Those of Caesar's household" could refer either to the highest officials in Roman government or the lowest servants in the emperor's household.[16] As a result, the allusions could point to Ephesus, Caesarea, or Rome. (4) From Paul's undisputed letters, we learn that Timothy was with Paul in Ephesus at the writing of 1 Corinthians (1 Cor 4:17; 16:10). From the secondary source of Acts we have one reference that Timothy accompanied him to Jerusalem (Acts 20:4). One can only deduce from this single reference that Timothy was possibly with Paul in Caesarea (Acts 24) and Rome (Acts 28). (5) Acts 19 presents a picture of busy evangelistic activity in Ephesus. Acts 21:8-10 alludes to the work of Philip the Evangelist with his daughters in Caesarea. Acts 28 refers to other Christians at Rome (v 15) and Paul's liberty to preach while under house arrest (vv 30-31). (6) Second Corinthians 1:16; 2:13; 7:5; and Acts 20:1-2 each mention Paul's subsequent travel through Macedonia after his ministry (and detention) in Ephesus. There is no evidence of Paul's returning to Macedonia after his Caesarean or Roman imprisonment. (7) Although sea and road travel had greatly improved in the Roman provinces, Ephesus is the closest and best location to explain the four or five trips presupposed in the Philippian correspondence.

Because points 4–7 argue favorably for it and points 1–3 support it as well as any other location, we favor Ephesus as the place of imprisonment from which Paul wrote Philippians and Philemon. Ephesus is also the most probable city toward which a runaway slave from nearby Colossae (i.e., Onesimus) would flee. Furthermore, if Paul were imprisoned in Rome or Caesarea, he would scarcely have entertained the prospect of a visit to distant Colossae in the immediate future (Phlm 22). The Ephesian origin would place the date of both Philippians and Philemon around AD 55.[17]

[15]J. B. Lightfoot, *St. Paul's Epistle to the Philippians* (London: Macmillan, 1913) 99–104.

[16]Lightfoot, *Philippians* 171–78.

[17]Paul's Ephesian imprisonment of AD 55 provides an even longer time frame for Paul's three letters to the Philippians than would the Macedonian setting of 56 for the last of Paul's Corinthian correspondence (2 Cor 1–7; 8; 9).

3. Philemon

The letter to Philemon[18] is the shortest of Paul's letters, consisting of 335 words in the original Greek. From our chapter on the letters of antiquity, we noted that Philemon shares more characteristics with the personal correspondence of ancient Egypt (e.g., letters of request and recommendations) than any other in the NT. John Knox stated that Philemon was a letter to a church embodied in a letter to an individual. He also believed that it was included in the NT canon because of the influence of Onesimus, the runaway slave in Philemon who later became bishop of Ephesus (according to patristic tradition). In this section, the above comments will be addressed as we examine the occasion, form, and rhetorical structure of Philemon

a. The Occasion

The occasion of the letter may be inferred from its contents. A slave named Onesimus had wronged his owner Philemon, a Christian living at Colossae (cf. the names in vv 1,2 with Col 4:9,17), and had run away. Somehow Onesimus had come into contact with Paul, either as a fellow prisoner or because he had sought refuge with the apostle's associates (a provision in Athenian law). It appears that Onesimus had stolen money and departed secretly (v 18). Roman law required that whoever gave hospitality to a runaway slave was liable to his master. This law may explain Paul's promise to pay back the amount (v 19). The primary purpose of the letter, therefore, is to ensure that Philemon will receive back the delinquent slave, although Paul may be hoping that Onesimus be returned to him (v 21).

[18]Most commentaries include Philemon with Colossians, see E. Lohse, *Colossians and Philemon*, Hermeneia, trans. W. Poehlmann et al. (Philadelphia: Fortress, 1971); P. T. O'Brien, *Colossians, Philemon,* WBC (Dallas: Word Books, 1982); A. G. Patzia, *Colossians, Philemon, Ephesians,* NIBC (Peabody, Mass.: Hendrickson, 1991). See also J. Knox, *Philemon among the Letters of Paul,* 2nd ed. (Nashville: Abingdon, 1959); L. A. Lewis, "An African American Appraisal of the Philemon-Paul-Onesimus Triangle," *Stony the Road We Trod* (Minneapolis: Fortress, 1991) 232–46. Martin, *NT Foundations* 2:310–16; M. L. Soards, "Some Neglected Theological Dimensions of Paul's Letter to Philemon," *PRS* 17 (1990) 209–19.

To show forgiveness to a criminal slave was a revolutionary act in contrast to the customary treatment of runaway slaves (e.g., imprisonment, flogging, crucifixion). Even though Paul does not request the slave's emancipation, v 16 brings us into an atmosphere in which the institution of slavery could only wilt and die.[19]

b. Philemon: The Genre

Paul employs the conventional letter writing format in Philemon. For example, a comparison of Paul's letter with that of Apion the soldier to his father Epimachus will establish this point. Extensive comparisons have also been made between Philemon and numerous papyri letters.[20]

The type of appeal made in Philemon has parallels in late antiquity. A good illustration of a plea for clemency on humanitarian grounds is seen in the younger Pliny's letters to Sabinianus (*Epistles* 9.21,24).[21] He intercedes for a young freedman who sought refuge in Pliny's home and is full of fear at the prospect of his master's wrath. Pliny grants the master's right to be angry but tries to steer Sabinianus in the direction of clemency because of the deserter's repentance, amendment of life, and his own request to be forgiven. From the second letter (9.24) it appears that Pliny's intercession was successful.

c. The Rhetorical Structure

Paul also appears to utilize the basic techniques of persuasion widely practiced in his day. A rhetorical analysis of Philemon, consulting the handbooks of Aristotle, Cicero, and Quintilian,

[19]F. F. Bruce, "St. Paul in Rome (2): The Epistle to Philemon," *BJRL* 48 (1965–66) 90.

[20]See our discussion of Philemon in ch 1, The Ancient Letter Genre. See also J. White, "The Structural Analysis of Philemon," SBLASP (Missoula, Mont.: Scholar's Press, 1971) 1–47; Chan-Hie Kim, *Form and Structure of the Familiar Greek Letter of Recommendation*, SBLDS 2 (Missoula, Mont.: Scholar's Press, 1972).

[21]*Pliny, Letters and Panegyricus*, 2 vols., trans. B. Radice, LCL (1975) 2:119–21, 126–7.

will verify this observation.[22] As in deliberative rhetoric, Paul is concerned with influencing a decision in the future concerning Onesimus that is fair, honorable, and beneficial for the whole community.

The Rhetorical Structure of Philemon

I. Epistolary prescript	vv 1-3
A. Senders	1a
B. Recipients	1b-2
C. Greeting	3
II. Exordium (or "Introduction")	vv 4-7
A. Paul secures the good will of Philemon (captatio benevolentiae)	v 4
B. Paul praises Philemon for those qualities upon which the outcome of the case depends (i.e. his love and koinonia)	vv 5-6
III. Confirmatio (or "Proof")	vv 8-16
A. Appeals to Paul's apostolic authority *(ethos)* and Philemon's compassion *(pathos)*	vv 8-10
B. Appeal to the motive of utility: the usefulness of Onesimus	v 11
C. Paul substitutes himself for Onesimus the offender	v 12
D. Appeal to honesty in the situation	v 13-14a
E. Appeal to the motive of honor: Philemon's opportunity to do a good deed	v 14b
F. Appeal to God's design in the situation	vv 15-16
IV. Peroration (reiteration of argument)	vv 17-22
A. Restates request with *pathos*: So if you consider me your partner (*koinōnon*) receive him as you would me.	v 17
B. Amplifies argument	vv 18-19
1. Paul anticipates Philemon's objections by offering restitution	vv 18-19
2. Paul reminds Philemon that he owes the apostle his very life	v 19b
C. Appeal to *pathos*: refresh my heart in Christ	v 20
D. Secures Philemon's favor	vv 21-22

[22]Our discussion and outline are adapted from: F. F. Church, "Rhetorical Structure and Design in Paul's Letter to Philemon," *HTR* 71 (1/2, 1978) 17–33.

V. Epistolary postscript	vv 23-25
A. Greetings from Paul's associates	vv 23-24
B. Benediction	v 25

Unlike Pliny's letter to Sabinianus, Philemon is not an appeal for clemency. It provides an opportunity to instruct Philemon and his community on practical Christian love. Although the letter is addressed to Philemon the slave owner, Apphia, Archippus, and their house church are also included. The tradition that this Onesimus is the one who later became bishop and was responsible for the preservation of this letter cannot be proven.[23]

4. Summary

In this chapter we looked at two of the so-called Prison Epistles of Paul. We first discussed Philippians. We noted that the city of Philippi was a Roman colony and military outpost which Paul visited on his first mission into Europe (Acts 16; Phil 1–2). After founding a community there he maintained contact with it through messengers, letters, and visits (Acts 19–20; Phil 2; 2 Cor 7:5-6). The opponents at Philippi appear to be of two types: Judaizers from without and Gnostics from within (Phil 3:2–4:3). Although Paul confronts the perfectionist notions and libertine practices of Gnosticism, he seems to have used traditions shared by the Gnostics in his description of the divine preexistence, earthly descent, and subsequent exaltation of Christ (Phil 2:6-11). Because of the presence of a startling polemical section (3:2–4:3) and delayed thanks for the church's gift (4:10-20), we believe that Philippians is a composite of three letters (A, 4:10-23; B, 1:1–3:1; 4:4-9; C, 3:2–4:3). The letters were probably written by Paul from prison in Ephesus around AD 54–55.

Philemon, the second Prison Epistle, is the shortest of Paul's letters. It shares many characteristics with the ancient papyri correspondence of Egypt. Its contents are similar to Pliny the

[23]Ignatius addressed Onesimus the church leader with a possible allusion to Phlm 20 (Ign Eph 2.2). On this basis J. Knox maintains that the above church leader must have been the same Onesimus addressed in Philemon.

Younger's letter to Sabinianus in which an appeal for clemency is made on behalf of a freedman. Paul's appeal on behalf of Onesimus, a runaway slave, uses the techniques of deliberative rhetoric to instruct Philemon and his community on the practice of Christian love. Within the epistolary format, the letter divides easily into exordium 4–7, securing goodwill and introducing points to be amplified in both the proof, 8–10 and peroration 17–22. In his proof, Paul appeals to the motives of utility, honesty, honor, and God's design, using much *ethos* and *pathos*. Paul restates and amplifies his argument in the peroration, using more *pathos* and securing Philemon's favor.

From a prison in Ephesus, it appears that Paul was still able to carry on an effective letter-writing ministry. Like the "Letter from A Birmingham Jail" (1963) by Martin Luther King, Jr., these captivity writings of Paul demonstrate the power of the pen in the hand of an incarcerated church leader.

7

The Thessalonian Correspondence

1. Introduction

The letters to the Thessalonians are considered by many to be the earliest Christian writings. They reveal some of the problems and aspirations of a young church. First Thessalonians, for example, is thought to have been written within twenty years of Jesus' ministry, shortly after Paul's founding of a community in Thessalonica, Macedonia (Acts 17; 1 Thes).

Despite the importance of these letters, difficulties arise when the two are compared and contrasted. How do we explain the close similarities and the sharp differences? Many arguments have also been posited against the Pauline authorship of 2 Thessalonians. In response to these problems, several theories have been presented concerning the destination, the chronological order, and editorial arrangement of the letters.

In our survey of 1 and 2 Thessalonians we will first look at background information, before examining the documents themselves. The background data consist of discussions on the city of Thessalonica, Paul's relationship to the church there, and the problems of the Thessalonian church. In our examination of the documents, we will deal with questions of authorship, destination, date, literary character, and rhetorical function.[1]

[1]Commentaries consulted in this study are: E. Best, *The First and Second Epistles to the Thessalonians* (London: Black, 1972); F. F. Bruce, *1 and 2 Thes-*

2. The City of Thessalonica

Unlike most cities that Paul visited, Thessalonica still exists as the modern Salonika. It also had a long history prior to Paul. It was first associated with the name, Therme, probably because of the nearby hot spring. It became a place of importance around 300 BC when it was rebuilt by Cassander, a general of Alexander the Great. He named the city, "Thessalonica" after his wife. Under Roman rule, Thessalonica was the capital of one of four Macedonian districts (167 BC). Later (146 BC) the Romans made Macedonia a province with Thessalonica its administrative center. In the first century, the local magistrates were called "politarchs," a title found in both Acts 17:6,8 and inscriptions from the site (e.g., Vardar Gate of Thessalonica).

Thessalonica was not only an administrative center, its location was beneficial for trade and commerce. It was situated on the Roman Via Egnatia, a main traffic artery between Rome and her eastern provinces. Thessalonica also possessed a fine natural harbor on the Thermaic Gulf (now, Gulf of Salonika).

3. The Church at Thessalonica

Our main sources for Paul's founding of a church at Thessalonica are Acts 17:1-10 and 1 Thessalonians. Allusions to "Macedonia" in Acts 19–20 and Paul's letters (1 and 2 Cor, Rom, Phil) assume subsequent visits and contacts with Thessalonica.

According to Acts 17:1-10, Thessalonica was the second European city in which Paul preached. In company with Silas (Silvanus?) and Timothy, Paul crossed the Aegean Sea from Asia. After visiting Philippi and a few small towns, the apostle arrived in Thessalonica (ca. AD 49).

salonians, WBC (Dallas: Word Books, 1982); J. Frame, *Epistles of Paul to the Thessalonians,* ICC (Edinburgh: T. & T. Clark, 1912); I. H. Marshall, *1 and 2 Thessalonians*, NCBC (Grand Rapids: Eerdmans, 1983); and L. Morris, *The First and Second Epistles to the Thessalonians*, NIC (Grand Rapids: Eerdmans, 1959 rev. ed. 1991). C. A. Wanamaker, *The Epistles to the Thessalonians: A Commentary on the Greek Text* NIGTC (Grand Rapids: Eerdmans, 1990); D. J. Williams, *1 and 2 Thessalonians* NIBC (Peabody, Mass.: Hendrickson, 1992). Special studies will be mentioned under the appropriate topics.

From Acts 17 we can note the following points. First, the church of Thessalonica was composed of Jews and Gentiles associated with the synagogue (vv 2,4). Second, Paul's preaching about Jesus as the Messiah who suffered and rose from the dead (vv 2-3) was misinterpreted to mean the announcement of a new ruler in opposition to the Roman emperor (v 7). Third, the persecution that ended Paul's three-week visit (v 2) was caused by the Jews (vv 5-6). Fourth, Paul left for Athens waiting for his associates who later rejoined him in Corinth (Acts 17:14-16; 18:1,5).

The allusions in 1 Thessalonians suggest a situation somewhat different from Acts. First, the addressees of 1 Thessalonians are converts from paganism not Judaism (1:9). There is no evidence of a Jewish community in 1 Thessalonians. Second, if 1 Thessalonians was written shortly after Paul's first visit (the majority opinion), a period longer than three weeks (Acts 17:2,10) is presupposed. The considerable follow-up ministry (1 Thes 2:9-12) and strong affection shown to the Thessalonians (2:8; 3:6-10) imply a stay of months, rather than weeks. Third, there is no indication in 1 Thessalonians that persecution was instigated by Jews. The reference in 1 Thes 2:14, probably an interpolation,[2] compares the situation of the Thessalonians to believers in Judea who suffered from the Jews. Fourth, according to 1 Thes 3:1-2, Paul was willing to be left behind in Athens while Timothy was sent back to Thessalonica. In Acts, neither Timothy nor Silas were with Paul in Athens, but rejoined him later in Corinth (Acts 17:14-16; 18:5).

Two explanations can be given for the discrepancies between Acts 17 and 1 Thessalonians. (1) Either the account of Acts gives an incomplete picture, or one that is presupposed but unmentioned in 1 Thessalonians. (2) The discrepancies are due to special Lukan concerns a generation after Paul.[3] For example, the mention of Jewish opponents was to show the Romans that Christianity was a harmless religion persecuted by the Jews and possibly to make

[2]B. Pearson, "1 Thes 2:13-16: A Deutero-Pauline Interpolation," *HTR* 64 (1971) 79–94.

[3]We are assuming here that Luke–Acts was written ca. AD 80–90. The author appears to be a third generation Christian (Lk 1:1-4) and not a companion of Paul. For further discussion, see W. G. Kümmel, *Introduction to the New Testament,* rev. ed. trans. H. C. Kee (Nashville: Abingdon, 1975) 150–51, 185–87.

the synagogue instead of the church the object of Roman consternation. This latter explanation seems more plausible and less naively harmonistic.

In agreement with 1 Thessalonians, however, Acts provides the following information. First, Paul's visit to Thessalonica had been preceded by a trip to Philippi, where they were "shamefully treated" (1 Thes 2:2; Acts 16:19-24). Second, Paul's stay in Thessalonica was attended by trouble and the persecution of converts (1 Thes 1:6; 2:14; Acts 17:5-9). Third, after leaving Thessalonica Paul went to Athens (1 Thes 3:1; Acts 17:14-16). Fourth, Paul writes to the Thessalonians when he is rejoined by Timothy and Silas/Silvanus (1 Thes 1:1; 3:6) which is probably in Corinth (Acts 18:1,5). It is at this time (AD 50) that Paul probably wrote 1 Thessalonians. Some argue that 2 Thessalonians was written shortly afterward.

Paul's continuing relations with Macedonia, which probably included Thessalonica, are alluded to in Acts 19–20 and also in Paul's Philippian, Corinthian, and Roman correspondences. From these references it appears that all was well. Paul commends them for their fidelity under persecution and their generous giving (Rom 15:26; 2 Cor 8:1-5). Toward the end of Paul's Ephesian ministry (AD 55) he planned to pass through Macedonia on his way to Corinth (1 Cor 16:5). Both 2 Cor 7:5 and Acts 20:1-6 indicate that Paul revisited Macedonia (AD 56) before his final trip to Jerusalem.

4. Church Problems

Defining the church problems Paul encountered at Thessalonica is a hypothetical enterprise. First, we cannot be sure if Paul's polemical or antithetical statements were occasioned by historical circumstances or are merely stock phrases which distinguish his ministry from others.[4] Second, we cannot be certain that both 1 and 2 Thessalonians reflect similar situations, since the authenticity of 2 Thessalonians is suspect. Nevertheless, we will exam-

[4]This latter possibility is developed in A. Malherbe, " 'Gentle as a Nurse,' the Cynic Background of 1 Thes 2," *Nov Test* 12 (2, 1970) 203–17.

ine some of the statements in each letter which could have been occasioned by historical circumstances and present our own explanations of the problems.

It appears that the Thessalonian church had undergone some type of "affliction" or "oppression" similar to that experienced by Paul and his associates (*thlipsis* 1:6; 3:3-4,7). The community also experienced the death of certain members which troubled them as they awaited the nearness of the Lord's return (4:13-18). Some were possibly doubting the near and sudden return of the Lord (5:1-11).

There also seem to have been problems of both sexual immorality (4:3-5) and social irresponsibility (4:11-12; 5:14; cf. 2:9). Perhaps there was even disrespect for Christian leaders (5:12) and some doubts about the credibility of Paul's ministry (2:3-8,10).

If there were problems of sexual license and social irresponsibility at Thessalonica this "libertinism" was characteristic of some later forms of Gnosticism (e.g., those attacked by Irenaeus and Epiphanius; possibly the Nicolaitans and the opponents in Jude).[5] Gnostics also disclaimed a future parousia by reinterpreting it in a present spiritual sense (e.g., Gospel of Thomas 51; 113).[6] It is also noteworthy that the affliction and death of certain members would be especially troubling to spiritual enthusiasts like those encountered by Paul at Corinth (e.g., 2 Cor 10–12).[7] Even if the problems faced by Paul in Thessalonica were merely the symptoms of Christianity in a pagan environment, it appears to be on a trajectory towards Gnosticism.

In 2 Thessalonians, which closely follows 1 Thessalonians, the following situation can be reconstructed. The recipients are des-

[5]For sources on libertine Gnosticism see Clement *Stromateis* 3, 7; Irenaeus *Against Heresies* 1.6, 2-3; Epiphanius *Panarion* 25–26; and probably Jude 4, 7, 8, 10, 12, 16, 18-19; 2 Pet 2:2, 10, 13-14, 18-19; Rev 2:6, 14-15, 20-22, 24.

[6]See also *Gospel of Philip* 73, 1-5; *Treatise on the Resurrection* 48, 4-7; 49, 10-17; and *Exegesis on the Soul* 134, 7-16. Schmithals, *Paul and the Gnostics* 123–218.

[7]This view is developed in R. Jewett, "Enthusiastic Radicalism and the Thessalonian Correspondence," *SBL 1972 Proceedings* 1:181–232. This type of enthusiastic radicalism may also have been an early form of Gnosticism as Jewett himself notes. See also R. Jewett, *The Thessalonian Correspondence* (Philadelphia: Fortress, 1986).

ignated as those enduring afflictions by unbelievers (1:4-8). They are shaken by the circulation of a pseudonymous letter announcing that the day of the Lord has arrived (2:2). There are those living in idleness who refuse to work for a living (3:6-12). Some also question the authority or credibility of the author of 2 Thessalonians (3:14-15,17).

If the above statements reflect actual problems in the community, it appears to be a type of libertine Gnosticism. There seem to be some in the community who have spiritually experienced a final resurrection which has subsequently freed them from the bondage of this world and all obligations connected with it.[8]

If there are any similarities between the two situations presupposed in 1 and 2 Thessalonians it is in the area of church problems. The recipients of both letters have experienced (1 Thes) or are experiencing (2 Thes) affliction. The clues for positing an early form of gnostic heresy in 1 Thessalonians are even more convincing in 2 Thessalonians.

5. *Authorship and Authenticity*

a. 1 Thessalonians

The Pauline authorship of 1 Thessalonians is no longer seriously challenged. Its characteristic grammar, spontaneity, and personal style point to Paul as its author. The papyrus manuscripts (p^{46} ca. AD 200; also p^{30}, p^{61}, p^{65}), every extant canonical list, the oldest versions of the NT, and the patristic citations from the second century onward mention the letter.

b. 2 Thessalonians

The authenticity of 2 Thessalonians is a more questionable matter.[9] Although 2 Thessalonians claims to be written by Paul (1:1; 3:17) and has some external and internal evidence to support it,

[8]See also our discussion of Gnosticism at Corinth in ch 4.

[9]See J. Bailey, "Who Wrote 2 Thessalonians?" *NTS* 25 (1979) 131–45; D. Schmidt, "The Authenticity of 2 Thessalonians: Linguistic Argument," *SBL 1983 Seminar Papers* 289–96; F. Beare, "Thessalonians, Second," *IDB* 4:626.

numerous problems challenge this contention. We will look at the support for its authenticity before examining its problems.

Arguments For Authenticity. By the second and third centuries, 2 Thessalonians received wide acceptance. For example, it is in one or two early papyri manuscripts (p^{30} ca. AD 300; prob. p^{46} ca. 200). It is also echoed in Polycarp *Letter to the Philippians* (ca. 140; 11.3/2 Thes 1:4; 11.4/2 Thes 3:15). Furthermore, it is listed in the Muratorian Fragment (2nd or 4th cent.) and included with 1 Thessalonians in Marcion's collection (ca. 140). Finally, Irenaeus quoted it by name (ca. 180), and both Clement of Alexandria and Tertullian of Carthage (3rd cent.) regarded it as authentic.

Now let us discuss the internal support. Second Thessalonians 2 shares a basic eschatological assumption with Paul's undisputed letters: the end has not yet come. Most of the language and style is also Pauline (e.g., "our gospel, give thanks, parousia, so then, finally, not anyone," parentheses like 1:10b). Finally, the letter structure of an opening with a lengthy thanksgiving, a body closing with a benediction, and a long parenesis is Pauline (e.g., 1 Thes, 1 and 2 Cor, Phil, Rom).

Despite the above statements favoring authenticity, there are at least four major arguments against the authenticity of 2 Thessalonians when it is compared with 1 Thessalonians. These four statements are: 2 Thessalonians is a close imitation of 1 Thessalonians; 1 and 2 Thessalonians have specific eschatological differences; there are distinct changes in mood; and a period of historical and theological development is presupposed in 2 Thessalonians.

Arguments Against Authenticity. The literary and structural parallels are outlined below:[10]

	2 Thes	*1 Thes*
A. Letter Opening	1:1-12	1:1-10
1. Prescript	1:1-2	1:1
2. Thanksgiving	1:3-12	1:2-10

[10]Bailey, "Who Wrote 2 Thes?" 133.

B. Body of Letter	2:1-16	2:1–3:13
1. Second thanksgiving	2:13	2:13
2. Closing benediction	2:16	3:11-13
C. Parenesis	3:1-15	4:1–5:22
D. Closing of Letter	3:16-18	5:23-28
1. Prayer of peace	3:16	5:23-25
2. Greetings	3:17	5:26
3. Benediction	3:18	5:28

Second Thessalonians has all the structural features of 1 Thessalonians, although it is hardly more than half as long. No other two Pauline prescripts are so similar (A 1). Both give thanks for the congregation and use similar vocabulary (A 2; e.g., "faith, love, endurance, affliction"). Both include the emphatic "we" in the body (B 1). The fact that 2 Thessalonians contains the second thanksgiving of 1 Thes 2:13-16, which is probably a later interpolation,[11] also casts doubts on its Pauline authorship.

The benediction (B 2) has the same two subjects, "God the Father" and "our Lord Jesus Christ" and the phrase "establish your hearts." At the end of the body (B) and the beginning of the parenesis (C) there are the same topics: handed down traditions, Paul's commands, "to establish." In the parenesis (C), both begin with "finally" and have similar vocabulary (e.g., "we exhort, brothers, in the Lord Jesus, live according to the traditions received by Paul"). After a similar prayer for peace (C,D 1), they close with almost identical benedictions (D 3). It is unusual for Paul to follow slavishly the structure of his previous letter.

Close thematic parallels also occur (e.g., 1 Thes 2:9/2 Thes 3:8; 1 Thes 4:7/2 Thes 2:13b-14). Concerning the first set (e.g., "remember our labor and toil") there are no other parallels in the Pauline corpus so close. Why would such a creative writer like Paul draw upon his previous work in such an unimaginative way?

The second argument against authenticity concerns the eschatological differences. First Thessalonians stresses the imminence of the parousia, whereas 2 Thessalonians states that the parousia will

[11]Pearson, "1 Thes 2:13-16," 79–94.

not take place until the "rebellion" occurs, the "man of lawlessness" appears and the "restrainer" is taken away. These two eschatologies appear contradictory. Either the end will come suddenly without warning (1 Thes) or it will be preceded by a series of apocalyptic events which warn of its coming (2 Thes). Although some apocalypses contain these contrasting features (e.g., Mt 24:3-35 and 36-44),[12] it is unusual for Paul to give two distinct types of advice to the same church at the same general time.[13]

When 2 Thessalonians is compared with 1 Thessalonians a more formal and official tone emerges. Except for 3:1,7–9, 2 Thessalonians lacks the personal style that is characteristic of 1 Thessalonians. Those verses are all that correspond to over thirty verses of personal remarks in 1 Thes 2:1–3:10. In contrast, the tone of 2 Thessalonians is official and formal. For example, instead of "we give thanks" (1 Thes 1:2); there is "we are *bound* to give thanks" (2 Thes 1:3; 2:13). Also, Paul writes of his desire to see and instruct the Thessalonians (1 Thes 3:10), but this desire is neither reiterated or alluded to in 2 Thessalonians.

In our comparison, an historical and theological development is presupposed in 2 Thessalonians. We will first look at passages implying a lengthy passage of time (2:2; 3:17), before mentioning the motifs and phrases that appear post-Pauline.

If the letter was written by Paul shortly after 1 Thessalonians (ca. 50), there are certain passages that seem to challenge this assumption. First, would it be necessary for Paul, at such an early date, to warn his readers against the advice of letters circulated in his name without his authority (2 Thes 2:2)? Would the circulation of false Pauline letters have been the tactic of Paul's opponents, who generally questioned his credentials and authority (e.g., 2 Cor 10:10; 11:5; Gal 1:10–11)? If the above tactic is improbable, why would Paul, therefore, feel obligated to guarantee the authenticity of his own letter (3:17)? A statement in this

[12]In our chapter on Matthew's Gospel, we argued that the author included both divergent and conflicting traditions in his Gospel to moderate between various opposing factions in his community. This situation of factions is not evident to us in the situation of Paul at Thessalonica (e.g., Acts 17; 1 Thes; cf. 2 Thes).

[13]This particular line of argument assumes that both letters were written within a few years of each other if 2 Thes is authentic. The problem is alleviated if each letter is addressed to a different audience at a different time.

passage is puzzling: "the mark in every letter" (*ho sēmeion en pasē epistolē* 3:17). How many letters had Paul written at this time? Only 1 Thes was previously written.[14] But the phrase "every letter" and the need to provide a mark of authenticity for each, seem to imply an extensive correspondence of many years (cf. 2:15).

The next point concerns the nature of the opposition presupposed in certain passages. Second Thessalonians 2:2 refers to a pseudonymous letter claiming that "the day of the Lord has come." If this teaching of a "realized eschatology" is gnostic, it also explains the additional problem addressed in 2 Thessalonians: idleness and disorderly conduct (3:6–13). Since these troublemakers have now experienced the final resurrection, they are freed from the bondage of this world and all obligations to it. This position would therefore be that of libertine Gnosticism. Although a nascent form of Gnosticism may have surfaced as early as the mid-first century, a period near the end of the first century is more likely because of the type of problem addressed in 2 Thessalonians.

Finally, let us look at some motifs that appear post-Pauline. In many passages we detect an increased importance of the "Lord Jesus" over "God," presupposing a high Christology of later generations (e.g., *1 Clem* 20.12; 21.6; Ign *Eph* 3.2; 18.2).

2 Thes	*1 Thes*
"beloved of the Lord," 2:13	"beloved of God," 1:4
"the Lord is faithful," 3:3	"God is faithful," 5:24
"the Lord of peace," 3:16	"the God of peace" 5:23

In another passage of 2 Thes, Christ is addressed as God (1:12). Paul could have addressed Christ in this manner (possibly in Rom 9:5), but it is primarily a characteristic of early catholicism (e.g., Ign *Eph* 18.2; Ign *Rom,* intro.).

Another post-Pauline feature of the letter is the idea of divine vengeance upon the persecutors of Christians (1:5–10). This conception seems to belong to a generation after Paul, expressed more

[14]In our chapter on Galatians, we argued that Galatians was not Paul's first letter, but was written around AD 54.

poetically in Rev 16:5–7 and 19:2. Also, the related motif of divine vengeance for the murder of Jesus and persecution of Christians is post-Pauline (e.g., Barn 16.5; Justin *Apology* 1.47; *Gospel of Peter* 7.25). This is one reason why 1 Thes 2:15-16 (which contains this theme) is regarded as Deutero-Pauline.[15]

6. Literary and Chronological Theories

In response to some of the literary and chronological problems connected with the Thessalonian correspondence, the following theories have been postulated. They are: different destinations, rearrangement of chronological order, and a composite work of more than two letters.

a. Different Destinations

The first destination theory is that 2 Thes was addressed to a separate house church of Jewish Christians in Thessalonica (A. Harnack, 1910). Early Christians worshipped in house churches (e.g., Rom 16:5; 1 Cor 16:19; Col 4:15; Acts 12:12) and there were usually several at each location (e.g., Rom 16:3-15). However, there are two problems with this theory. Why would so much of 1 Thessalonians be repeated in 2 Thessalonians if the former letter was to be circulated to "all the brethren" (5:27)? Also, why is no reference to 1 Thessalonians made in 2 Thessalonians? Second Thessalonians 2:2 refers to a pseudonymous letter, not 1 Thessalonians.

A second destination theory is that 2 Thessalonians was misnamed and formerly addressed to the Philippians (E. Schweizer, 1945). Titles for the NT books were not given until the second century and it is possible that some were misnamed. However, the only data for this theory are two passages in Polycarp, *Letter to the Philippians*. One reveals Polycarp's acquaintance with 2 Thes 1:4 (Pol *Phil* 11.3) and the other mentions that Paul wrote "letters" (plural) to the Philippians (3.2). The theory supposes that 2 Thes-

[15]Pearson, "1 Thes 2:13-16," 84.

salonians was the second letter to the Philippians. It lacks sufficient evidence.

b. Reversal of Order Theory

The major theory of chronological rearrangement argues that 2 Thessalonians was written before 1 Thessalonians (Manson, 1953). The reversal of order could have been due to the tendency to place longer letters first. For example, the NT order of books from Rom to 2 Thessalonians is according to size with the longest first. This procedure is evident in the fourth century lists. Second Thessalonians also appears to have a cruder eschatology and anticipates persecution, whereas 1 Thessalonians has a more developed eschatology and views persecution as past. Finally, specific topics discussed in 1 Thes 4:9,13; 5:1 might be interpreted as responses to questions raised from reading 2 Thessalonians (e.g., 2 Thes 3/1 Thes 4:9-12; 2 Thes 2/1 Thes 5:1). For example, the *peri* sections in 1 Thes 4:9–5:11 ("concerning the") are said to concern problems arising from a previous letter (cf. 1 Cor 7:1; 8:1).

There are, however, a number of problems connected with the above rearrangement of the Thessalonian letters. First, our earliest lists of NT books were not arranged according to size or length (e.g., Marcion, Clem of Alexandria). Second, why is there no specific mention of a previous letter in 1 Thessalonians? Paul usually refers to his previous correspondences (e.g., 1 Cor 5:9; 2 Cor 2:3-4). Third, the "more primitive" eschatology of 2 Thes can be explained by its greater dependence on more traditional apocalypticism, as in Revelation. Fourth, in 1 Thessalonians Paul speaks of persecution as a *continuous* threat (3:3) as well as a past event. Fifth, there are no specific points of correlation between topics discussed in 1 Thessalonians and what is already mentioned in 2 Thessalonians.[16] For example, it is difficult to see how 1 Thes 4:9 specifically deals with the reluctance of the church to apply the harsh discipline commanded in 2 Thes 3:6-15. Also, 1 Thes

[16]For further discussion and critiques, see Best, *Thes* 42–45; D. Guthrie, *New Testament Introduction,* 3rd ed. (Downers Grove, IL: InterVarsity Press, 1970) 575–78; and Marshall, *Thes* 11–16.

5:1-11 need not presuppose a previous discussion of the parousia set forth in 2 Thes 2. The death of Christians (1 Thes 5) would be a shock to any congregation that believed it would live to see the Lord's return.[17]

c. *The Composite Letter Theory*

The most influential composite theory of the Thessalonian correspondence is outlined below.[18]

A. 2 Thes 1:1-12; 3:6-16 (first letter sent on hearing news of gnostic enthusiasm in the church)

B. 1 Thes 1:1–2:12; 4:2–5:28 (an attempt to counter gnostic charges against the credibility of his ministry)

C. 2 Thes 2:13-14; 2:1-12; 2:15–3:3,5,17-18 (Paul's reply to news that a letter ascribed to him has been circulated and has encouraged eschatological fanaticism)

D. 1 Thes 2:13–4:1 (Paul's joyful letter after Timothy has returned from Thessalonica with a good report)

This composite theory is based on the following views: (a) an earlier letter fragment in 1 Thessalonians (2:13-4:1); (b) 2 Thessalonians, or a fragment of it, preceding 1 Thessalonians; (c) 2 Thessalonians is comprised of two letters written by Paul; and (d) the Thessalonian correspondence countered a unified opposition of gnostic enthusiasm. Although an interpolation exists in 1 Thes 2:13-16, there are insufficient reasons to challenge the letter as a unified composition.[19] The problems with the chronological priority and Pauline authenticity of 2 Thessalonians have already been emphasized. Finally, we have argued that 1 and 2 Thessalonians, even though they address related problems of "gnosis," are separated historically from each other. Although we favored elsewhere a composite theory for Phil (ch 6), the evi-

[17]Jewett, "Enthusiastic Radicalism," *SBL* (1972) 1:190–91.

[18]Schmithals, *Paul and the Gnostics* 123–218. It is discussed and refuted in Best, *Thes* 17–19 and Marshall, *Thes* 15-16.

[19]For extensive argumentation, see Best, *Thes* 30–35.

dence here is insufficient to endorse a similar theory for the Thessalonian correspondence.

7. The Date and Place of Composition

Based on our previous discussion in this chapter, 1 Thessalonians was written about AD 50 from Corinth, shortly after the founding of the community there. In 1 Thessalonians, Paul is addressing a Gentile community that is both troubled by the death of some of its members and persecuted by non-Christian neighbors. To complicate matters there are also some spiritual enthusiasts who believe themselves to be liberated from the world and its obligations. Although he addresses these problems, the apostle makes a special effort to show his affection and appreciation for the congregation.

Second Thessalonians, as we have argued, was written near the end of the first century, probably to a Macedonian community by a follower of the Apostle Paul. First Thessalonians is utilized in this letter to counter some form of libertine Gnosticism. The author writes in the name of his revered teacher to a new generation of readers.

8. Genre and Rhetorical Function

a. Ancient Letter Genre

From our comparisons of 1 and 2 Thessalonians and earlier discussion (ch 1), it is clear that both writings are early Christian letters. In 1 Thessalonians, Paul is concerned with securing the goodwill and favor of his readers (1:1-10; 5:23-28), affirming the credibility of his ministry (2:1-12),[20] maintaining personal contact through an emissary (Timothy, 2:17–3:13), and exhorting the

[20]This section where Paul distinguishes his ministry from other Hellenistic preachers, (1 Thes 2), has many parallels with Dio Chrysostom's *Oration 32* (LCL, vol. 3); Malherbe, "Gentle as a Nurse," 203–17.

congregation on various issues confronting them (4:1–5:22).[21] The letter attempts to secure church sentiment and support (chs 1–3), before expedient advice is given to the congregation (chs 4–5).

b. Deliberative Rhetorical Function

Both 1 and 2 Thessalonians seem to function as advisory rhetoric (e.g., 1 Cor 5–16; 2 Cor 1–9; Phlm), but 1 Thessalonians is more persuasive and 2 Thessalonians more dissuasive. Note the following comparisons of 1 Thessalonians with similar NT texts of persuasive rhetoric: e.g., 1 Thes 3:6-10/2 Cor 1:3-11; 1 Thes 4:9f./1 Cor 13:4-7; 1 Thes 5:1-11/1 Cor 7:25-31 and Phil 2:14-18; 1 Thes 5:12-22/1 Cor 16:15-18. The major concerns of these texts are constructive persuasion and positive exhortation. Now let us examine the more dissuasive emphasis in 2 Thessalonians. For example, the passage of 2 Thes 2:1-7 is countering rumors that "the day of the Lord has come" with the presentation of an apocalyptic time-table of events preceding the end. Also, the exhortations in 3:6-16 warn against a form of libertinism probably related to the apocalyptic fanaticism countered in 2 Thes 2. Furthermore, both the warning in 2 Thes 4:14 and the mark of authenticity in v 17 confirm this dissuasive concern. Therefore, despite the fact that both have deliberative functions, 2 Thessalonians contains more warnings against heresy, whereas 1 Thessalonians contains more constructive exhortations for its readers.

9. Summary

In our survey of the Thessalonian letters, we looked at both the background situation and the books themselves. In the back-

[21]For further elaboration, see H. Boers, "The Form Critical Study of Paul's Letters. 1 Thes as a Case Study," *NTS* 22 (1975–76) 140–58. In this article also 1 Thes 2:13-16 is regarded as a Deutero-Pauline interpolation. See also F. W. Hughes, *Early Christian Rhetoric and 2 Thes* (Sheffield: JSOT Press, 1989); B.C. Johanson, *To All the Brethren. A Text-Linguistic and Rhetorical Approach to 1 Thes* (Stockholm: Almquist & Wiksell International, 1987); J. L. Sumney, "The Bearing of a Pauline Rhetorical Pattern on the Integrity of 2 Thes," *ZNTW* 81 (1990) 192–204.

ground discussion we noted that Thessalonica was both the provincial headquarters and an important trade center in Macedonia. Paul visited the city on his first European mission (ca. 49). The Christian community founded by the apostle appears to be primarily Gentile, and they were facing some persecution from their neighbors. Paul maintained a healthy relationship with the Thessalonians up to his final trip to Jerusalem.

The following comments can be made concerning the Thessalonian books themselves. Even though the authenticity of 1 Thessalonians is unquestioned, the Pauline authorship ascribed to 2 Thessalonians is disputed. Why would Paul so slavishly imitate a previous letter to the same congregation a few years later? The theology and historical situation also suggest a period after Paul (late 1st cent.). The various destination, rearrangement, and composite theories of the letters, although noteworthy, are all based on insufficient evidence. First Thessalonians was written by Paul around AD 50 from Corinth, shortly after founding the church. Second Thessalonians was probably written near the end of the first century to a Macedonian community by a follower of the Apostle Paul. Both 1 and 2 Thessalonians are early Christian letters. In 1 Thessalonians, Paul seeks to secure the goodwill of this readers and establish the credibility of his ministry, before addressing important issues concerning eschatology and social responsibility. Second Thessalonians, as an imitation of 1 Thessalonians, contains similar advisory concerns but has a more dissuasive emphasis, i.e., warnings against heresy. It appears to be countering the teachings of libertine Gnostics who have spiritually experienced the final resurrection and have consequently shirked all earthly responsibilities. It was for this reason that the Pauline disciple "resurrected" Paul's letter (1 Thes) to address a new situation of readers.

8

Colossians and Ephesians

1. Introduction

Colossians and Ephesians are literary siblings. Almost one-third of the former book appears in the latter, and approximately one-half of the sentences in the latter book include language from the former.[1] Although Colossians and Ephesians are often classed with Phil and Phlm as Paul's Prison Epistles, authorship problems raise some doubts about this classification. First we will look at Colossians, then Ephesians, noting the questions of authorship, historical setting, literary characteristics, genre, and structure.

2. Colossians

In 1961 at the World Council of Churches Assembly at New Delhi, Joseph Sittler caused an international sensation with his lecture on "The Cosmic Christ." Using Col 1:15-20, he asserted that Christian salvation permeates the entire world because both

[1]Roetzel, *Letters* (1982) 100. See esp.: T. Abbott, *Epistles to the Ephesians and Colossians*, ICC (Edinburgh: T. & T. Clark, 1897) xxiii–xxiv; N. Perrin and D. Duling, *The New Testament: An Introduction* 2nd ed. (New York: Harcourt, Brace, Jovanovich, 1982) 218–20.

nature and grace are one in Christ.[2] Reactions to Sittler's controversial presentation were mixed; nevertheless, it aroused some interest in this text and the book of Colossians.

During the past thirty years the whole letter of Colossians has become a theological battleground. Who wrote it? Against whom was the letter written? What kind of letter or literary type is it? These are some of the questions that this section will address.

a. Authorship

Of the disputed Pauline letters, Colossians, like 2 Thessalonians, makes a strong claim to be genuine. But since the mid-nineteenth century doubts about the authenticity of Colossians have been voiced.[3] Both the claims and counterclaims will be presented.

Arguments Supporting Authenticity. There is good external and noteworthy internal evidence for maintaining that the apostle Paul was the author. Colossians is alluded to in the writings of Ignatius (Ign *Eph* 10.3/Col 1:23) and Justin Martyr (*Dialogues* 85/Col 1:15). Also, both Marcion and Origen regarded it as authentic. Internal similarities with Phlm also lend support for the authenticity of Colossians:

(1) Both contain Timothy's name with Paul's in the opening greeting (Col 1:1; Phlm 1).

(2) Greetings are sent in both letters from Aristarchus, Mark, Epaphras, Luke, and Demas, who are clearly with Paul at the time (Col 4:10-14; Phlm 23, 24).

(3) In Phlm 2, Archippus is called "fellow soldier," and in Col 4:17 he is directed to fulfill his ministry.

(4) Onesimus, the slave about whom Paul writes to Philemon, is mentioned in Col 4:4 as being sent along with Tychicus and is described as "one of you."

[2]Statement from: J. Sampley, et al. *Eph, Col, 2 Thes, Past.* (Philadelphia: Fortress, 1978) 41.

[3]The following work first raised the issue: E. Mayerhoff, *Der Brief an die Colosser* (Berlin, 1838). See also Lohse, *Colossians and Philemon*, Hermeneia, trans. W. Poehlmann and R. Karris (Philadelphia: Fortress, 1971); Perrin and Duling, *NTIntro* 209–12; Sampley, *Eph, Col* 69–71; Kümmel, *Introduction* 340–46.

Finally, there are some stylistic idiosyncrasies shared with the undisputed letters: (a) the construction of *kai* after *dio touto* ("for this reason also," Col 1:9; cf. 1 Thes 2:13; 3:5; Rom 13:6), (b) *charizesthai* ("forgive," Col 2:13; 3:13; 2 Cor 2:7,10; 12:13), (c) *en merei* ("with regard to," Col 2:16; 2 Cor 3:10; 9:3), and (d) "every good work" (Col 1:10; 2 Cor 9:8; Rom 2:7; 13:3; Phil 1:6).

Arguments Against Authenticity. Despite the convincing claims for Pauline authorship, there is sufficient evidence to counter it. First, Colossians has a distinctive vocabulary and style. Twenty-five words do not occur in Paul's other letters, and thirty-four are not found elsewhere in the NT. Synonyms are heaped together (e.g., "praying and asking" 1:9; "holy and blameless" 1:22), genitives are linked together (e.g., "of the mystery of God, of Christ," 2:2 cf. 2:12). The style is often cumbersome, wordy, and overloaded almost to obscurity with dependent clauses, participial and infinitive constructions, or substantives with *en* ("in"). For example, in the Greek both 1:9-20 and 2:9-15 are only one sentence each.[4]

A second point disputing Pauline authorship is the absence of concepts characteristic of Paul. Themes like righteousness, justification, law, salvation, revelation, fellow Christians as "brethren" (apart from the letter greeting), are noticeably absent in Colossians. Paul's sense of urgency in his apostolic mission is also missing. No longer is the apostle driven to complete his work before time runs out. No longer does he write under the shadow of the world's denouement. The future dimension of salvation almost disappears (e.g., Col 1:13,22; 2:12,13).

A third claim countering the Pauline authorship of Colossians is the occurrence of concepts either new in the Pauline corpus or representing a significant development after it. We will look at the following themes: Christology, apostleship, ministry, and baptism.

The Christology of Col 1:15-23, for example, is more advanced than anything found earlier. In Col 1:15, Christ is "the image of the invisible God, the first born of all creation." No longer does Christ reflect a likeness to which others can be conformed

[4]Kümmel, *Introduction* 341.

(e.g., Rom 8:29), but he is now seen as a true representation of God, making visible what heretofore was invisible. Moreover, Christ is the goal of all creation (Col 1:16), whereas in 1 Cor 8:6, this title is only applied to God. In Col 1:18, Christ is the head of the body, where the "body" is a cosmic reality (1:18,24; 2:19; 3:15), but in Rom 7:4; 12:5; 1 Cor 12:12-31, it is a metaphorical way of expressing mutual interdependence of Christians in the local church. Christ as the "head" of the body was also never used in the earlier writings. In Col 2:6, moving towards early catholicism, "Christ Jesus" is the subject of the authoritative tradition that the believer "receives" and in which he "lives" (Col 2:6). This is a step beyond Paul's view of tradition (1 Cor 7:10; 11:23-26).[5]

Concerning the concept of apostleship in Colossians, we note also a development beyond the undisputed Pauline letters. Although Paul represents himself as the apostle to the Gentiles who shares in the sufferings of Christ, the apostle in Colossians gladly suffers for the sake of the readers (1:24). Through Paul's preaching and *suffering* he takes the gospel to every creature (1:23). Here the suffering of the apostle compliments the vicarious suffering of Christ. In 2 Corinthians, Paul scoffs at those who claim to be mature (3:1-4). In Colossians, Paul appears as the apostle to the nations, whose message given "in all wisdom" (1:28) serves to make everyone "perfect" in Christ.[6]

In Colossians we do not find a charismatic view of ministry, but a more institutionalized formulation of it. Epaphras is a "faithful minister of Christ on our behalf" and Paul's ministry is a "divine office" (1:7,23,25). In the Corinthian correspondence, however, Paul and others are referred to as "servants" of God or Christ, with no specific office indicated (1 Cor 3:5; 2 Cor 6:4; 11:23).

One last point is the distinct role of baptism. In Col 2:11 baptism is the Christian equivalent of Jewish circumcision; it is the formal sign of membership in the community. In the earlier letters circumcision is a Jewish rite now abandoned by Christians

[5]Perrin and Duling, *NTIntro* 211–12.

[6]Roetzel, *Letters* (1982) 94–96.

(Rom 2:25-29; 3:1,30; 4:9-12) and baptism is a dynamic means of entry into a new and different life (Rom 6:3-11). The eschatological baptismal language of Rom is also missing from Colossians.

Conclusions. The above linguistic and theological departures from the undisputed letters can be interpreted in a number of ways. It is possible that: (a) changes occurred in Paul's thinking through the years, (b) new vocabulary and theology were used to address a new situation, (c) a new secretary or amanuensis was employed, or (d) a post-Pauline author is responsible for the work.

In support of post-Pauline authorship, the departures from the undisputed letters seem to point in a specific direction: toward emerging orthodoxy.[7] They are too unique to be explained as simply a change in Paul's thinking or his addressing a new situation. If a new secretary was employed, his/her influence was so dominant that it would be more appropriate to identify this secretary as the author. Furthermore, just as each person has distinctive fingerprints and even a "voice-print" which cannot be imitated by someone else, so each person has a "language print."[8]

Because of the distinctive vocabulary, style, and theology, it is more plausible that Colossians was the work of a later interpreter who sought to update the Pauline tradition for a new situation, i.e., Deutero-Pauline authorship. Since Ignatius was acquainted with it by the early second century, Colossians was written earlier, probably the late first century. Familiarity with Phlm may point to the province of Asia as the general place of origin for the letter.

[7]See E. Käsemann, "Paul and Early Catholicism" in idem, *NT Questions Today*, trans. W. Montague (Philadelphia: Fortress, 1979) 236–51; I. H. Marshall, " 'Early Catholicism' in the NT," in R. Longnecker, ed. *New Dimensions in NT Study* (Grand Rapids: Zondervan, 1974); R. Kraft, "The Development of the Concept of 'Orthodoxy,' " in G. Hawthorne, *Current Issues in Biblical and Patristic Interpretation* (Grand Rapids: Eerdmans, 1975) 48–56; W. Bauer, *Orthdoxy and Heresy in Earliest Christianity,* trans. R. Kraft, et al. (Philadelphia: Fortress, 1971); C. B. Puskas, *An Introduction to the New Testament* (Peabody, Mass.: Hendrickson, 1989) 223–52.

[8]Sampley, *Eph, Col* 69.

b. The City and the Church at Colossae[9]

Colossae was located in the Lycus river valley of Phrygia (western Asia Minor) east of Ephesus. It was near Laodicea and Hieropolis, where there were other churches (Col 4:13-17). From the letter it appears that the church of Colossae was composed mainly of Gentiles (1:21,27; 2:13). We have no evidence that the Apostle Paul ever visited the city.

c. The False Teachers

A major problem that occasioned the writing of Colossians was that of false teachers. They were propagating a way of life that was contrary to the author's own position and thus were viewed as a harmful influence on his or her readers. It is unclear to what extent these false teachers had already influenced the author's audience.

Their Philosophy. Their identity is much debated, but the letter does reveal something about their "philosophy" (2:8). This philosophy is not concerned with logical thought or speculation but a revealed knowledge through which the meaning of the world was known. It was specifically concerned with the powers or "elemental spirits of the universe" (2:8; cf. Gal 4:3). The "worship of angels" (objective genitive? Col 2:18) probably refers to the reverence given to these "principalities and powers" (1:16; 2:15). By attaining a proper relationship with these cosmic powers, one could experience divine fullness (*plērōma*). As possessors of this divine fullness,the opponents claimed special "visions" (2:18). It could be that they were even revered by some of the Colossians as the perfect ones (*teleioi*). This "philosophy" was also

[9]For further study, see C. E. Arnold, "Colossae" *ABD* 1:1089–90. Francis and Meeks, *Conflict at Colossae*; V. P. Furnish, "Colossians, Epistle to the" *ABD* 1:1090–96; Gunther, *Opponents*; P. T. O'Brien, *Colossians, Philemon*, WBC (Dallas: Word, 1982) xxx–xli; M. J. Harris, *Colossians and Philemon.* EGGNT (Grand Rapids: Eerdmans, 1991); P. Pokorny, *Colossians: A Commentary,* trans. S. Schatzmann (Peabody, Mass.: Hendrickson, 1991); P. T. O'Brien, *Colossians, Philemon,* WBC (Dallas: Word, 1982); A.G. Patzia, *Ephesians, Colossians, Philemon,* NIBC (Peabody, Mass.: Hendrickson, 1991); Roetzel *Letters* 97–99; Perrin and Duling, *NTIntro* 212–14.

ascetic or world-denying. The commands, "do not handle, do not taste, do not touch" (2:21) promoted a certain "rigor of discipline, self-abasement and severity of the body," (v 23). Certain judgments were also passed on "food and drink" and the observance of "a festival or a new moon or sabbath days" (2:16).

Mystery Cult Devotees? Who were these false teachers? Their generalized portrait in Colossians has prompted numerous theories on the subject. One advocated that they were devotees of a pagan mystery cult.[10] This theory interpreted the Greek word for "enter into, take one's stand" (*embateuō*, Col 2:18) as describing an initiate entering the sanctuary of a mystery cult to consult an oracle. This view was based on inscriptions discovered in the sanctuary of Apollo at Claros (near Ephesus). It argued that certain Colossian Christians joined with certain pagan mystagogues in a cultic life devoted to the "elemental spirits." Early forms of Gnosticism were also present in the cult.

Jewish-Christian Ascetics? A second theory regarded the Colossian heresy as a form of Jewish-Christian mystical asceticism.[11] It interpreted *ha heoraken embateuō* (2:18) as "entry into the heavenly sanctuary that he saw in a state of ecstasy," *thrēskeia tōn angelōn* as the "angelic worship" of God (subjective genitive, 2:18), and *tapeinophrosynē* ("humility" 2:18,23) as denoting ascetic practices. In this view the observance of certain rituals and ascetic practices gained for the devotee an entry into heaven which climaxed in joining the angels in the worship of God. Parallels to such a view would be at Qumran, where members believed that they would not only fellowship with angels in the future life, but also in the present join with them in the common praise of God (e.g., 1QH 3.21-23; 11:10-14). The Qumran community also observed their own calendar, followed sabbath regulations, had certain food distinctions, and observed numerous ascetic practices (e.g., CD 10.14-11.18; 12.11-22; 16.2-6). The par-

[10]M. Dibelius, "The Isis Initiation in Apuleius and Related Initiatory Rites," in Francis and Meeks, *Conflict at Colossae* 61–121. For interpretations of *embateuō*, see *BAGD* 254

[11]F. O. Francis, "Humility and Angelic Worship in Col 2:18," in Francis and Meeks, *Conflict at Colossae* 163–95.

allels from Qumran have lead many to believe that a similar form of sectarian Judaism was combatted at Colossae.[12]

Early Jewish Gnostics? A third and widely held theory is that the Colossian opponents adhered to an early form of Gnosticism.[13] The language of "wisdom," "knowledge," and "fullness," the boasting and arrogance of the adherents, world-negating asceticism, and the appearance of a "Redeemer myth" in Col 1:5-20[14] support this view. The Nag Hammadi writings also contain books reflecting an early form of non-Christian *Jewish* Gnosticism (e.g., *Eugnostos, Apocalypse of Adam, Paraphrase of Shem, Thunder*). The entire collection advocates a world-denying asceticism. Furthermore, the Gospel of Truth, a Christian-Gnostic writing from Nag Hammadi, uses language that is characteristic of Colossians. It mentions "knowledge" of the savior who came from the "pleroma" (16.3–17.4), the superior status of those who possess this revealed knowledge (22.3-19), and the eternal origins of the Redeemer who came from the Father (41.4-20).[15] Thus, it seems plausible that the Colossian opponents practiced an early form of Gnosticism, containing certain Jewish elements (Col 2:16-17). We favor this last view over the previous two.

d. The Author's Response

In response to his opponents, the author provides a corrective that reflects considerable interaction with Gnosticism. He utilizes the hymn that speaks of the creation of the powers through Christ (1:15-20), agrees that Christ is head of the powers (2:10), but argues that Christ's death on the cross has disarmed and publicly

[12]The following work provides a survey and critique of this view: E. Yamauchi, "Sectarian Parallels. Qumran and Colossae," *BSac* 121 (1964) 141–52.

[13]Lohse, *Colossians and Philemon* 120–30. The following scholars have detected elements of Gnosticism at Colossae: J. B. Lightfoot, M. Dibelius, G. Bornkamm and S. Lyonnet, as cited in Francis and Meeks, *Conflict at Colossae.*

[14]Gnostic parallels to Col 1:15-20 are the preexistence of the Redeemer (*First Apoc of James* 24; *Treatise on the Resurrection* 44; *Sophia* 94), the title of "Pleroma" (*Peter to Philip* 136) and the subjection of the rulers (*The Archons* 144-45; [Col 2:15] *Seth* 56; *Truth* 25-26). In the wisdom traditions of Hellenistic Judaism there are also parallels (e.g., Wis 6–9; Prov 8; Sir 1; 24).

[15]Statements from: Robinson, *Nag Hammadi* 37–49.

disgraced them (2:15). The author exhorts his readers to "seek the things that are above, where Christ is seated at God's right hand" (3:1), and not focus on the lower regions where the powers are relegated. Through Christ's death, the author writes, the church is already holy (1:22) and needs no further purification (1:22). The commands of the law are only human precepts (2:22-23). Borrowing household duties from popular Hellenistic ethics,[16] the author promotes an ethical behavior that takes a positive view of the world (3:18–4:1); a perspective that is free from the control of powers and principalities, and "hid with God in Christ" (3:3).[17]

e. The Genre

It is apparent that Colossians follows the basic pattern of early Christian letters.[18] There is a letter opening with senders, addressees, and greetings (1:1-2). It is followed by a thanksgiving section that contains a prayer of intercession, and ends with an eschatological note (1:3-11). The letter body (1:12–2:23) includes christological hymns, ethical exhortations, and polemics against false teaching. The lengthy parenesis (3:1–4:6) contains moral injunctions and lists of household duties. The letter closing (4:7-18) has recommendations of Tychicus and Onesimus (vv 7-9), greetings from various co-workers (vv 10-15), closing instructions (vv 16-17), and both a personal signature and benediction (v 18).

The Colossians letter also has an official and public character. The senders are identified as the apostle Paul and his associate Timothy (1:1), making it an official pronouncement. The public character is further indicated by the directive to circulate the letter to the church of the Laodiceans (4:16). Finally, the identification of co-workers who will deliver the letter (4:7) and the implication that an amanuensis or executive secretary was em-

[16]For Greco-Roman examples, see Philodemus, *Concerning Household Management* 29-30,38; Areius Didymus, *Epitome* 148–49; Seneca, *Epistles* 89, 94–95. See also C. J. Martin, "The *Haustafeln* (Household Codes) in African American Biblical Interpretation," in C. Felder, ed. *Stony the Road We Trod* (Minneapolis: Fortress, 1991) 206–31.

[17]H. Koester, *Introduction to the NT* (Philadelphia: Fortress, 1982) 2:265–66.

[18]See ch 1, The Ancient Letter Genre.

ployed in the letter body (4:18) enhance the apostolic authority of the sender.

f. The Rhetorical Structure of Colossians

The rhetorical function of the letter is epideictic. Although the anti-gnostic polemics in 2:8-23 have the appearance of forensic rhetoric, they lack reference to any specific wrongdoing committed in the past (e.g., Gal 1:6f.; 3:1-5; 4:8-20; 5:7). The rhetorical questions in 2:20-21 possibly reflect a particular situation, but are probably literary devices (cf. Gal 4:8-11) used to convey *pathos* at the conclusion of the argument in ch 2. The panegyric creation hymn (1:15-20) and the encomium of Christ the Lord (2:6-15) promote the (anti-gnostic) beliefs of Deutero-Pauline Christianity. The lengthy parenetic section (3:1–4:6) also displays the common virtues and values of Hellenistic Christianity. As shown in our studies of Romans and 2 Timothy, demonstrative rhetoric includes both the praise of common values and the censure of unacceptable practices. Even Paul's epideictic letter to the Romans includes invectives against opponents (e.g., 16:17-20). Therefore, the author of Colossians seeks to intensify adherence to the common faith, employing both praise and censure (e.g., thesis statement in Col 2:8).

The Rhetorical Structure of Colossians

I. Epistolary prescript	1:1-2
Senders	1:1
Addressees and Greetings	v 2
II. Proem: The apostolic message of Christ's cosmic lordship (theological foundation for diegesis)	1:3–2:5
A. Thanksgiving for their faith and love	1:3-8
*commendation of Epaphras as faithful minister of Christ	v 7
B. Intercession for their growth in Christ	1:9-11
C. Encomium of Christ's cosmic lordship	1:12-23
1. Introduction[19]	1:12-14

[19]See the following works which designate 1:12-14 as the introduction to the Christ hymn of Col 1:15-20, Lohse, *Colossians and Philemon* 32–33; E. Schweizer, *The Letter to the Colossians*, trans. A. Chester (Minneapolis: Augsburg, 1982) 45–49.

2. Encomium: Lord of the cosmos and the church 1:15-20
3. Hortatory application (peroration) 1:21-23

D. The apostolic office which proclaims Christ's cosmic lordship 1:24–2:5
1. General mission: to make known to everyone the revelation of the mystery 1:24-29
2. Specific example of Paul's relations with Colossae 2:1-5

E. Hortatory application functioning as peroration of proem 2:6-7

III. Diegesis (Statement of Case): Submit to Christ's lordship, not human traditions and the elemental spirits 2:8-23
A. Thesis to be demonstrated 2:8
B. Enthymeme supporting the relevance of Christ's lordship in Christian life and faith 2:9-15
C. Conclusion of enthymeme: therefore do not subject yourself to human ordinances and angelic worship 2:16-19
D. Peroration (recapitulation of section II) 2:20-23
1. Union with Christ frees us from the elemental spirits and human regulations 2:20-22
2. These human regulations have no real value v 23

IV. Apodeixis (practical demonstration of evidence): How to live in union with risen Christ 3:1–4:6
A. Introduction: Seek Christ who is above, not the powers below 3:1-4
1. Protasis: "if then you have been raised . . ." v 1a
2. Apodosis: "Seek . . . set your mind . . . " vv 1b-2
3. Enthymeme: "For you have died . . . " vv 3-4
B. Topic one: personal ethics in Christ, "put on the new nature" (a metaphor from Christian baptism) 3:5-17
1. Negative exhortation: put to death the vices of the old nature vv 5-11
2. Positive exhortation: put on the virtues of the new nature vv 12-17
C. Topic two: Christian social ethics (world-affirming household rules of Hellenism) 3:18–4:6
1. Exhortations to wives and husbands vv 18-19
2. Exhortations to children and parents vv 20-21

3. Exhortations to slaves and masters	3:22–4:1
4. General exhortations (peroration of topic two)	4:2-6
V. Epistolary postscript	4:7-18
A. Peroration (summary of arguments)	vv 7-17
1. Paul commends Tychicus and Onesimus who are "faithful ministers" and "beloved brothers" (cf. 1:7,23)	vv 7-9
2. Greetings from Aristarchus, Mark, and Jesus, "men of circumcision" (cf. 2:11-13) who are Paul's co-workers for God's kingdom (cf. 2:11-13)	vv 10-11
3. Greetings from their leader Epaphras (cf. 1:7) whose prayer is also that they may stand perfect and fully matured in all the will of God (cf. 1:9, 28), also his commendation from the apostle	4:12-13
4. Other greetings topoi and accompanying exhortations	4:14-17
B. Signature and benediction (allusion to chains, cf. 4:3)	4:18

3. Ephesians

The book entitled "The Letter of Paul to the Ephesians" is both prestigious and puzzling for the modern reader. It ranks high among the NT letters because of its emphasis on Christ and the church. Martin Luther favored it as the "true kernel and marrow" of the NT. C. H. Dodd bestowed on it the lofty title, "the crown of the Pauline writings."[20]

Ephesians is also a puzzle, for the following reasons. First, we do not know who were the intended recipients. The earliest Greek manuscripts omit "in Ephesus" from 1:1. Second, we are not certain who wrote the book. The vocabulary, style, and theology of Ephesians differ considerably from Paul's undisputed letters. Third, we cannot be sure why Ephesians was written. Paul's let-

[20]Quotes from C. L. Mitton, *Ephesians*, NCBC (Grand Rapids: Eerdmans, 1976) 2; see also N. Alexander, "The Epistle for Today," in *Biblical Studies in Honor of W. Barclay*, ed., J. McKay and J. Miller (Philadelphia: Westminster, 1976) 112–18.

ters usually respond to some specific historical situation, which is lacking in Ephesians. Fourth, we are uncertain about what type of document is Ephesians. Although it begins and ends like a Pauline letter, its contents are more characteristic of a treatise or homily. In this section we will explore the above issues, as well as the thought milieu, rhetorical function, and structure of the book.[21]

a. The Recipients

The words "in Ephesus" are absent from two early Greek manuscripts (p^{46} B), some old codices that were known to Basil of Cappadocia, and the Greek text used by Origen. Marcion (AD 140) labeled it the letter "To the Laodiceans" (cf. Col 4:16), although there is no evidence to support it. The impersonal character of the book and its lack of reference to specific situations, support the omission.

Because of the omission of "in Ephesus," it has been argued that the document was a circular letter to churches in a broad region. Asia Minor would have been the most likely location since the book has literary ties to Colossians. It was probably carried from one place to another by a courier (e.g., Tychicus, Eph 6:21).[22] The letter's general character and distinct emphasis on the universal church (e.g., 1:22; 2:19-22; 5:23-25) also support this view. Furthermore, certain genres (e.g., the homily) were also incorporated into a circular letter form.

Another theory connected with the destination of the letter is that Ephesians was a cover letter for Paul's body of writings.[23]

[21]For commentaries and other studies on Ephesians, see Abbott, *Ephesians and Colossians*; M. Barth, *Ephesians*, 2 vols., AB 34, 34A (New York: Doubleday, 1974); V. P. Furnish, "Ephesians, Epistle to the," *ABD* 2:535–42; E. J. Goodspeed, *The Meaning of Ephesians* (Chicago: University Press, 1933); A. T. Lincoln, *Ephesians* WBC (Dallas: Word, 1990); A. G. Patzia, *Ephesians, Colossians, Philemon* (1991); Mitton, *Ephesians*; Sampley, *Eph, Col* 9-40.

[22]The related suggestion that Tychicus was the courier and that a blank was left in the letter for him to fill in the name of each church that he visited, is merely a conjecture (Guthrie, *Introduction* 510–11).

[23]This theory was developed in Goodspeed, *The Meaning of Ephesians* (1933), and qualified in Mitton, *Ephesians* 7–18. The view that Onesimus (of Phlm) is

According to this view, Ephesians served as an introductory letter for the collection of Paul's writings near the end of the first century after the publication of Acts renewed an interest in Paul. As an introduction to the Pauline corpus, Ephesians summarizes much of Paul's teaching in the undisputed letters (e.g., Rom, 1 and 2 Cor, Gal, 1 Thes). However, in contrast to the explicit reference in Pol Phil 13.2, Ephesians does not refer to itself as a cover letter. Further evaluation of this theory will also be made in our discussion of genre and rhetorical function.

b. Authorship

Arguments Supporting Authenticity. The case for authenticity seems strong at first. Ephesians claims to be written by Paul (1:1; 3:1; cf. 4:1). His favorite themes of grace, priority of faith over works (2:8-9), body of Christ, Spirit, and election (4:4-6) surface again, and even the hymn of 1:3-14 recalls similar poems in 1 Cor 13 and Phil 2. The letter was known by Polycarp, Ignatius, and Marcion in the early second century. Both Irenaeus and Clement of Alexandria assumed that Paul was the author. It was not until the time of Erasmus (16th cent.) that the Pauline authorship of Ephesians was questioned.

Arguments against Authenticity. The authenticity of Ephesians is called into question on the following points: its distinct language and style, dependency on Colossians, and advanced theology.

Concerning its special language and style, there are 38 words in Ephesians not found elsewhere in the NT and 44 additional words not used in Paul's undisputed writings. The stylistic peculiarities are more noticeable. Erasmus was the first to call attention to the long ponderous sentences (e.g., 1:3-10, 15-23; 3:1-7; 4:11-16 in KJV or Greek text). Others have noted the many relative clauses, the piling up of synonyms (e.g., 1:19 four separate words for "power"), use of contrasting parallel phrases (e.g., 4:12,16-17), and the constant use of prepositions, especially "in" (e.g., 1:3-10). All of these traits seem far removed from the pas-

the same person who became bishop (in Ignatius' letters) and collects Paul's letters, is a conjecture with little support.

toral approach of Paul, whose letter-writing habits are known to us from the undisputed writings (e.g., personal appeals, rhetorical questions, straightforward approach).[24]

The literary dependence of Ephesians on Colossians, outlined in the next section, argues further against Pauline authorship. Why would Paul borrow so many phrases from a book like Colossians and invest them with different meanings for a new situation? For example, Christ as head of the cosmos (Col 2:19) is changed to Christ as head of the church (Eph 4:15-16). Similar changes have also occurred with "stewardship" and "mystery" in Colossians and Ephesians. Additional examples are found in the next section. The plausibility of Paul's borrowing from Colossians is further weakened when we consider the many arguments against the Pauline authorship of Colossians (mentioned earlier in this ch).

The theology of Ephesians reflects a period in the church after the time of Paul. The use of "church" in Ephesians as universal (1:22; 3:10,21; 5:24-25,27) resembles early catholic conceptions of the Great Church, not Paul's perspective. In the undisputed Pauline writings (and Col), "church" refers to the local congregation, with only a few exceptions (e.g., 1 Cor 3:17; 12:12-13; cf. Col 1:18). In Eph 3:4-6, the "mystery of Christ" is the unity of Jews and Gentiles in the body of Christ, a cause for which Paul was still fighting (e.g., Rom 9–11).

As in 2 Thessalonians the divine actions once attributed to God in Paul's undisputed writings are ascribed to Christ in Ephesians: e.g., Christ reconciles Jew and Gentile (Eph 2:16)/God reconciles (Rom 5:10); Christ appoints apostles and prophets (Eph 4:11)/God appoints (1 Cor 12:28). Special prominence is also given to apostles and prophets in Ephesians. For examples, they are the foundation of the church (Eph 2:20; cf. Christ is the foundation in 1 Cor 3:11) and reference is made to "holy apostles" as recipients of God's revelation (Eph 3:4-5). Because of the well-developed themes, dependency on Colossians, and distinctive vocabulary, the author of Ephesians seems to be living in a situation after that of the apostles.

[24]R. Martin, *NT Foundations* (Grand Rapids: Eerdmans, 1978) 2:226; Abbott, *Ephesians and Colossians* xiv–xx.

c. A Comparative Study of Ephesians

A Comparison of Themes. Related to the concerns of authorship, purpose, and literary character is the question of the relationship of Ephesians to other NT books. We will first note the extensive parallels between Ephesians and Colossians, next, significant comparisons with the undisputed Pauline letters, then suggestive parallels between Luke-Acts and 1 Peter.

Topic[25]	*Eph*	*Col*
(1) Redemption, forgiveness	1:7	1:14,20
(2) The all-inclusive Christ	1:10	1:20
(3) Intercession for the readers	1:15-17	1:3-4,9
(4) Riches of a glorious inheritance	1:18	1:27 (hope of glory)
(5) Christ's dominion	1:21-22	1:16-18
(6) You he made alive	2:5	2:13
(7) Aliens brought near	2:12-13	1:21-22
(8) Abolishing the commandments	2:15	2:14
(9) Paul the prisoner	3:1	1:24
(10) Divine mystery made known to Paul	3:2-3	1:25-26
(11) Paul, minister of universal gospel	3:7	1:23,25
(12) Paul to make known the mystery to all	3:8-9	1:27
(13) Lead a life worthy of your calling	4:1	1:10
(14) With all lowliness, meekness, patience forbearing one another	4:2	3:12-13
(15) Christ unites members of church	4:15-16	2:19
(16) Put off old nature and put on new nature	4:22-32	3:5-10,12f.
(17) No immorality among you	5:3-6	3:5-9
(18) Walk wisely and make the most of the time	5:15	4:5
(19) Sing songs, hymns, and spiritual songs, giving thanks to God	5:19-20	3:16-17
(20) Tables of household duties for husbands, wives, children, parents, slaves, and masters	5:21–6:9	3:18–4:1

[25]The "topics" are derived from Ephesians and follow its order. Certain deviations from Ephesians are noted in far right column.

(21)	Paul the prisoner exhorts persistence in prayer	6:18-20	4:2-3
(22)	Tychicus sent to inform church about Paul and to encourage them	6:21-22	4:7-8

The dependency of Ephesians on Colossians best accounts for the evidence. Words and phrases from Colossians appear in Ephesians clothed with new meaning (e.g., parallels 10,15). There are also places where passages from Colossians seem conflated (combined) in Ephesians (parallels 1,3,11). It seems that the author of Ephesians was so familiar with Colossians that he even followed the basic argument of the letter and brought together passages that were scattered in the earlier book. Now we will note the parallels between Ephesians and the undisputed letters of Paul.

Ephesians and Romans

Topic		*Eph*	*Rom*
(1)	Elected to be holy	1:4-5	8:29
(2)	God's will accomplishes all	1:11	8:28
(3)	Not saved by works	2:8-9	4:2
(4)	We have access to God through faith	2:18; 3:11-12	5:1-2
(5)	The gift of God's grace	3:7; 4:7	5:15; 12:3
(6)	Their senseless minds were darkened and they gave themselves over to immorality	4:17-19	1:21-22,24
(7)	The acceptable will of the Lord	5:10,17	12:2
(8)	Have no fellowship with the works of darkness	5:11	13:12
(9)	God shows no partiality	6:9	2:11

Ephesians and 1 Corinthians

Topic		*Eph*	*1 Cor*
(1)	Church as a building and temple with a foundation, which God causes to grow	2:20-21	3:6,9,11-12, 16
(2)	Paul, least of all saints, enabled by God's grace to preach	3:8	15:9-11

(3) God has given apostles, prophets and teachers for the church	4:11	12:28
(4) Let him labor, working with his hands	4:28	4:12
(5) Be imitators of God	5:1	4:14,16 (be imitators of me)
(6) Immoral people will not inherit God's kingdom	5:5	6:9-10
(7) Husband is head of wife, Christ is head of church	5:23–11:3	(Christ is head of man)
(8) We are members of Christ's body; Gen 2:24	5:30-31	6:15-16

Ephesians and 2 Corinthians

Topic	*Eph*	*2 Cor*
(1) Paul an apostle of Jesus Christ by the will of God to the saints	1:1-2	1:1-2
(2) Blessed be the God and Father of our Lord Jesus Christ	1:3	1:3
(3) The seal of the Holy Spirit	4:30	1:22
(4) Paul, an ambassador in chains speaks boldly	6:20	5:20 (ambassadors for Christ)

Ephesians and Galatians

Topic	*Eph*	*Gal*
(1) In the fullness of times	1:10	4:4
(2) The promise of the Spirit	1:13	3:14
(3) Saved by faith not works	2:8-9	2:16
(4) Christ who loved us and gave himself up for us	5:2, 25	2:20
(5) Do not be "menpleasers" but servants of Christ	6:6	1:10

Ephesians and Philippians

Topic	*Eph*	*Phil*
(1) An offering and sacrifice to God; what is acceptable to the Lord	5:2,10	4:18

(2) Pray always with all prayer and supplication	6:18	4:6

Ephesians and 1 Thessalonians

Topic	*Eph*	*1 Thes*
(1) The redemption we are to obtain	1:14	5:9 (2 Thes 2:14)
(2) Those having no hope	2:12	4:13
(3) Lead a life worthy of your calling	4:1	2:12 (worthy of God)
(4) Put on the breastplate of righteousness and the helmet of salvation	6:14-16	5:8 (breastplate of faith and love)

Ephesians and Philemon

Topic	*Eph*	*Phlm*
(1) Paul, a prisoner for Christ Jesus	3:1	v 1
(2) I am an ambassador in chains	6:20	v 9 (an ambassador and now prisoner)

The above parallels of Ephesians with Paul's undisputed letters are so close at points and the changes so subtle yet profound, that an acquaintance with these writings is probably presupposed. The parallels also argue favorably for Ephesians as an introductory letter for the Pauline corpus, that summarizes much of its teachings (see earlier discussion). Now we will compare Ephesians with the other NT books of Luke-Acts and 1 Peter.

Ephesians and Luke-Acts

Topic	*Eph*	*Luke-Acts*
(1) "Inheritance among the saints"	1:18	Acts 20:32
(2) "God raised him up and appointed him to sit at his right hand"	1:20	Acts 2:32-35; 7:55
(3) "With all humility"	4:2	Acts 20:28

(4)	Pastors, evangelists	4:11	Acts 20:28; 21:8
(5)	"In holiness and righteousness"	4:24	Lk 1:75
(6)	Devil (*diabolos*)	4:27	Acts 13:10
(7)	Be filled with the Spirit	5:18	Acts 2:4,15
(8)	"Serving the Lord"	6:7	Acts 20:28
(9)	"Able to withstand"	6:13	Lk 21:15
(10)	"Your loins girded"	6:14	Lk 12:35

Ephesians and 1 Peter

Topic		*Eph*	*1 Pet*
(1)	"Blessed be the God and Father of our Lord Jesus Christ"	1:3	1:3
(2)	God raised Jesus, set him at his right hand, above all rulers and authorities and put all things under his feet.	1:20-22	3:22
(3)	You are fellow citizens, members of God's household, build upon a foundation with Christ as cornerstone; a holy temple and dwelling place of God in the Spirit	2:19-22	2:4–6,9
(4)	God's mystery hidden for generations is now revealed to his holy apostles and prophets	3:2-6	1:10-12

The literary dependency of Ephesians upon both 1 Peter and Luke-Acts is doubtful. It is plausible that 1 Peter made use of Ephesians and probable that Ephesians and Luke-Acts both reflect similar concerns of the late first century. The latter conclusion involving Luke-Acts, further weakens the case for Pauline authorship of Ephesians.

Ephesians and the Qumran Literature. Some of the themes in Ephesians coincide with the teaching of the Dead Sea Scrolls (140 BC–AD 68) discovered at Khirbet Qumran (1947). Although the author of Ephesians probably would not have agreed with the apocalyptic, exclusivistic, and legalistic tendencies of the Qumran community, he seems to share other basic beliefs with the group. The following are some of the common themes and concerns:[26]

Qumran and Ephesians

Topics	*Eph*	*Qumran*
(1) Divine predestination and election	1:4-5, 11;	1QS 4.22-26
(2) Conflicting spirits of light and darkness	5:8-14;	1QS 3.21-4.1; 1QM 1; 3-4
(3) Spiritual warfare of humankind	6:10-17;	1QM 1; 3-4; 7; 1QS 3.13-4.26
(4) Special role of house or people of God	2:19-22;	1QS 5.2-7; CD 8.21; 19.16
(5) Emphasis on unity and community	1:10; 2:13-16, 19; 4:3-6,13	CD *hay-yahad* or "unity" in CD and 1QS 1; 5.2-7
(6) The disclosure of God's secret plan	1:9; 3:3-4; 6:19	1QS 3.13-4.26; 1QH 1; 5; CD 2.2-13; 3.18-19
(7) Awareness of God's revelation as a privilege of the faithful	1:9,17-18; 3:3-5,9	1QH 12.11-12; 1QS 9.16-19; 1QpHab 7.1-8
(8) Exhortations to forsake evil and do good	4:17-5:20	1QS 1.2-18; 5.1-2
(9) Rules for marriage, women, and children	5:21–6:4	1QSa 1.4-12; CD 7.6-9

[26]Abbreviations for the Qumran literature signify the following: CD = Damascus Document, 1QS = Manual of Discipline, 1QM = War Scroll, 1QH = Thanksgiving Hymns, 1QSa = Order of Congregation, 1QpHab = Habakkuk Commentary. Qumran passages have been cited from: T. Gaster (ed.) *Dead Sea Scrolls*,

There are general similarities in the above parallels but numerous specific differences. Note the following differences: no concerns at Qumran to make known God's mystery to the Gentiles (Eph 3:8-9) and no human/divine analogies exalting the ideal of marriage (Eph 5:21-33). Also, the "mystery of God's plan" has more diverse semantic associations at Qumran (e.g., order of cosmos, salvation, kingdom of Belial, nature of man) than in Ephesians (1:9; 3:3-4,9; 5:32; 6:19). Therefore, the general similarities are best explained as originating from a common Near Eastern thought-milieu, rather than as indicators of a common pre-70 date or a specific Palestinian setting.

Ephesians and Gnosticism. Comparisons with the Nag Hammadi Codices (AD 300) and other gnostic writings reveal possible gnostic and anti-gnostic influences. These are evident in the gnostic-like vocabulary, the Christ hymns of earthly descent and heavenly ascent, the heavenly marriage motif, the call to awake, and the realized eschatology. Anti-gnostic motifs are possibly found in the exhortations to responsible ethics in the world (*contra* libertinism), the view of God the Father (not the Demiurge) as creator of the world, and the exalted view of earthly marriage renounced by many Gnostics. We will outline each point below.[27]

Vocabulary/Topic	*Ephesians*	*Gnosticism*
(1) Knowledge of divine mysteries	1:9; 3:3-4; 6:19	*Tripartite Tractate* 126 *Gospel of Truth* 21-23; 24.28-25.19; Valentinianism in Irenaeus *Against Heresies* 1.21.4
(2) *Plērōma*, the fullness	1:10, 23; 3:19; 4:13	*Plērōma*, the realm of the unknown God; *Gospel*

3rd ed. (Garden City, N.Y.: Doubleday, 1976). Note the importance of comparing contexts and viewpoints, as well as vocabulary in S. Sandmel, "Parallelomania," *JBL* 81:1 (1962) 1–13; and H. Ringgren, "Qumran and Gnosticism," in U. Bianchi, ed., *The Origins of Gnosticism* (Leiden: Brill, 1970) 379–84.

[27]Sources for Gnosticism are from: J. M. Robinson, ed. *The Nag Hammadi Library in English* (San Francisco: Harper & Row, 1977); K. Rudolph, *Gnosis: The Nature and History of Gnosticism,* trans. R. Wilson (San Francisco: Harper & Row, 1983); and Jonas, *Gnostic Religion.*

		of Truth 16.31-37; 43.10-22 *Tripartite Tractate* 125.30-36; 136.21-25
(3) Principalities (*archai*) and powers in the heavenlies	1:21; 3:10; 6:12	*Archons* or spirits who inhabit lower heavenly spheres above earth. *On the Origin of the World* 100.1-11; 102.20-24; 104.14-27; 111.20-25; *Apocryphon of John* 4; 18-21
(4) Perfection and unity a goal of redemption	4:13 ("perfect man")	*Gospel of Philip* 70.10-18; as *Gospel of Truth* 24-25; ("perfect man" *Gos Phil* 76.23-25; *Apocryphon of John* 8.29-34)
(5) "middle wall of partition" (barrier)	2:14-15 (between Jews and Gentiles)	Barrier separating hostile powers from heavenly pleroma: Valentinianism in Irenaeus *Against Heresies* 1.3.5
(6) Earthly descent and heavenly ascent of the redeemer	4:8-10	*Tripartite Tractate* 123-26 *Gospel of Truth* 21.26-22.12; 34.36-41.15
(7) Call for sleepers to awake	5:14	*The Concept of Our Great Power* 39.33-40.7; *Gospel of Truth* 22.2-19; *Acts of Thomas* 110.43
(8) Heavenly marriage motif	5:22-32 (human and heavenly marriages)	Gnostic bridal chamber *Gospel of Philip* 69.1-71.35; 76.7-36
(9) Union of Christ and Church	5:25-27,29, 32	*syzygies* or unions of aeons (pairs of angelic spirits emanating from the unbegotten Father): Valentinianism in Irenaeus, *Against Heresies* 1.21.2 (e.g., Nous-Truth, Christ-

			Holy Spirit, Man-Church); *Apocryphon of John* 36.16-39.4
(10)	Concept of spiritual man with cosmic "body" and "head," along with motif of growth	1:22-23; 4:15-16	So-called 'Naassene Sermon' in Hippolytus *Refutation of All Heresies* 5.7-8 (astrology)
(11)	Realized eschatology	2:1, 6	*Exegesis of the Soul* 134.7-16; *Gospel of Philip* 73.1-5; *Treatise on Resurrection* 49.10-17

Many of the above parallels are general similarities, which are interpreted differently in both writings (e.g., "*gnōsis, plērōma*, perfect man"). Therefore, whatever gnostic concepts are found in Ephesians have been Christianized in a manner suitable to emerging orthodoxy. Ephesians also contains themes which appear anti-gnostic (see below). The late date of the gnostic writings and their generalized similarities with Ephesians, rule out any direct dependence of this Deutero-Pauline writing on any extant gnostic book. The parallels suggest, however, a similar lexicon of vocabulary and images used by the author of Ephesians and certain Gnostics. Note also the differences:

(1) Ephesians has a positive concept of human marriage (5:22-33) in contrast to Gnostics who rejected it as proof of one's membership in heavenly world (e.g., Saturlinus in Irenaeus, *Against Heresies* 1.24.2 and Severus in Epiphanius, *Panarion* 42.2.1).

(2) The exhortations to responsible personal and social ethics in the Roman world (Eph 2:10; 4:1-2; 4:17-5:20; 5:21–6:9) are in opposition to the stance of libertine Gnostics who believed that redemption frees one from all worldly obligations (e.g., in Irenaeus, *Against Heresies* 1.6.2–3; Epiphanius, *Panarion* 25-26; 40.34).

(3) References to God as Creator (3:9) and his plan to redeem the world (1:9-10) are in contrast to Gnosticism which ascribed the creation of the world to an inferior deity, the Demiurge (*Apocryphon of John* 39.4-44.18; *On the Origin of the World*

100.29-103.2). The redemption of the material world is not found in any gnostic systems (e.g., *On the Origin of the World* 99.2-22).

The above themes in Ephesians inherently conflict with gnostic thought. There is no *explicit* evidence that gnostic groups are opposed in the book. However, since Ephesians is Deutero-Pauline, it was common for such early catholic writings to define their beliefs and practices vis-à-vis their opponents. Therefore the author of Ephesians may be outlining his beliefs and practices which have been defined (by him and others) in general opposition to Gnosticism.

d. The Genre

There are numerous liturgical and hortatory features in Ephesians. Comparisons of Ephesians with Qumran and Gnosticism have already highlighted the traditional hymnic and confessional material (e.g., 1:3-14, 20-23; 2:4-7,10,14-18,20-22; 3:5,20-21; 4:4-8,11-13; 5:2,14,25-27).[28] Both Colossians and Ephesians testify to the use of "psalms and hymns" in their worship (Col 3:16/Eph 5:19-20). The lengthy blessing in Eph 1:3-14 is reminiscent of the beginning of the "Eighteen Benedictions" used in the Jewish synagogue service.[29] The prayers for wisdom (1:15-23) and spiritual maturity (3:14-19) are formal enough to be recited in worship. The teaching about spiritual death/spiritual life (2:1-10) and the exhortations to put off the old nature/put on the new nature, mirror some baptismal liturgy (cf. 1 Pet 1:22–2:3; Justin Martyr, *First Apology* 61; Hippolytus, *Apostolic Tradition* 20). The list of household duties from Hellenistic Christianity (Eph 5:21-6:9/Col 3:18–4:1) are conveniently placed after the exhortations to righteous living (possibly added later).

The numerous liturgical and hortatory features in Ephesians make a plausible case for regarding it as a baptismal homily adapted for general circulation.[30] Another NT book, 1 Peter, is

[28]See discussions of hymnic material in M. Barth, *Ephesians* 1:6-10, 97–104; Martin, *NT Foundations* 2:248–75.

[29]See Barrett, *NTB* 162.

[30]A qualification of the thesis is in Meeks, *Writings* 121–22.

regarded by some as an early baptismal liturgy.[31] Although the distinct features of a baptismal liturgy have been less evident with Ephesians than 1 Pet. The liturgical aspects of Ephesians are more evident, however, when the Pauline epistolary features are removed (1:1-2,15-23; 3:1-13; 4:1; 6:21-22).

The epistolary features of Ephesians may indicate that the baptismal homily was eventually placed in letter form. This adaptation from homily to letter was either the work of the speaker/author or an editor from the same community, since a similar style pervades the book. The absence of specific addressees indicates that the letter was intended for several congregations, probably Pauline communities in western Asia Minor.

The parallels with Colossians and the undisputed letters indicate that Ephesians is a product of Pauline Christianity. The author and his community were probably familiar with Colossians (also from the province of Asia) and a collection of Paul's letters.[32] It is plausible to conclude, therefore, that Ephesians was a baptismal homily from a Pauline community, placed in letter form for general circulation among the churches of western Asia.

e. The Rhetorical Function

The view that Ephesians is an adapted form of a baptismal homily finds some support in the book's rhetorical function. Although the parenetic section (4:1–6:20) has an advisory aspect (to dissuade and persuade), it is subordinate to the epideictic function of the book: to extol the common values of Pauline Christianity and intensify adherence to them. The opening blessing (1:3-14), formal prayers (1:15-23; 3:14-19), and other hymnic materials (2:4-8,10,14-18; 3:5,20-21; 4:4-6,8,11-13,22-24; 5:2,14) support this encomiastic function. In the parenetic section, Eph 4:17–5:20 function as specific exhortations to new converts, Eph 5:21–6:9 can be viewed as general exhortations to the community, and 6:10-20 as closing admonitions. In the context of the

[31]For 1 Peter as a baptismal liturgy see J. N. D. Kelly, *The Epistles of Peter and Jude*, HNTC (New York: Harper & Row, 1969) 15–20; F. L. Cross, *I Peter: A Paschal Liturgy* (London: A. R. Mowbray and Co., 1954).

[32]See our comparison in this chapter under c. Ephesians: A Comparative Study.

book, the above exhortations do not appear to be prompted by specific questions or problems of a particular congregation (cf. 1 Cor 7). They are stereotyped pareneses (Eph 5:21–6:8) and contain baptismal imagery (4:17–5:20). In our discussion of Hebrews, we mention the epideictic influence of both hymns and OT imagery on early Christian sermons.

f. The Structure of Ephesians

Even though Ephesians follows the basic pattern of Colossians with doctrinal exposition followed by practical exhortation, it lacks the polemical material of the former book. The rhetorical function of Ephesians is to extol the common values of Deutero-Pauline Christianity and intensify adherence to them (cf. Rom). The liturgical and homiletical characteristics of Ephesians support this function.[33]

The Rhetorical Structure of Ephesians

I. Epistolary prescript (added later)	1:1-2
II. Baptismal liturgy for new converts	1:3–3:21
A. Opening praise to God for blessings and privileges received through Christ	1:3-14
B. Intercessory prayer for initiates, closing with a hymn about Christ's headship over the church	1:15-23
C. Exhortations for newly baptized converts	2:1-22
1. The significance of the baptismal act explained and proclaimed	2:1-10
2. A reminder of their shameful past without Christ	vv 11-12
3. A reminder of how Christ has put right these disadvantages (hymn sung or chanted, vv 14-18)	vv 13-22
D. Presence of Paul mediated to converts in apostolic address (3:1-13) and prayer (vv 14-19) [possibly added later with epistolary features]	3:1-19
E. Doxology and Amen	3:20-21

[33]Structure derived from the translation of Ephesians and discussions of style and hymnic features in Barth, *Ephesians* 1:xxvii–10.

III. Baptismal homily addressed to new converts and congregation 4:1–6:20
- A. Proem: Apostolic admonitions for personal responsibility and Christian unity 4:1-16
  1. Hymn extolling unity of the faith 4:4-6
  2. Text on ascending messiah 4:8
  3. Exposition of text 4:7,9-10
  4. Hymn on Messiah appointing officers for the church 4:11-13
  5. Reiteration of theme vv 14-16
- B. Address to new converts on righteous living 4:17–5:20
  1. Opening remarks about their former lives as Gentiles 4:17-21
  2. Analogy from baptismal act: Strip off old nature, put on new nature vv 22-24
  3. Negative aspect of analogy expounded: Put away immorality vv 25-31
  4. Positive aspect of analogy expounded: Walk in love 4:32–5:2
  5. Deeds of darkness and deeds of light 5:3-14
     hymnic call to awake v 14
- C. Recapitulation of proem and address to new converts 5:15-20
  Admonitions to continue in Christian worship vv 19-20
- D. Address to households in the congregation (possibly added later with epistolary features) 5:21–6:9
  1. Admonitions to wives and husbands based on analogy between the church and Christ 5:21-33
  2. Admonitions to children and parents 6:1-4
  3. Admonitions to slaves and masters 6:5-9
- E. Apostolic admonition to entire congregation 6:10-20
  1. Put on God's armor for the spiritual warfare (baptismal allusion?) 6:10-17
  2. Recapitulation of apostolic admonitions to congregation (cf. 4:1) 6:18-20

IV. Epistolary postscript (added later) 6:21-24
- A. Personal remarks about the sending of Tychicus vv 21-22
- B. Closing salutation and benediction 6:23-24
  (reiteration of themes from opening hymn 1:3 and proem of baptismal homily 4:1-2)

4. Summary

In this chapter on Colossians and Ephesians we discussed the question of authorship, historical setting, literary features, genre, and structure. Because the linguistics and theology appeared post-Pauline, we favored the view that both books were the products of a Deutero-Pauline School, composed after the apostle's death. The parallels between Colossians and Ephesians were so extensive, that dependency of the latter on the former is favored. Both books also seem to have similar epideictic functions, even though Colossians contains polemics against some form of Jewish Gnosticism. Ephesians expressly extols the virtues and values of Deutero-Pauline Christianity, probably for baptismal converts. Despite the fact that both works reflect the situation of emerging orthodoxy, they seem to incorporate and Christianize traditions from Gnosticism and other Near Eastern religions. Colossians presents us with a lofty vision of the cosmic Christ, whereas Ephesians concentrates on those enduring truths which bring healing and harmony within the Christian community.

9

Hebrews

1. Introduction

It has become fashionable to characterize Hebrews by its own description of Melchizedek, "without father or mother or genealogy" (7:3), because there is so much doubt about who wrote it, who received it, and when.[1] The early Christian theologian Origen tersely summed up the authorship question with the statement: "only God knows who wrote this epistle."[2] Even the literary form is a mystery since it begins like a treatise, proceeds like a sermon, and closes like a letter. Let us now examine the following topics better to understand the document: genre, rhetorical structure, religious context, authorship, place of composition, audience, destination, and date.

2. The Genre

Like John's Gospel and 1 John, Hebrews opens with a majestic prose introduction of the divine Son of God (1:1-4). It proceeds with further doctrinal expositions of religious themes (indirect discourse 1:5-14; 2:5–3:6; 5:1-10; 7:1–10:18; 11:1-40;

[1]The statement, originally attributed to Franz Overbeck (1875), is from: R. E. Brown and J. Meier, *Antioch and Rome, NT Cradles of Catholic Christianity* (New York: Paulist, 1979) 139.

[2]Cited in Eusebius, *Eccl Hist* 6.25.14.

12:18-24; 13:8,10-12), that are interchanged with practical exhortations (direct discourse 2:1-4; 3:7-4:16; 5:11–6:20; 10:19-39; 12:1-17; 13:1-23). Then, it concludes as an early Christian letter: *parenesis* (exhortation 13:1-19), closing prayer and doxology (vv 20-21), postscript with a "personal" word (v 22), brief travelogue (v 23), final greeting (v 24), and benediction (v 25).[3]

Despite the likelihood that Hebrews was put into written form for circulation among the author's readers (e.g., 13:12, "I have written to you"), it lacks too many epistolary features to be classed as a letter. There is no letter opening, no sender identified, no addressee designated (the title "to the Hebrews" was added later), and the epistolary closing is a postscript.

Clues in the text suggest that Hebrews was originally a spoken address, probably a sermon or collection of sermons. First, the author seems to identify his document as a "word of exhortation" (13:22). In Acts, a homily (or sermon) given in a synagogue after the reading of Scripture is identified as a "word of exhortation" (13:15).[4] Second, allusions to speaking and hearing in Hebrews, support this oratorical nature. Here are examples: "about this matter we have much to say that is hard to explain since you have become dull of hearing" (5:11), "though we speak this" (6:9), "now the main point in what we are saying is this" (8:1; cf. 2:1,5; 9:5; 11:32). All of these statements exemplify direct address between the speaker and his audience.

A third clue concerning the hortatory nature of Hebrews is that it contains many practical exhortations that are typical of early Jewish and Christian homilies. In the Greek text they are distinctly marked by the use of the first person plural hortatory subjunctive, "let us" (4:1,11,14,16; 6:1; 10:22,23,24; 12:1,28; 13:13,15). Also, these practical exhortations are combined with doctrinal expositions that are based on passages from the Hebrew Scriptures (e.g., Heb 2:1-9/Ps 8:4-6; Heb 3:7–4:3/Ps 95; Heb 7/Gen 14 and Ps 110; Heb 8/Jer 31:31-4).

[3]The First Letter of Peter ends in a similar manner: parenesis (5:6-10), doxology (v 11), postscript with personal comments (v 12), and final greeting (vv 13-14).

[4]If Acts 13:15 reflects the situation of the narrator instead of that which is narrated, it is a contemporary parallel to Heb 13:22. This comment assumes that the author of Hebrews wrote in the late first century as also did the author of Luke-Acts.

The combinations in Hebrews of doctrinal exposition of Scripture with practical exhortation is characteristic of Jewish and Christian homilies of late antiquity. This practice occurs in a variety of Jewish hortatory literature: e.g., *T 12 Patr;* the intro. to Wis 1–5; Tob 4; the opening exhortations in the Damascus Document of Qumran, CD 1-8. It is not only characteristic of the speeches in Acts (e.g., Acts 2:14-36; 3:12-26; 7:2-53; 10:34-43; 13:15-43; 17:22-31) but also of early Christian homilies (e.g., 1 Pet, *2 Clem,* closing homily in *Epistle of Diognetus* 11-12).

Therefore, because of the hortatory clues in the text, Hebrews should be classed with early Christian sermons like 1 Peter, 2 Clement, Diognetus 11-12, and the kerygmatic speeches of Acts. There are least four reasons for this classification. (1) All make use of the Jewish Scriptures to expound their Christian doctrines. (2) Each combines doctrinal exposition derived from the Scriptures with practical exhortations. (3) Each has the deliberative rhetorical function to persuade or dissuade the listeners/readers.[5] (4) All presuppose an oratorical setting (real or fictional) between the speaker and his audience.[6]

The classification of Hebrews as an early Christian sermon, however, does not undervalue the diverse influences that produced this hortatory genre. The sections of biblical exposition have affinities with both rabbinic argumentation[7] and the pesher exegesis of Qumran.[8] Furthermore, Jewish missionary propaganda (e.g., Philo, *Sibylline Oracles,* Aristobulus[9]) and Hellenistic rheto-

[5]Acts 7:2-53 may be a judicial speech, which denounces the unbelieving Jews.

[6]By "fictional" we mean that certain speeches and their settings, like those in Acts, are primarily the work of the author.

[7]For e.g., the rabbinic inference from minor to major (*qal vahomer*) seems to be used in Heb 9:14; 12:9, 25 (cf. Lk 11:13; 12:28) and the rabbinic argumentation of similar but subordinate analogy (*gezeira sheva*) in Heb 4:3-4,10 (Israel's "rest" and God's "Sabbath").

[8]Hebrews and Qumran are discussed in this chapter under 4. Hebrews: The Religious Context, c. The Qumran Community.

[9]For discussion of Philo, see in this chapter, 4. b. Alexandrian Judaism. An excellent introduction and translation of the *Sibylline Oracles* is found in Charlesworth, *OTP* 1:317–472. Some of the teachings of Aristobulus, the Jewish teacher of Ptolemy (2 Macc 1:10) are mentioned in Eusebius *The Preparation of the Gospel* vii. 14; xiii. 12.

ric (e.g., Aristotle, Cynic-Stoic dialogues) both influenced it. Finally, hymns and *kerygma* concerning Jesus, the Greek OT (e.g., Pss 2; 22; 110; Jer 31; Isa; Dt), and Near Eastern wisdom traditions also determined the Christian hortatory genre.

3. The Rhetorical Structure

Now that Hebrews has been identified as early Christian homily, we will consider its rhetorical structure. Although much of its doctrinal sections contain *encomia*, praising Christ or the virtues of famous people, the exhortations give Hebrews a deliberative function: to persuade its readers in the faith and dissuade them from unacceptable views and practices. As with 1 Cor 7–16 and 2 Cor 8–9, Hebrews focuses on expedient courses of action for the future, although praiseworthy virtues in the present (*encomium*) are included. The types of rhetoric employed in Hebrews will be helpful in determining its function and purpose, as well as its structure. In our outline of the rhetorical structure, attention will be given to both the doctrinal prose sections and the hortatory discourses (which often overlap).

The Rhetorical Structure of Hebrews

I. Proem: Christ as a superior mediator — 1:1–4:16
  A. Doctrine
    1. A final revelation of God — 1:1-3
    2. Superior to the angels — 1:4–2:18
      Hortatory application (2:1-4)
      Appeal to necessity of correct action (2:3a)
      First *prolepsis*[10] on a faithful high priest (2:17)
    3. Superior to Moses — 3:1-6
      Second *prolepsis* on Jesus the high priest (3:1)

[10]The word *prolepsis* (Gk., "taking beforehand") is used here to denote a statement which anticipates some objection or precedes further clarification and amplification.

B. Ethical exhortations on heeding God's voice and entering his heavenly rest	3:7–4:16
Exposition of Psalm 95 (3:7-11,15)	
Rhetorical questions (3:16-18)	
Third *prolepsis* on a great high priest (4:14-15)	
II. Diegesis (statement of case): The superior high priesthood of Christ	5:1–6:20
A. Doctrine: Christ and the qualifications of the priesthood	5:1-10
First *prolepsis* on Melchizedek (v 10)	
Topics to be developed later (5:11) in chs 7–10	
B. Exhortations on maturity (5:12–6:3), apostasy (6:4-8), Christian service (vv. 9-12), and hope (vv 13-20)	5:12–6:20
First *prolepsis* on heroes of faith (6:13-18; cf. ch 11)	
Second *prolepsis* of Melchizedek (v 20)	
III. Apodeixis or demonstration of evidence concerning Christ's superiority over the Levitical system	7:1–10:18
Doctrine (development of topics)	
A. On the priesthood of Melchizedek: A superior order	7:1-28
1. It continues for ever and is superior to that of the Levites	vv 3-11
2. It is not based on physical descent, since Christ also belongs to this order	vv 12-22
3. Christ, who offered the ultimate sacrifice for sin, holds this office permanently	vv 23-28
B. Christ serves as high priest of the heavenly sanctuary and is the mediator of the new covenant	8:1-13
C. The worship conducted in the wilderness tent was imperfect and temporary	9:1-10
D. Christ as high priest and mediator of the new covenant offered himself as the eternal sacrifice for sin	9:11–10:18
1. Thesis: He performed a final sacrifice in a more perfect tent for eternal redemption (vv 11-12) and his death ratifies the new covenant (vv 15-22)	vv 11-22
2. Amplification of thesis (in 9:11-22)	9:23–10:18

IV. Epilogue (peroration): Summary of arguments	10:19–13:21
A. First recapitulation of exhortations	10:19-32
1. We have direct access through Jesus the high priest (cf. 4:14-16)	vv 19-22
2. Let us hold fast to our confession (cf. 4:14,16)	v 23
3. The apocalyptic dangers of apostasy (cf. 6:1-6)	vv 26-31
B. Encomium of faith in the context of community affliction and hortatory applications	10:32–12:17
1. Prelude to encomium: exhortations to a community formerly afflicted	10:32-38
2. Doctrine: encomium on the virtues of those who have faith	11
3. Exhortations derived from encomium on faith	12:1-17
C. Second recapitulation of exhortations	12:18–13:17
1. Direct access through Jesus (cf. 4:14-16; 10:19-22)	12:18-24
2. The apocalyptic dangers of apostasy (cf. 6:1-6; 10:26-31)	12:25-29
3. Christian service and compassion (cf. 6:10; 10:24,34)	13:1-3,16
4. Respect your leaders/teachers (cf. 5:12)	13:7,17
5. Do not be mislead by human regulations (cf. 9:9-10)	v 9
6. We seek a heavenly city (11:10,16; 12:22)	v 14
7. Offer spiritual sacrifices (cf. 10:8-10)	vv 15-16
D. *Ethos*: author appeals to his own conscientious and honorable behavior	vv 18-19
E. Prayer and Doxology	vv 20-21
F. Epistolary Postscript	vv 22-25
Final appeal to listen willingly to this "word of exhortation" 13:23 (cf. 3:13)	

The proem introduces the reader to Jesus Christ, God's final revelation who is superior both to the angels (intermediaries between God and humanity) and Moses (leader of God's people). Next, the reader is introduced to Jesus Christ the high priest (to be discussed in the *diegesis* and *apodeixis*). Then the reader is exhorted to heed God's word and to seek entry into God's heavenly rest.

The *diegesis* first develops the doctrine of Christ's priesthood by an analogy with Aaron (5:4). Numerous exhortations are also presented here (5:12–6:20) which will be repeated later in the book (10:19-39; 12:18–13:17). Finally, statements are made concerning Melchizedek (5:10; 6:20) anticipating further discussion.

The *apodeixis* displays the proofs concerning Christ's superiority over the Levitical system (7:1–10:18). It is the book's longest doctrinal section. Hebrews 9:11-22 introduce topics which are expounded in more detail immediately after this pericope (i.e., 9:23–10:18).

The *epilogue* consists of: recapitulations of earlier exhortations (cf. 10:19-32; 12:18–13:17); an *encomium* on the virtues of the faithful (ch 11) in the context of the community's afflictions (10:32-39) and with its accompanying exhortations (12:1-17); the author's appeal to his own Christian character (12:18-19); and a prayer with a doxology (vv 20-21). Then, it ends with an epistolary postscript (vv 22-25).

The special attention given in the *epilogue* to the exhortations, by means of recapitulation and elaboration, confirms the deliberative function of the book. Hebrews seeks to persuade its readers to continue in the faith and to dissuade them from wavering in their beliefs, as a result of their doubts, discouragements, and exposure to false teachings.

4. The Religious Thought-World

An examination of the thought-milieu of Hebrews provides some helpful clues for understanding other questions relating to the book's content, authorship, and addressees. In this section we will look at the following aspects of the religious thought-world of Hebrews: the author's dependence on the Jewish Scriptures (LXX); possible influences from Alexandrian Judaism, Qumran, and Gnosticism; and finally, the author's relationship to Hellenistic Christianity.

a. The Jewish Scriptures

Along with the many allusions to the Jewish Scriptures, one study lists 20 quotations from the Pentateuch, 11 from the Hebrew Prophets division, and 28 from the Hebrew writings (26 from the Pss including repetitions of preferred passages).[11] Favorite texts in Hebrews are Pss 2 (kingship), 95 (wilderness testings), 110 (kingship and Melchizedek reference), and Jer 31:31-34 (new covenant). Although the LXX was the primary text of the author, there are about six textual deviations due to either the author's own free renderings or his use of text versions no longer extant.

According to the author, the Jewish Scriptures are replete with meaning and significance for Christ and his church. Hebrew prophecies find their fulfillment in the time of Jesus and his people. Israel's life and worship are viewed as preparatory for the coming of Christ. One could even assert that Christ is viewed here as the complete solution to the enigma of Israel's history, ritual, and ideals.[12] How the author interpreted the Jewish Scriptures to support his beliefs will be discussed in the following sections.

b. Alexandrian Judaism

It has been argued that Hebrews reflects the Alexandrian school of "Jewish Platonism" and has its closest parallels with Philo of Alexandria.[13] Plato's dualistic view of the material world as only a shadow of the true realm of ideas was attractive to Greek-speaking Jews. Philo (AD 40) for example, who was convinced that Judaism fulfilled all Hellenistic aspirations, interpreted the Scriptures allegorically to support this conviction. This form of interpretation perceived deeper, hidden meanings conveyed in the familiar biblical stories. Examples of this mystical exegesis include: Abraham's journey into unknown Canaan, which became an example of the soul's migration from human bondage (*Migration of Abraham*). Melchizedek the priest of Salem (Gen 14), in Philo, refers to reason which rules with justice over the body and soul

[11]R. G. Bratcher, ed., *Old Testament Quotations in the NT* (New York; London: United Bible Societies, 1961) 57–67. Note: Hebrew Prophets Division includes Joshua, Judges, Samuel, and Kings along with major and minor prophets.

[12]B. F. Westcott, *The Epistle to the Hebrews* (London: Macmillan, 1889) 493.

[13]J. Moffatt, *Epistle to the Hebrews* ICC (Edinburgh: T. & T. Clark, 1924) xxx–iv; C. Spicq, *L'Epitre aux Hebreux* (Paris, 1952) 1:39-91. Note: Texts of Philo are from the Loeb Classical Library, 1929–53, ten volumes.

(*Allegorical Interpretation* 3.79f.). Egypt is the place of material bondage (*Agriculture* 89). Moses was the perfect hero-king who revealed in himself the unwritten law behind the Torah (*Life of Moses*). Judaism was revealed to Moses as the true mystery religion. The plans for building the wilderness tent were immaterial forms which Moses saw with the eyes of his soul (*Life of Moses* 2.73f.). All of these examples reflect Philo's dualistic views from Platonism.

Does not Hebrews reflect this allegorical interpretation from a Platonist standpoint?[14] Are not the human priest, sanctuary, and sacrifices of ancient Israel merely the "shadowy copy" of the reality manifested in Jesus Christ and his sacrificial death? Are not the author's analogies between shadow and reality (8:5; 10:1), earthly and heavenly (8:1-4; 9:23-24), created and uncreated (9:11), transitory and enduring (7:23-24; 10:34; 13:14), obvious indicators of Platonic dualism? Do not the invisible heavenly future things (11:1,16; 12:22; 13:14) constitute the true reality in Hebrews? Do not unusual etymological interpretations (e.g., "Melchizedek," 7:2) and stark metaphorical associations (e.g., "curtain" = "flesh," 10:20; also 3:6; 13:14) signify a form of exegesis like that of Philo? Besides a similar dualistic world-view and allegorical interpretation, both Hebrews and Philo make use of the LXX and share both common vocabulary (e.g., *athlēsis*, *dysermeneutos*) and topics (e.g., Melchizedek, wilderness tabernacle, faith, angels, Abraham).

Even though similarities are numerous, the differences are profound. First, the dualism in Hebrews is grounded in a two ages scheme of redemptive history, i.e., the former age of the old covenant (Israel) and the new age of last days (messianic age). Comparisons between old Levitical worship and the work of Christ must be viewed in this framework. Second, because Hebrews maintains this scheme of salvation history, its exegesis presupposes a typological correspondence of persons and events in history. For example, the mysterious and preeminent priesthood of Melchizedek is a type of Christ's office. Some correspondence

[14]See Montefiore, *Hebrews* (1964) 6–11; R. Williamson, *Philo And the Epistle to the Hebrews* (Leiden: Brill, 1970) 11–81, 142–233; Williamson, however, argues *against* the Philonic character of Hebrews.

of these two personages in history is presupposed (7:2-3). Third, Hebrews uses the vocabulary and topics common to Philo in a different and independent manner. For example, Abraham's journey into Canaan is portrayed as a historical example of faith, not as the soul's migration from human bondage in Philo. Therefore, even though Hebrews and Philo may share a common heritage of Hellenistic Judaism, possibly Alexandrian, there are insufficient parallels to establish Hebrews as Philonic or Platonic.[15]

It must be added, however, that Hebrews shares literary and thematic features with other works that probably originated from Alexandria, the home of Philo. For example, the "famous people of faith" chapter of Heb 11 has numerous parallels with 4 Macc 17 and Sir 44–49. Hebrews also shares features with the Wisdom of Solomon (e.g., wisdom motifs, blend of doctrine and exhortation, eschatology) and the Christian letter of Barnabas (e.g., polemics against Jewish legalism, use of typology, blend of doctrine and exhortation.). None of these "Alexandrian" writings, however, are as Platonic in emphasis as Philo's works.

c. *The Qumran Community*

Because of its apparent polemics against certain forms of Jewish speculation and legalism, it has been suggested that Hebrews was addressed to former members of the Qumran community (Essene-Christians?).[16] Let us look at the following similarities between Hebrews and the Dead Sea Scrolls of Qumran: the method of biblical interpretation and four themes of purification, sacrifice, apostasy, and messianism.

In both its method of interpretation and the texts it employed, Hebrews has remarkable similarities to the Qumran writings. The biblical exegeses in both documents presuppose a life-situation in the last days of the messianic age when the veiled meanings

[15]The Greek terms in Heb 8:5; 9:23; 10:1, which sound Platonic (*hypodeigma, skia, antitypos*) can be translated by a number of less Platonic sounding synonyms, see L. Hurst "How 'Platonic' Are Heb 8:5 and 9:23f.?" *JTS* 34 (1, 1983) 156–68.

[16]Y. Yadin, "The Scrolls and The Epistle to the Hebrews," *Aspects of the Dead Sea Scrolls*, eds. Ch. Rabin and Y. Yadin (Jerusalem: Magnes, 1958) 36–55. Note: sources for Qumran writings are Vermes, *Scrolls*; Gaster, *Dead Sea Scriptures*.

of the Hebrew prophecies would be fully understood. This form of "pesher" interpretation assumed that the Hebrew prophecies spoke to the contemporary situation in an exclusive manner (e.g., Heb 8:8-13/CD 8.19-20; Heb 10:38-39/1Qp Hab 8.1-3). Furthermore, the same texts are used by both in this manner: e.g., Dt 29:16; 32; 2 Sam 7:14; Jer 31:31-34; Hab 2:3-4; Pss 95; 110.

Let us look at some of the common themes. Although the ceremonial washings criticized in Hebrews (6:1-2; 9:10) recall the teachings and practices of Qumran (1QS 3.4-6,8-9; 4.20-21), these Essene "waters of purification" could only benefit those of "an upright and humble spirit." Such qualifications would not be condemned in Hebrews. Since the Qumran community did not participate in the ritual sacrifices of the Jerusalem temple, it advocated the offering of "spiritual sacrifices" to God (Heb 13:15-16/1QS 9.3-5). As in Hebrews (6:4-6; 10:26-27), the Qumran community offered little hope of forgiveness for the apostates (1QS 2.13-14). Finally, the preeminence of Christ as apostle and high priest (Heb 3:1-6) might be viewed as a corrective to the messiahs of Qumran: e.g., the rise of the prophet alongside the messiahs of Israel and Aaron (1QS 9.11).

The similarities with the Qumran scrolls provide a number of insights for understanding Hebrews. They clarify many of the author's interpretations of Scripture texts. They also provide a context for understanding the liturgical motifs, messianic speculations, and Jewish polemics in the Christian book. However, a clear association of the readers of Hebrews with the Qumran community lacks sufficient proof. If the readers are attracted to a sect of Judaism it might be the type of Judaism represented by the Essenes of Qumran, but not restricted to this group.[17]

d. Gnosticism

Like John's Gospel, Hebrews uses numerous images and motifs similar to Gnosticism.[18] We will look at the following: the

[17]F. F. Bruce, " 'To the Hebrews' or 'To the Essenes,' " *NTS* 9 (3, 1963) 217–32 (esp. 232); idem, *The Epistle to the Hebrews* NICT, rev. ed. (Grand Rapids: Eerdmans, 1990).

[18]Sources for Gnosticism are from: Robinson, *Nag Hammadi; Acts of Thomas* and *Pseudo-Clementines* in Hennecke and Schneemelcher, *NTA* 2:425-570; Odes

preexistence of the Gnostic Redeemer, his descent to earth through heavenly realms, the common origin of both the Redeemer and the redeemed, pilgrimage to heavenly home, and gnostic rebuttals.

The preexistence of the Redeemer is assumed in both writings (e.g., Heb 1:2-3; 2:10; 9:26/*1 Apoc Jas* 24.21-25; 33.21-24; *Treatise on Resurrection* 44.33-36) and the Redeemer's descent to earth through the heavenly realms (Heb 2:9,14-18; 5:7-8; 9:11-14,24/*Seth* 59.20-25; *Shem* 15.29-36) to destroy the powers of death and darkness (Heb 2:9, 14-15; 9:13-14/*Archons* 97.6-13; *1 Apoc Jas* 25.10,21). The divine origins and descent of the Primal Man is also found in gnostic writings like *Poimandres* (Hermetic writings 1.12-15). The common origin of both the Redeemer and redeemed is also presupposed in both writings (Heb 2:11; 5:9/*Truth* 34.28-35.23; *Peter to Philip* 136.16-28).

Another major motif is the pilgrimage of believers to their heavenly home (Heb 3:11,18; 4:1,3,5,10-11). This theme in Hebrews has parallels with the motif of the ascent of the soul to its heavenly home in gnostic writings (*Treatise on Resurrection* 45.36-39; *Seth* 58.30-59.11; *Shem* 41.21-43.30; 45.31-46.3; 47.6-48.9). Accounts of the heavenly journey of the soul are also given in the *Odes of Solomon* (35.5-7; 38.1-3), *Poimandres* (Hermetic writing 1.24-26), the *Acts of Thomas* (22-28,80,85), and the *Pseudo-Clementine Homilies* (3.20).

Certain emphases in Hebrews may also be viewed as rebuttals of Gnosticism. Appeals to the suffering and death of the Redeemer on earth (Heb 2:9-10,14,17-18; 4:15; 5:7-8; 9:12-14,22) might be viewed as attempts to counter gnostic teaching that Christ did not actually suffer and die (*1 Apoc Jas* 31.15-26; *Seth* 55.9-56.19; *Apoc Peter* 81.3-82.14). Also, Hebrews from the beginning (1:5–2:18) excludes any mediation of salvation through angelic powers, which might be a reaction to the elaborate cosmologies of syzygies (e.g., Nous-Truth) emanating from the Unbegotten Father (e.g., Valentinian system).[19] Finally, the apocalyptic view of the future in Hebrews (1:2; 2:5; 6:5; 9:26-28; 10:35-37; 13:14; cf. Qumran)

of Solomon, Hermetic, and Mandean writings in W. Barnstone, ed., *The Other Bible* (San Francisco: Harper & Row, 1984) 267–85, 567–80, 696–704; Rudolph, *Gnosis.*

[19]Valentinian system according to Hippolytus, *Refutation of All Heresies* 29–36, or Irenaeus, *Against Heresies* 1–8.

may be an attempt to balance the gnostic extreme of realized eschatology (i.e., resurrection = release of soul from body).[20]

Despite these general similarities of motifs and images, there are some problems in the comparison of Hebrews and gnostic writings. First, the theme of the promised heavenly rest is not the goal of the celestial journey of the soul in Hebrews, but of the wanderings of the historical people of God on earth. (Hebrews, however, may be correcting this gnostic view.) Second, the author of Hebrews places too much emphasis on the Levitical culture and priesthood for it to be merely a defense of the salvific significance of Jesus' death *only* against Gnosticism. The readers must have been attracted to some form of Jewish legalism. Third, the author's (pesher) interpretation of Scripture has little in common with the esoteric and mystical explanations of the gnostic writings. Fourth, the late dating of many of our gnostic sources (e.g., Hermetica, Mandean) continues to raise problems whenever comparisons are made with the NT. It is a difficult enterprise to distinguish the earlier gnostic traditions from later Christian redactions. Despite these difficulties it is possible that the author of Hebrews shared some motifs and images with later Gnosticism, even though they are used in a context different from what we know to be "gnostic." As a result, there does not appear to be sufficient proof for postulating Hebrews as an anti-gnostic writing.

e. Hellenistic Christianity

With what movement of early Christianity might we classify the book of Hebrews? To formulate a plausible answer, we must look at its internal evidence: its language, style, historical allusions, and its conceptual similarities with other early Christian writings. This evidence will also provide further information about the author.

The language and style of both Hebrews and Luke-Acts are nearest to literary Koine Greek (e.g., writings of Epictetus, Josephus, Philo). The author of Hebrews employs a rich and di-

[20] *Exegesis of the Soul* 134.7-16; *Gospel of Philip* 73.1-5; *Treatise on Resurrection* 49.10-17.

verse vocabulary (e.g., 157 words not used elsewhere in the NT).[21] The author appears to be acquainted with the classical standards of rhythmic prose (e.g., Heb 1:1-3; Aristotle *Rhetoric* 3.8.6-7). Like the rhetoricians he employed assonance or similar sounding words (e.g., *parakaleite* . . . . *kaleitai*, 3:13; *emathen* . . . . *epathen*, 5:8; *kalou* . . . . *kakou*, 5:14), alliteration (*polumeros kai polutropos palai* . . . . *patrasin* . . . . *prophetais*, 1:1; *apator, ametor agenalogetos*, 7:3), and rich sounding compound words (e.g., *misthapodosia*, 2:2; 10:35; *euperistatos*, 12:1). His skillful use of grammar and his complex sentence structure also betray some acquaintance with Attic Greek.[22] Obviously at home in the Hellenistic tradition of the literary Koine, the author of Hebrews does not reveal any knowledge of the classical Hebrew or Aramaic dialects.[23] Instead, he relies heavily upon the LXX in his biblical quotations.

Sparse historical allusions in Hebrews indicate that the author and his readers belonged to the second Christian generation (2:3), were acquainted with Timothy the associate of the Apostle Paul (13:23), had experienced past persecution (10:32-34, under Nero?), and awaited more persecution (12:4, under Domitian?).

Let us now look at the similarities of Hebrews with other early Christian writings. Although it is clearly different from Paul's writings in language, style, and theological emphasis,[24] Hebrews contains some general Pauline themes. In Christology, both Hebrews and Pauline Christianity speak of Christ as the image of God (Heb 1:3; 2 Cor 4:4), his agency over creation (Heb 1:2; Col 1:16), and of his obedience (Heb 5:8; Phil 2:8). Both writ-

[21]These *hapax legomena* are listed and discussed in R. Williamson, *Philo and Hebrews* 11–18.

[22]For more information, consult: J. Moulton and W. Howard, *A Grammar of New Testament Greek*, 4 vols. (Edinburgh: T. & T. Clark, 1920, 1968) 2:24-25; Moffatt, *Hebrews* (1924) lvi–lxiv.

[23]Moulton and Howard, *Grammar* 2:24-25; Moffatt, *Hebrews* lvi–lxiv. There are only 6 textual deviations from the LXX which could have been due either to the author's own free renderings or Greek text versions no longer extant. See also Longenecker, *Biblical Exegesis in the Apostolic Period* (Grand Rapids: Eerdmans, 1975) 169–70; Westcott, *Epistle to the Hebrews* 481.

[24]Paul could not have written Hebrews, see D. Guthrie, *New Testament Introduction* 3rd ed. (Downers Grove, Ill.: InterVarsity Press, 1970) 688–90; Moffatt, *Hebrews* xvii–xxi. In Hebrews there is the absence of typical Pauline abruptness, digressions of thought, and emotional pathos.

ings discuss the new covenant (Heb 9:15; 2 Cor 3:6) and the administration of the Spirit's gifts (Heb 2:4; 1 Cor 12:11). "Faith" with Abraham as the leading model (Heb 11; Rom 4) and Habakkuk 2:4 as a major text (Heb 10:38; Rom 1:17; Gal 3:11) is mutually discussed. Finally, Israel's disobedience in the wilderness is used as an example of warning (Heb 3:7–4:10; 1 Cor 10:1-11). Although the above themes are employed differently for different reasons, the similarities may reveal that either Hebrews and Pauline Christianity shared a common collection of religious themes or that the author of Hebrews was familiar with some form of Pauline Christianity. In support of the latter possibility, the author and his readers were acquainted with Paul's associate Timothy, who seems to be living at the time of writing (13:23).[25]

In distinction from Pauline Christianity, the author of Hebrews takes a more radical stance against the "old covenant" religion. Even though Paul opposed Jewish legalism as a precondition for Gentile salvation (e.g., Gal), the apostle spoke Hebrew (as well as Greek) and maintained cultural and historical ties with both Jerusalem ("the collection") and Judaism (Rom 9:1-4; 2 Cor 11:22). The author of Hebrews would probably agree with Paul's stance against Jewish legalism but goes beyond Paul in having no apparent acquaintance with the Hebrew language and maintaining no ties with Jerusalem or contemporary Judaism. The author's only apparent understanding of Judaism concerns the ancient Israel of the Greek OT.

If we interpret correctly the "Hebrews" and "Hellenists" of Acts 6:1 as referring to Hebrew and Greek-speaking Jewish Christians respectively, Hebrews would be classed with the latter group ("Hellenists") and Paul with the liberal wing of the former ("Hebrews").[26] Let us examine these "Hellenists" in Acts to discern any similarities with the book of Hebrews. According to Acts, the Hellenist movement began at Jerusalem and was associated with Stephen (6:1-5, 8-14). The group was scattered throughout Judea after Stephen's death (8:1), and it spread to Samaria with

[25]"Timothy" is probably Paul's friend of that name, see Bruce, *Hebrews* 414.

[26]For more information, see Brown and Meier, *Antioch* 1-9; M. Hengel, *Between Jesus and Paul,* trans. J. Bowden (Philadelphia: Fortress, 1974) 1–29. See also C. C. Hill, *Hellenists and Hebrews* (Minneapolis: Fortress, 1992).

Philip (8:4-6), onward to Phoenicia, Cyprus, Antioch (11:19-20), and eventually to Ephesus and Rome. This group of Greek-speaking Jewish Christians did not converse in Hebrew or Aramaic (6:1). They not only opposed Jewish legalism for Gentiles but also saw no abiding significance in the worship at the Jerusalem temple (7:47-51).

Since Stephen is the main exponent of Hellenistic Christianity in Acts, a comparison of Stephen's speech with Hebrews would be instructive.[27] First, even though both regard the tabernacle as built by Moses according to a divine pattern ("*typos*," Acts 7:44/Heb 8:5), it is still an imperfect structure (Acts 7:39-46/Heb 7:18-19; 8:7,13; 9:11). Second, the patriarchs and their descendants are portrayed in both writings as the wandering people of God (Acts 7:3-4,6,29,34,36-38,42/Heb 3:16-17; 11:8-16,22,27,29,38; 13:4). Third, both speak of Israel leaving Egypt under Moses and of its rebellion in the wilderness (Acts 7:36,39-40/ Heb 3:16-17). Fourth, both speak of Joshua and the promise of rest (*katapausis*, Acts 7:44-45,49; Heb 3:7–4:10). Fifth, each one speaks of the call of Abraham (Gen 12) and mentions Abraham's non-possession of the land (Acts 7:3-5/Heb 11:8-10, 13-14). Sixth, both the Stephen speech and Hebrews focus on Jesus as the goal of salvation history (Acts 7:55-56/Heb 12:2). Finally, both speak of the angels as ordainers of God's law (Acts 7:53/Heb 2:2) and of God's word as "living" (*zōe*, Acts 7:38/Heb 4:12).[28] Although these topical similarities are interpreted differently, they reflect a radical stance against the Jewish religious heritage.[29]

[27]Although the speeches of Acts are primarily Lukan creations, they often contain historical information that can be corroborated with other writings (e.g., Acts 22:3/Gal 1:14; Acts 13:46/Rom 1:16; Acts 18:26-27/Rom 11:7-8). Furthermore, like most literary men of antiquity, Luke knew that his speeches had to be realistic and appropriate to the different speakers and occasions. On the comparison of Stephen's Speech and Heb, see W. Manson, *The Epistle to the Hebrews* (London: Hodder and Stoughton, 1951) 36, 50, 159–97.

[28]See also similar typological use of the LXX (e.g., Gen 12 in Acts 7 and Heb 11; Ex 25 in Acts 7 and Heb 8) and a fondness for the same OT characters as heroes and saints (e.g., Abraham, Joseph, Moses, and the prophets in Acts 7 and Heb 11).

[29]Such a position expressed by Stephen and the Hellenists appears to run counter to Luke's own concern to present Jesus and his followers as faithful Jews loyal to the law (e.g., Lk 2:21-24,41-43; Acts 3:1-2; 5:12-13; 18:18; 20:16). Could not

Even though Hebrews does not mention the Jerusalem temple, its emphasis on the preeminence of Jesus as great high priest makes it agree by implication with the anti-temple motif in the Stephen speech: "the Most High does not dwell in houses made with hands" (Acts 7:48; cf. Heb 9:11). The Gospel of John more directly agrees with this anti-temple statement, since the body of Jesus replaces the temple (Jn 2:19-21; cf. 4:21). The Gospel of Mark's portrait of Jesus abrogating Jewish law and tradition (Mk 2:15–3:6; 7:1-13) also classes it with this type of Hellenistic Christianity. All of these writings with their profound criticisms of the Jewish cult and ritual conform to a Hellenistic type of Christianity which is transcending much of its Jewish heritage (e.g., Heb 10:8-10). In the second century, this form of Christianity will evidence a further hardening against Jewish ritual. This latter tendency is seen in the *Letter of Barnabas* and *Letter to Diognetus,* both of which have stylistic similarities to Hebrews.

5. The Authorship

We will first look at the external and internal evidence for the authorship of Hebrews. Then we will draw our own conclusions based partly on the previous study of its religious thought world.

a. External Evidence

Despite the fact that Clement of Rome (AD 95) is the first to quote from Hebrews (*1 Clem* 36.2-5; 17.1) no mention is made of its author. Clement of Alexandria (ca. 200) was the first to ascribe it to Paul. The apostle supposedly wrote it in the Hebrew language and it was translated by Luke into Greek. According to Clement, Paul did not identify himself in the book because he was the apostle to the Gentiles, not to the Hebrews.[30] Origen,

this distinctive portrait of Stephen and the Hellenists signify Luke's attempt to portray the beliefs of a historical group that is different theologically from his own more moderate views? Such an approach would be in keeping with Luke's technique of versatility in which he composed speeches that were realistic appropriate to the different speakers and occasions.

[30]Clement of Alexandria according to Eusebius, *Eccl Hist* 4.14.2-3.

Clement's successor in Alexandria, stated that the thoughts were the apostle's but the diction and phraseology belonged to someone else, possibly Clement of Rome. Origen concludes, however: "But who it was that really wrote the epistle, God only knows."[31] Tertullian (ca. 210) attributed it to Barnabas, the companion of Paul (*On Purity* 20). Martin Luther (1537) separated Hebrews from the Pauline letters and attributed the book to Apollos (cf. Acts 18:24).[32] Other candidates for the authorship of Hebrews have been: Silas (1 Pet 5:13), Philip the Evangelist (Acts 21:8), and Priscilla (Acts 18:26).[33]

b. Internal Evidence

The internal evidence for the authorship of Hebrews is sparse. As we have noted earlier, the author wrote in polished literary Koine Greek. Although he shares certain themes with Paul (e.g., faith, new covenant), he writes differently, argues differently, and thinks differently than the apostle.[34] The thought forms of Hebrews have some resemblance to Alexandrian Judaism, but not enough to regard it as a Philonic writing or a book written by Apollos the Alexandrian (Acts 18:24-28; 1 Cor 1-4).[35] Hebrews also employs some motifs that are similar to Gnosticism (e.g., Redeemer, journey motif), yet one cannot call it a gnostic work (cf. *Acts of Thomas*) and there is insufficient proof to describe it as a polemic against Gnosticism.[36] The polemics of Hebrews,

[31]Origen according to Eusebius, *Eccl Hist* 6.25.11-12; see also Eusebius, *Eccl Hist* 3.38 (Clement as author of Hebrews).

[32]See Martin Luther, "Lectures on Genesis," in *Luther's Works*, ed. J. Pelikan (St. Louis: Concordia, 1966) 8:178; T. Zahn, *Introduction to the NT*, trans. J. Trout (Grand Rapids: Kregal, 1953) 2:364.

[33]See Guthrie, *Introduction* 694–7.

[34]Guthrie, *Introduction* 688–94.

[35]H. Montefiore, *A Commentary on the Epistle to the Hebrews* (London: Black, 1964) 6–11 argues for the Philonic character of Hebrews and Apollos as its author. R. Williamson, *Philo and Hebrews* argues against the Philonic character of Hebrews and weakens the argument for Apollos as its author.

[36]Although the emphasis of Hebrews on both the humanity and suffering of Jesus (2; 4:15; 5:7-8; 9) and its apocalyptic view of the future (1:2; 2:5; 6:5) would place it with so-called early catholic Christianity.

however, envision a type of Jewish sectarianism like that at Qumran (e.g., Heb 6:1-2; 9:10; Manual of Discipline 1QS 3-4).[37]

The Christian viewpoint of the author is that of Hellenistic Christianity. He (or she) is a representative of a Greek-speaking Christianity, linguistically and culturally separated from Judaism. The author is a second generation Christian (2:3) and only casually acquainted with Pauline Christianity (despite 13:23). His (or her) viewpoint regarding the obsoleteness of Jewish tradition is similar to that of Mark, John, Barnabas, and Diognetus.

6. The Place of Composition

The place of composition for the writing might be any urban center of Hellenism, where an influx of Gnosticism, ancient Near Eastern wisdom, and Essene teaching could be found. Candidates for the place of authorship might be: Alexandria of Egypt, Antioch of Syria, or Ephesus of Asia. Rome does not appear to be a likely location because of Heb 13:24, "those who are *from Italy* salute you."[38] Palestine is not a probable location because the author shows no acquaintance with the Jerusalem or Palestine of his day.[39] His knowledge of Palestine seems to be derived from the LXX.

7. The Audience

The title "To the Hebrews" was not supplied by the author. By AD 200 the designation was found in an early Greek manuscript (p^{46}). Clement of Alexandria claims that his teacher, Pantaenus (180), knew it by this title, and Tertullian (210) refers to

[37]The author of Hebrews also appears to share some common themes and exegetical techniques like those at Qumran (e.g., spiritual sacrifices, apostasy, pesher interpretation of Scripture). From Josephus we learn that Essenes like those at Qumran lived in other areas of Palestine.

[38]Heb 13:24 will be further discussed in this chapter under 7. Audience and 8. Destination.

[39]The author's lack of acquaintance with the Palestine of his day may also raise doubts about Antioch of Syria, near Palestine, as the place of origin.

it in this manner.[40] The superscription "to the Hebrews" probably originated from an analysis of the book itself, since it seems to be addressed to Jews who were lapsing from their faith in Jesus.

Some, in disagreement with the traditional title, argue that the book was addressed to Gentiles, not Hebrews. Since the LXX, used in Hebrews, was the Bible of early Christianity, both Gentile and Jewish believers would have been acquainted with it. The author does not deal with the Judaism of his day or any Jewish-Gentile controversies, only OT Israel. The statements about falling away from the "living God" (3:12) and the mention of "dead works" (6:1; 9:14) sound like the author is combating a return to pagan idolatry. Finally, those who stress the gnostic motifs and polemics in Hebrews maintain that the book argues against the gnostic denial of the significance of Jesus' death for salvation, and not against Judaism.[41]

The reasons for maintaining a gentile audience for Hebrews, however, are not convincing. First, the appeal to the Greek OT would be meaningless to gentile Christians relapsing into paganism. Second, the omission of Jewish-Gentile controversies (e.g., circumcision in Gal) is understandable if addressed to a Jewish audience. Third, the imagery of falling away from the "living God" (3:12) is adduced from Israelite disobedience in the wilderness (Ps 95) and is certainly relevant for Jews of the first century AD. Hebrews 6:1-2 and 9:13-15 seem to imply the Jewish antecedents of the readers. Fourth, the argument that Hebrews concerns gnostic, not Jewish, polemics lacks conclusive data. It does not account for the Qumran parallels (e.g., ceremonial washings, purification, pesher interpretation) and the amount of space devoted to Levitical sacrifice and priesthood which still have significance for the readers (e.g., Heb 7:11).[42]

The audience of Hebrews was probably a group of Jewish Christians that was attempting to merge with a form of Judaism to which it had previously belonged. This act of apostasy (as the

[40]Pantaenus is cited by Clement of Alexandria in Eusebius, *Eccl Hist* 6.14.3-4; Tertullian entitles the book "To the Hebrews" in *On Purity* 20.

[41]Koester, *Introduction* 2:276.

[42]For further critique of the theory of a Gentile audience for Hebrews, see Bruce, *Hebrews* xxvi–xxviii.

author views it) may have resulted from both the pressures of Roman persecution (10:32-34) and the uncertainties resulting from the delay of the Lord's return (vv 35-37).

Even though the readers are probably Greek-speaking Jews, they seem attracted to a type of sectarian Judaism similar to that practiced at Qumran (e.g., Heb 6:1-2; 9:10/1 QS 3-4). Perhaps there were some converted Jewish priests in their midst (cf. Acts 6:7) who had a natural interest in the ritual details that our author criticized. Whatever form of Judaism they were attracted to, these Jewish Christians had concerns similar to those original "Hebrews" of the Jerusalem church (Acts 6:1).[43] This conservative wing of Hebrew Christianity was also interested in upholding certain Jewish traditions, like the food and purity laws (e.g., Acts 10:9-20; 15:19-20; 21:25). The writer of Hebrews, representing the liberal group of Hellenistic Christianity (e.g., Acts 7; John) warns his readers against apostasy and argues that Judaism is now superseded by Christianity.[44]

8. The Destination

Various locations for the destination of Hebrews have been postulated.[45] We will examine the two major localities: Jerusalem and Rome.

It has been argued by some that Hebrews was addressed to readers in Jerusalem or Palestine. Either location would be a likely place for the readers to be enticed back to Judaism. It was in the Jerusalem church that a distinction was first made between "Hebrews" and "Hellenists" (Acts 6:1), although we do not know how long it lasted. In Acts 8:16, the Hellenists were driven out.

[43]Despite the harsh statements on "apostasy" by the author of Hebrews, the readers may have only been interested in practicing a more judaistic form of Christianity, not forsaking the Christian faith altogether.

[44]See Manson, *Hebrews* 159–72.

[45]For example Colossae or Lycus Valley (similar problems of angelic intermediaries, Heb 1-4/Col 2:18 and ritual tendencies, Heb 5-10/Col 2:14-15), Alexandria (parallels with Wisdom, 4 Maccabees and Philo, although these reflect more of the *author's* situation).

The statements in Hebrews of "serving the saints" and helping the poor or afflicted (6:10; 10:34; 13:16) may be allusions to assisting the poor in Jerusalem (e.g., Rom 15:26). In the rural areas outside Jerusalem, there would have been numerous Essene communities, like Khirbet Qumran, which represented a type of sectarian Judaism to which the readers may have been attracted. References to the former sufferings of the readers (Heb 10:32; 12:4) may denote persecution from the Jerusalem Jews (e.g., Acts 4:1-2; 8:16) or the tragedies resulting from Jerusalem's destruction (Josephus, *War* 6.220-357).

Jerusalem as the destination of Hebrews has problems. First, the religious situation in Jerusalem was dominated by the temple, to which no explicit reference is made. Second, the statements of needing "someone to teach you" (5:12) and remembering "your leaders who spoke to you the word of God" (13:7) seem inappropriate for the earliest Christian community, the Jerusalem church. Third, if a post-70 AD date is maintained for Hebrews, it weakens considerably the likelihood of a Jerusalem destination since the temple was destroyed and the city no longer was the center for Judaism after this date. Most of these objections are removed if the destination was to somewhere else in Palestine (e.g., Caesarea, Samaria).

The destination of Hebrews favored by most is Rome. Several reasons can be provided. First, it was in Rome that Hebrews was first known (1 Clem 9:4; 12:1; 36:1-2; Rome, AD 95). Second, the concluding salutation in Heb 13:24 seems more naturally understood as Italians who are away from Italy who are sending greetings home, than of Italians sending greetings to some non-Italian destination.[46] Third, Timothy (Heb 13:23) was probably known to Roman Christians.[47] Fourth, the persecutions of Heb 10:32-34 and 12:4 could refer to those under Nero. Fifth, the Roman church appears to be comprised of both Jewish and Gentile believers (e.g., Rom 4:1; 11:13) who met in separate house churches (Rom 16:5,14,15). Hebrews was probably addressed to a particular house church within the Roman community that was

[46]There are problems with this verse. Do "they of Italy" simply mean "Aquila and Priscilla" (Acts 18:1-2). Can we be sure it is a specific historical reference?

[47]Again, it must be asked if this "Timothy" was the associate of Paul.

comprised of conservative Jewish Christians with Judaistic leanings (cf. Rom 2:17-29?).[48]

Although we favor a Roman destination for Hebrews, the position also has its shortcomings. First, Clement of Rome was also familiar with letters of Paul that were not addressed to Rome (e.g., 1 Cor). Moreover, it is difficult to pinpoint the specific nature of the persecutions in Heb 10:32-35. Finally, the apparent concerns of the Jewish Christians deduced from Paul's rhetoric in Romans (e.g., 2; 9-11) are different from those in Hebrews (although a later date for Hebrews might account for the differences).

9. The Date

The latest possible date for Hebrews would be around AD 95, the date of 1 Clement, which first cites the work. A date prior to AD 70 cannot be inferred either from the silence concerning the catastrophe of AD 70 or references to an imminent crisis (8:13; 10:25). The persecutions which the community has experienced (10:32-34, Neronian?) and the spiritual proximity to John's Gospel (e.g., Hellenistic Christianity, Jewish polemics) point to a post-Pauline period. The writer and readers are probably second generation Christians (2:3). The new suffering which threatens the readers (12:3-11) may point to the time of Domitian (81-96). Therefore, Hebrews was probably written around AD 90.[49]

10. Summary

In our study of Hebrews, we looked at its literary genre, rhetorical structure, religious thought-world, authorship, addressees, place of destination, and date. First, we argued that Hebrews was

[48]For more information on this view, see Bruce, *Hebrews* xxxv; Manson, *Hebrews* 159–62, 172–89, 187–92. Heed, however, our precautions about deriving too much data on the Roman church from the rhetoric of Paul's Letter to the Romans, in ch 5 of this book.

[49]See the following work for a post-70 date: Kümmel, *Introduction* 403; and the following for a pre-70 date: Guthrie, *Introduction* 716–18.

an early Christian sermon put into written form for a distant audience. Like other Christian homilies, it combines doctrine and exhortation to persuade or dissuade its audience. Second, we outlined Hebrews as a form of deliberative persuasion, concerned with future issues of expedience. Hebrews contains a proem (1:1–4:12), statement of the case (4:13–6:20), a demonstration of evidence (7:1–10:18), an epilogue summarizing the arguments (10:19–13:21), and an epistolary postscript (13:22-25). Third, we noted the author's dependence on the LXX, his common heritage of Hellenism with Alexandrian Judaism, his affinity with both Qumran eschatology and pesher interpretation of Scripture, his utilization of motifs also found in Gnosticism (e.g., heavenly Redeemer, wandering motif), and his religious proximity to the Hellenistic Christianity of Stephen, Mark, and John.

Fourth, we deduced from the book that the author was skilled in Hellenistic style and diction, and conversant with traditions of Alexandrian Judaism, Gnosticism, and Qumran. He represents a type of Hellenistic Christian that was separate from Judaism and viewed its traditions as obsolete for Christianity (cf. John's Gospel). It is pure guesswork to assign a name to the author of Hebrews. Fifth, the addressees appear to be Hellenistic Jews attracted to a form of sectarian Judaism like that at Qumran. Their concerns reflect those of the earlier Hebrew Christians of Jerusalem who sought to retain their Jewish traditions. Sixth, both Jerusalem and Rome are the most promising candidates for the place of destination. Rome is favored because Hebrews was first known there, it best accounts for the closing greeting of those "from Italy" (13:24), the Roman church had both Jewish and Gentile believers there, and the theory is less threatened by a post-70 AD date. Finally, because the book is a product of second generation Christianity, it has religious affinities with John's Gospel, reflects early persecutions and anticipates more, and can be dated no later than 1 Clement, a date of composition for Hebrews around AD 90 is plausible.

The book of Hebrews provides us with a distinctly Christian interpretation of the Jewish Scriptures for faith and practice. It also presents a bold and articulate statement about the superiority and finality of Christ for believers, and it reveals the wide gap already existing between church and synagogue.

10

The Pastoral Letters

1. Introduction

The letters of Paul to Timothy and Titus have been labeled the "Pastoral Epistles" since the eighteenth century. They were given this title because of their usefulness for instructing Christian leaders.[1] But the designation may be inadequate. The contents

[1]Professor Paul Anton at the University of Halle (1726) was the first to give all three books this technical designation, although Thomas Aquinas (1270) also used the word "Pastoral" in his discussion of these books, see P. N. Harrison, *The Problem of the Pastoral Epistles* (London: Oxford University Press, 1921) 13–16.

For commentaries and other studies, see M. Dibelius and H. Conzelmann, *The Pastoral Epistles*, Hermeneia, trans. P. Buttolph et al. (Philadelphia: Fortress, 1972); B. S. Easton, *Pastoral Epistles* (New York: Scribner's Sons, 1948); G. D. Fee, *1 and 2 Timothy, Titus* Good News (San Francisco: Harper & Row, 1984); B. Fiore, *The Function of Personal Example in the Socratic and Pastoral Epistles* (Rome: Biblical Institute Press, 1986); D. Guthrie, *The Pastoral Epistles and the Mind of Paul* (London: Tyndale, 1956); A. T. Hanson, *The Pastoral Epistles*, NCB (Grand Rapids: Eerdmans, 1982); idem, *The Pastoral Letters* (Cambridge: University Press, 1966); A. J. Hultgren and R. Aus, *I–II Timothy, Titus, II Thess*, ACNT (Minneapolis, Minn.: Augsburg, 1984); R. J. Karris, *The Pastoral Epistles*, NTM 17 (Wilmington, Del.: Michael Glazier, 1979); idem, "The Background and Significance of the Polemic of the Pastoral Epistles," *JBL* 92 (1973) 549–64; J. N. D. Kelly, *A Commentary on the Pastoral Epistles*, HNTC (New York: Harper & Row, 1963); G. W. Knight, *The Faithful Sayings in the Pastoral Letters* (Grand Rapids: Baker, 1979); J. D. Quinn, "The Pastoral Epistles," *BibToday* 23 (4, 1985) 228–38; idem, *The Letter to Titus: A New Transl. with Notes and Commentary and an Intro. to Titus, 1 and 2 Timothy* (New York: Doubleday, 1990); D. C. Verner, *The Household of God. The Social World of the Pastoral Epistles,*

are much more than private correspondences from a senior pastor (Paul) to younger pastors (Timothy, Titus). First Timothy and Titus also contain advice for the "regulation of church discipline" (Muratorian Fragment). Second Timothy also seems to have a separate rhetorical function as a final testament of the apostle Paul. Nevertheless, all three writings share such noteworthy similarities that they form a separate group among the so-called Pauline corpus. In this chapter we will observe how their distinctiveness affects questions of authorship, setting, and date. Our examination of the literary character and rhetorical structure of the books will also point out their similarities with other writings of late antiquity.

2. Authorship

The authorship question of the Pastorals is enigmatic. First, external evidence for the use of the Pastorals before AD 150 is disputed. Second, a clear gap exists between the explicit Pauline claims of these books and their numerous differences with the undisputed Pauline writings (i.e., 1 Thes, Gal, 1 and 2 Cor, Phil, Phlm, Rom).

a. Arguments for Authenticity

Although the early witnesses of 1 Clement (95), Ignatius, and Polycarp (early 2nd cent.) have linguistic similarities with the Pastorals, it is difficult to prove their dependence on the Pastorals. All seem to stand in the same ecclesiastical and cultural tradition.[2]

It is also difficult to ascertain whether the Pastorals were either unknown or omitted by other early witnesses. They do not appear in Marcion's collection of Scripture (140), even though Marcion could have rejected them (as alleged in Tertullian *Against Marcion* 5.21). The Pastorals are also absent from the Chester

SBLDS 71 (Chico, Calif.: Scholars Press, 1983); S. G. Wilson, *Luke and the Pastoral Epistles* (London: SPCK, 1979).

[2]Kümmel, *Introduction* 370; Dibelius and Conzelmann, *Pastoral Epistles* 1–2, 84–86.

Beatty Papyrus, p^{46} (ca. 200), although it breaks off before the end of the codex (at 1 Thes 5:5). It seems likely, however, that Tatian of Syria (160) rejected 1 and 2 Timothy but not Titus.[3]

Mention of the Pastorals appears in the Muratorian Fragment, but the second-century date of this document is questioned[4] and the Pastorals appear in the Muratorian list as an appendix to the other Pauline letters. Nevertheless, it was from the time of Irenaeus (180) until the nineteenth century, that 1 and 2 Timothy and Titus were cited without dispute as authentic letters of Paul.[5]

The internal claims of Pauline authorship are explicit. The author identifies himself in all the epistolary prescripts as "*Paulos apostolos.*" His addressees are Timothy (e.g., 2 Cor 1:1; Phil 1:1) and Titus (2 Cor 2:13; Gal 2:1), two well-known co-workers in Paul's undisputed letters. First Timothy purports to have been written after Paul had left Ephesus on his way to Macedonia in the hopes of rejoining Timothy there (1 Tim 1:3; 3:14; 4:13; cf. 2 Cor 2:12-13; 7:5-6). In the letter to Titus he writes to his co-worker whom he had left behind in Crete (Tit 1:5; cf. Acts 27:7,12-13,21). In 2 Timothy, Paul is a prisoner at Rome (2 Tim 1:17; cf. Acts 28). Facing martyrdom, he appoints Timothy as a successor (2 Tim 1:8,11; 2:3,9; 4:6-8; cf. Acts 20:17-38). In the Pastorals, the names of certain individuals (e.g., Prisca, Aquila, Apollos, Tychicus) and localities (e.g., Antioch, Iconium, Lystra, Miletus) are also known from Paul's letters and Acts. The Pauline identifications, the mention of his co-workers, and his travels in familiar territory all give one the impression that these are letters composed by Paul.

[3]Dibelius and Conzelmann, *Pastoral Epistles* 2.

[4]See A. C. Sundberg, "Canon Muratori: A Fourth Century List," *HTR* 66 (1973) 1–41 and "Muratorian Fragment," *IDBSup* 609–610.

[5]For support of the Pauline authorship of the Pastorals, see Tertullian; Eusebius, *Eccl Hist* 2.22; 3.4; Athanasius; Jerome. It was not until the early 1800s (J. E. C. Schmidt, 1804; F. Schleiermacher, 1807) that the Pauline authorship of the Pastorals was disputed on stylistic grounds. On Schleiermacher and his study of 1 Timothy, see M. Redeker, *Schleiermacher: Life and Thought* (Philadelphia: Fortress, 1973) 79. For current discussion, see E. E. Ellis, "The Authorship of the Pastoral Epistles: A Resume and Assessment of Recent Trends," *Paul and His Recent Interpreters* (Grand Rapids: Eerdmans, 1961) 49–57; C. F. D. Moule, "The Problem of the Pastoral Epistles: A Reappraisal," *BJRL* 47 (1965) 430–52.

b. Arguments against Pauline Authorship

There are four main difficulties with Pauline authorship of the Pastorals: chronological, linguistic, doctrinal, and ecclesiastical. After all four problem areas are considered, conclusions will be made.

Chronological Problems. The activities of Paul in the Pastorals raise chronological problems because none fit well with the life of Paul as we know it from both the undisputed letters and Acts. We will first state the discrepancies before examining the attempts to harmonize the data.

According to 1 Tim 1:3, Paul left Timothy in Ephesus and went to Macedonia, hoping to rejoin him in Ephesus (3:14; 4:13). In the book of Acts, however, Paul left Ephesus for Macedonia (ca. AD 55) where he is joined by Timothy there (Acts 19:1,21-22). The apostle intends to return to Corinth and Jerusalem, but *not* Ephesus (20:25,38). According to Acts, not even Timothy returns to Ephesus but accompanies the apostle on his final trip to Jerusalem (20:4)! Acts provides no confirmation of a proposed Ephesian rendezvous between Paul and Timothy as stated in 1 Tim 1:3.

In Titus, Paul and Titus have been working in Crete and the apostle leaves him there to appoint elders (Ti 1:5). After the arrival of Tychicus or Artemas, he is to join Paul at Nicopolis (3:12). According to Acts, however, Paul stops at Crete as a prisoner en route to Rome (Acts 27:7,12-13,21) and has neither the time nor liberty to organize a church there. Did Paul stay at Crete before his final Jerusalem trip (Acts 20:3)? We have insufficient data to be certain.

The information in 2 Timothy raises problems concerning the place of Paul's writing and the location of the addressee. Was Paul writing as a prisoner from Rome? It is clear that he was a prisoner (1:8; 2:9) and nearing the end of his life (4:6-8). Although 2 Tim 1:16-17 assumes that Paul had been in Rome, it is unclear if he is currently residing there as a prisoner.

Could Paul have been writing as a prisoner in Caesarea? According to the apostle's activities in 2 Timothy, Paul had recently visited Troas (4:13), Corinth, and Miletus (v 20). In Acts 20:2,6,15, these are the same locations he visited en route to Jerusalem (AD 57). In the holy city, Paul was brought before the

Sanhedrin, but he escaped injury (Acts 23:1-11). Could 2 Tim 4:16-17 be referring to this event? Compare Acts 23:11 with 2 Tim 4:17. Could Paul's imprisonment in Caesarea (Acts 23:31-33) have been the occasion for the departure of certain associates for Thessalonica, Galatia, Dalmatia (2 Tim 4:10), and Ephesus (4:12)? Unfortunately, at this time (AD 57-58), Paul had not yet been to Rome, which is presupposed in 2 Tim 1:17. If Paul's activities were contrived by another author, he might have been acquainted with the above episodes in Acts.

Was Paul writing to Timothy in Ephesus? It is clear that Timothy was in Ephesus (1:18) and that Aquila and Priscilla who are with him (4:19) had also resided there (Acts 18:18-19,26; 1 Cor 16:19). It is unusual, however, that Paul would say, "I have sent Tychicus to Ephesus" (4:12) instead of "to you" (Timothy). Also, why would the apostle need to report that he left Trophimus ill at Miletus (4:20), when the location is only thirty-two miles south of Ephesus, where Timothy was supposed to be residing? These problems raise questions about its destination and author.

In response to the above difficulties the question might be raised: is only that which can be harmonized with Acts and Paul's letters considered authentic? There are certainly events in Paul's life not recorded in these sources.

From patristic allusions, some have argued for the following sequence of events: Paul was released from his first Roman imprisonment (Acts 28:16-31), engaged in brief missionary activity (the activities in the Pastorals and possibly Spain), was arrested and imprisoned a second time in Rome, where he was finally executed (AD 64 or 67). The clearest statement of this hypothesis is found in Eusebius, *Eccl Hist* 2.22.2. Unfortunately, we cannot be certain that Eusebius was not influenced by Paul's letter to Romans, where the apostle discloses his plans to go to Spain (16:28) and by the scanty allusions in 2 Timothy, with which he was probably familiar. Clement of Rome (AD 95) mentions a mission of Paul "to the extreme west" before his martyrdom (1 Clem 5.7), but we are unsure if this is Spain and he mentions no release and second imprisonment. The Muratorian Fragment alludes to Paul's departure from Rome for Spain, but no second imprisonment.

These patristic allusions are meager and questionable. The Pastorals also supply no clear evidence for a second Roman imprisonment. "My first defense" (2 Tim 4:16) could be an allusion to Paul's hearing in Jerusalem (Acts 23) or Caesarea (Acts 24–26) rather than a "first" hearing in Rome.

Linguistic Problems. Although there is disagreement on the methodology and significance of some conclusions, linguistic studies have established the disharmony of the Pastorals with the other Pauline writings.

The Pastorals have 335 out of 3484 total words peculiar to them, 175 of them appear no where else in the NT. The use of such special vocabulary occurs two and one half times more frequently than in a cross section of Paul's undisputed letters.[6]

The distinctive vocabulary of the Pastorals is more characteristic of popular Hellenistic religion than of Paul's letters. Note the following examples: "piety" (*eusebeia*, 2 Tim 3:5), "sound teaching" (*hygiainousē didaskalia*, 1 Tim 1:10), "sound-minded" (*sōphron*, Ti 1:8), "self-controlled" (*enkratēs*, Ti 1:8), "irreligious" (*anosios*, 2 Tim 3:2), "manifestation" (*epiphaneia*, 1 Tim 6:14), "way of life" (*agogē*, 2 Tim 3:10), "loving good" (*philagathos*, Ti 1:8), "truth" (*alētheia*, 2 Tim 2:15), "Savior" (*sōter*, Ti 2:13).

Some of the typical Pauline language is also absent from the Pastorals. For example, the following Pauline words are absent: "to proclaim good news (*euangelizesthai*)," "spiritual," "to die," "body," and "uncircumcised." Also important religious concepts like "righteousness" (45 times) and "in Christ" (48) appear only a few times with altered meanings.

[6]The statistical research of Grayston and Herdan has revised the earlier work of Harrison (1921) and confirmed the studies of Morgenthaler (1958), see K. Grayston and G. Herdan, "The Authorship of the Pastorals in the Light of Statistical Linguistics," *NTS* 6 (October, 1959) 1–15; Harrison, *The Problem of the Pastoral Epistles*; R. Morgenthaler, *Statistik des Neutestamentlichen Wörtschatzes* (Zurich: Gotthelf, 1958) 30, 38–39. The following work, however, places certain limitations on the statistical analysis of NT words: B. M. Metzger, "A Reconsideration of Certain Arguments against the Pauline Authorship of the Pastoral Epistles," *ExpT* 70 (1958–59) 91–94.

Stylistic Problems. There is, finally, a clear difference of style in the Pastorals. Much of Paul's dramatic writing style—its spirited energy, emotional intensity, and impassioned argumentation—is lacking in the Pastorals. What predominates, instead, is a monotonous style of repetition and a prudish concern for preciseness. These dissimilarities are most evident by the differences in grammar (e.g., considerable use of prepositions, conjunctions, pronouns, definite articles).

Doctrinal Problems. Even though the Pastorals contain some Pauline-sounding themes, most of its teaching is foreign to Pauline thought. Statements corresponding to Paul's teaching, but phrased differently, are: "Christ came to save sinners" (1 Tim 1:15), salvation by grace not works (2 Tim 1:9; Ti 3:5), justified by his grace to be heirs in the hope of eternal life (Ti 3:7), and "to believe on him for eternal life" (1 Tim 1:16). Much of the grammar in these statements is different from that in the recognized letters. Many of them are confessional statements or are elaborated upon with lengthy epithets of God and Christ. Even some of the Pauline-sounding phrases convey a different meaning than they did for Paul. For example, "justification by grace" seems to be the fruit of baptism attained by God's power (Ti 3:4-7).[7]

Hellenistic statements that appear alien to Paul are: "for the grace of God has appeared (*epiphanē*) bringing salvation to all men" (Ti 2:11); "when the kindness and benevolence (*philanthrōpia*) of God our Savior (*sotērōs*) appeared" (3:4); "waiting for the blessed hope and the appearance of the glory of our great God and Savior (*tou megalou theou kai sotērōs*), Jesus Christ" (2:13); "the blessed and only Sovereign (*dynastēs*), the King of kings and Lord of lords, who alone has immortality (*athanasian*) and dwells in unapproachable light" (1 Tim 6:15-16). The elaborate epithets ascribed to God and Christ with language from Hellenistic piety are distinctive features not found in the undisputed letters of Paul.

Ecclesiastical Views. In the Pastorals and Paul's recognized letters, we have two different versions of the apostle's ecclesiastical

[7]For baptismal imagery in Titus 3 with Greco-Roman parallels, see Dibelius and Conzelmann, *Pastoral Epistles* 148–50.

views and concerns. Although the general portrait of Paul in the Pastorals as an apostolic "pastor" concerned with the welfare of the churches he founded finds agreement in the undisputed letters, the differences are apparent when we compare the specific views in both sets of writings. We will examine, for example: the church's nature and mission, and its organization and ethics.

In the Pastorals the church is more institutionalized and defensive, whereas in Paul it is more charismatic and expansive. In 1 and 2 Timothy, the church is to maintain ethical and doctrinal order as "God's household" (1 Tim 3:5,15; 2 Tim 2:20-22) and "guard the deposit of the faith" (1 Tim 6:20; 2 Tim 1:14) as the "pillar and bulwark of the truth" (1 Tim 3:15). It seems that these concepts and directives envision one universal church rather than the concerns of local churches in Ephesus and Crete.

In Paul's undisputed writings, the church is the body of Christ, whose "members" manifest diverse gifts of the Spirit (1 Cor 12). It is also God's holy temple (1 Cor 3:17) whose members must be holy and pure before God. The churches were encouraged to proclaim the faith to everyone as Paul himself did (1 Thes 1:8; Rom 1:8). Although his metaphors encompassed one church of Jews and Gentiles, Paul was mainly concerned with the issues and activities of the local churches he founded (e.g., 1 Thes; 1 and 2 Cor).

In the Pastorals, we have an institutionalized view of leadership and congregational behavior. In the undisputed letters of Paul, we have a charismatic view of leadership and eschatological ethics for believers.

Unlike other NT writings, the Pastorals list specific qualifications for the church offices of bishop (Ti 1:7-9; 1 Tim 3:1-7), elder (Ti 1:5-6; 1 Tim 5:17-22; cf. Jas 5:14; 1 Pet 5:1) and deacon (1 Tim 3:8-13). These were appointed offices (Ti 1:5; 1 Tim 5:22) following the precedent of the apostle Paul's appointment of Timothy (2 Tim 1:6; cf. 1 Tim 4:14). It appears that both bishops and elders were assigned the responsibilities of teaching and ruling the church, whereas the deacons were probably in charge of finance and relief work.[8] Most charismatic activities were now

[8]Sampley, *Eph, Col* 107–15; J. P. Meier, "*Presbyteros* in the Pastoral Epistles," *CBQ* 35 (1973) 323–45; R. E. Brown, "*Episkopē* and *Episkopos*: the NT Evidence," *TS* 41 (1980) 322–38.

connected with the appointed office (2 Tim 1:6; 1 Tim 1:18; 4:14; cf. Jas 5:14).

Like the Deutero-Pauline writings and 1 Peter, attention is given in the Pastorals to household and community rules (Ti 2:1-10; 1 Tim 2; 5:1–6:2; cf. Col 3:18–4:1; Eph 5:21–6:9; 1 Pet 2:13–3:7). These are ethical standards and social relationships expected of all good citizens in the Roman world. They presuppose a situation where the church no longer has an imminent end-time expectation, but is settling down to life in the Roman world.[9] In this context both faith and works were important (Ti 3:5,8) and Greco-Roman social ethics were to be transformed by Christian love.[10]

In Paul's authentic letters, we find a different view of leadership and ethics. In the Pauline congregations, leaders arose when they manifested the appropriate gifts of ruling and teaching (e.g., 1 Cor 12:27-30; 16:15; Rom 12:3-8). It is in this context that the early reference in Philippians to "overseers and helpers" (1:1, our trans.) should be understood. Under the supervision of Paul and his co-workers, leaders probably arose in all his churches (e.g., 1 Cor 16:15-16). These leaders were appointed *by God* (1 Cor 12:28). It is unlikely that Paul himself was concerned with appointing "elders . . . in every church" (Acts 14:23). This reference probably reflects the later perspective of the author of Luke-Acts. It is plausible, however, that an elder system was developed in the Jerusalem church, patterned after the Sanhedrin and synagogue (Gal 2; Acts 15).[11]

Paul, like the post-apostolic writers, also employed Hellenistic ethical instructions, but his rationale for using them was different. First, they were ethics practiced in preparation for the soon

[9]P. Rogers, "The Pastoral Epistles as Deutero-Pauline," *ITQ* 45 (1978) 248–60; Käsemann, *NT Questions* 236–51; E. Schweizer, *Church Order in the NT*, SBT 32 (London: SCM, 1961) 77–88. M. Y. McDonald, *The Pauline Churches: A Socio-historical Study of the Institutionalization in the Pauline and Deutero-Pauline Writings* (New York/Cambridge: Cambridge Univ. Press, 1988).

[10]N. J. McEleney, "The Vice Lists of the Pastoral Epistles," *CBQ* 36 (1974) 203–19; C. J. Martin, "The *Haustafeln* (Household Codes) in African American Biblical Interpretation," in *Stony the Road,* ed. C. Felder (Minneapolis: Fortress, 1991) 206–31. Sampley, *Eph, Col* 117; Verner, *Household of God.*

[11]Sampley, *Eph, Col* 111.

approaching day of the Lord (1 Thes 5:1-11; 1 Cor 7:29-31). Vice lists were descriptions of those who would not inherit the kingdom of God (Gal 5:19-21; 1 Cor 6:9-10). Paul's exhortations on subordination to earthly governments (Rom 13:1-10) and his caution about changes in social status (1 Cor 7:17-24) were also conditioned by his imminent end-time expectation (Rom 13:11-14; 1 Cor 7:29-31). Second, Paul's list of virtues were to be manifestations of the believer's new status in union with Christ. They were to demonstrate the believer's death to sin and awakened life to righteousness, symbolized in Christian baptism (Rom 6:5-11). They were also to be the signs of the Spirit who dwells in the believer (Gal 5:16,22-26; 1 Cor 6:19-20). The ethics of both the Deutero-Pauline letters and the Pastorals lack Paul's eschatological perspective and mystical dimension.

c. Conclusions

Taken together, the chronological, linguistic, doctrinal, and ecclesiastical differences of the Pastorals compared with the undisputed Pauline letters are so decisive that the "burden of proof" on the authorship question seems to have shifted from the opponents of Pauline authorship to its proponents.

3. Historical Setting

The concerns of the Pastorals coincide well with those of emerging orthodoxy.[12] In the Pastorals we discover conflicts with false teachings, a fixed organizational structure, preservation of the apostolic tradition, credal statements and confessions of faith, and normative Christian ethics.

a. False Teaching

It is unclear if any specific heresy is confronted in the Pastorals because the polemics seem directed against both Judaistic (Ti

[12]See my discussion of characteristics of emerging orthodoxy in C. B. Puskas, *An Introduction to the New Testament* (Peabody, Mass.: Hendrickson, 1989) 223–52. See also W. Bauer, *Orthodoxy and Heresy in Earliest Christianity* (Philadelphia: Fortress, 1971); E. Käsemann, "Paul and Early Catholicism" in idem, *NT Questions Today* (Philadelphia: Fortress, 1979) 236–51.

1:10,14; 1 Tim 1:7-11; 4:3) and gnostic views (Ti 3:9; 1 Tim 4:3-5,7; 6:20; 2 Tim 2:18). These errors are also not confronted by forceful debate, as in Paul's letters (Gal 3; 2 Cor 11), but are merely labeled as foolish and contrasted to the truth (e.g., 1 Tim 1:3-7). Perhaps one of the functions of the Pastorals is to enable churches to identify heresies by their vices and thus reject them without entering into polemical debates.[13]

In the second and third centuries, we know of Judaistic Christians, called the Ebionites, who maintained a rigid adherence to the law of Moses (cf. 1 Tim 1:7-11) and viewed Christ as a great human prophet (*Pseudo-Clementine Homilies;* The *Gospel of the Hebrews;* Eusebius, *Eccl Hist* 3.27). Perhaps early manifestations of this group were surfacing at the time of the Pastorals.

Also by the second century, we learn of the Valentinian and Basilidian Gnostics with elaborate mythical schemes of the cosmos (cf. "myths and endless genealogies" 1 Tim 1:4; 4:7). Such groups also advocated ascetic practices (cf. 1 Tim 4:3-4) and maintained the belief that a spiritual resurrection had already taken place (cf. 2 Tim 2:18).[14]

Possible references to Marcionite heresy can also be found in the Pastorals. The mention of "contradictions (*antitheses*) of the false *gnosis*" (1 Tim 6:20) seems to refer to the *Antitheses* written by Marcion (140).[15] In it, Christ's abolishment of human traditions and Paul's teaching of freedom from the law are posited against both the Creator God and Mosaic law of the Jewish Scriptures. Perhaps the appeal to the goodness of God's creation (1 Tim 4:4) and the mention of "all Scripture is God-breathed" (2 Tim 3:16) might be viewed as a polemic against Marcion.

The heresies of the Pastorals seem to coincide with those of the second and third centuries (e.g., Justin Martyr, *First Apology*; Irenaeus, *Against Heresies*; the polemics of Tertullian, Hippolytus, and Epiphanius). Based on the clues in the texts

[13]Koester, *Introduction* 2:304; McEleney, "Vice Lists," 203–19.

[14]Further information on 2nd-cent. Gnosticism can be found in Irenaeus *Against Heresies* 1–8; 24; Hippolytus *Refutation* 7; 29–36; Jonas, *Gnostic Religion;* Rudolph, *Gnosis, Nag Hammadi, Gnosticism, and Early Christianity,* ed. C. W. Hedrick and R. Hodgson (Peabody, Mass.: Hendrickson, 1986).

[15]For a reconstruction of Marcion's *Antitheses*, see W. Meeks, *The Writings of St. Paul* (New York: Norton, 1972) 180–90.

themselves, it is likely that early forms of these later heresies were surfacing when the Pastorals were written.

b. Fixed Hierarchy

A system of appointed bishops, elders, and deacons has already been noted. Excluding the reference to a plurality of elders and one bishop in Titus 1:5-7, there is no evidence of a single bishop supported by a council of elders and assisted by deacons (e.g., Ign *Smyrn* 8:1; *Magn* 6.1; *Trall* 7.2). Either the Pastorals preceded this early second-century monepiscopal structure or it had not yet been instituted in the localities they addressed. The admonition that a bishop "must not be a new convert" (1 Tim 3:6) and the extensive lists of household and community rules (e.g., Ti 2; 1 Tim 3) presuppose a developed church structure of second and third generation Christians (e.g., 2 Tim 2:1-2).

c. Preservation of Apostolic Tradition

The dominant themes of teaching "sound doctrine" (1 Tim 1:10; 6:3; 2 Tim 1:13; 4:3; Ti 1:9,13; 2:1,8) and guarding the "deposit of the faith" (1 Tim 6:20; 2 Tim 1:14) reflect an early catholic concern to preserve the apostolic tradition. In 2 Tim 2:1-2, Paul entrusts Timothy with apostolic traditions and he must pass them on to "faithful men" who must hand it down to "others." This process, presupposes possibly four generations: Paul, Timothy, faithful men, others (if "others" refers to a subsequent generation). The apostolic succession of tradition is characteristic of Christianity in the late first and early second centuries (1 Clem 42; Ign *Magn* 13; Justin Martyr, *Apology* 1.66-67).

d. Creeds and Confessions

Credal statements and confessions are also evident in the Pastorals (e.g., 1 Tim 3:16; 6:11-16; 2 Tim 2:5-6,11-13; Ti 3:4-7). Even though some probably originated as hymns in earlier worship settings (e.g., 1 Tim 3:16), they became a dominant feature of early catholic Christianity (e.g., Eph 2:14-16; 1 Pet 3:18-19,22; Ign *Magn* 9; 13; Ign *Smyrn* 1-2; Irenaeus, *Against Heresies* 3.4.2; Tertullian, *Against Praxeas*).

e. *Normative Ethics*

In order to ensure sound doctrine ("orthodoxy"), the Pastorals emphasize the importance of right living ("orthopraxy"). These ethical norms for every member and class in the congregation (Ti 2; 1 Tim 3) are found in numerous early catholic writings (e.g., 1 Pet 2:13–3:7; *Did* 4.9-11; *Barn* 19.5-7; *1 Clem* 21.6-9; Pol *Phil* 4.2–6.3).

4. *The Destinations*

Because of the general nature of the polemics and church rules, it is not necessary to restrict the setting of the addressees to Ephesus and Crete. The author was most familiar with the Aegean Sea region. Probably he and his addressees lived somewhere in this area. Since the Pastorals do not presuppose a monepiscopal system, their origin and destination may have been outside the sphere of Ignatius. Macedonia, Achaia, or Crete would therefore be suitable localities.

5. *The Dates*

Conjectures on the dates of the Pastorals as post-apostolic writings range from late first to mid-second century. An early second-century date is plausible because of the advanced forms of heresy, organizational structure, and normative ethics detected in the Pastorals. The influence of Marcion in the churches (if he is opposed in the Pastorals) probably preceded his arrival in Rome (ca. 140; birth ca. AD 85). The monepiscopal system in Ignatius (98–117) was probably not yet adopted by the churches addressed in the Pastorals, although Ti 1:5-7 may suggest a movement in this direction.

6. *The Genre and Rhetorical Function*

a. Titus and 1 Timothy

The books of Titus and 1 Timothy contain most of the literary forms found in the Deutero-Pauline and so-called General Epistles. They both begin and end like letters. Both contain household and community rules. When the qualifications for appointed church leaders are considered, Titus and 1 Timothy have the appearance of a church manual, like the Didache (ca. 100), which also has warnings against false prophets. Because they anticipate problems in the future and their parenetic emphasis has an advisory aim, Titus and 1 Timothy have a deliberative function. Like 1 Cor 7–16, 2 Cor 8–9, and Hebrews, they are concerned with the expedient goal of persuading their readers in the faith and dissuading them from unacceptable views and practices. Most parenetic literature has this deliberative aim. Details supporting this view will be given in the outline.

b. 2 Timothy

With Acts 20:17-38 and 2 Peter (for Peter),[16] 2 Timothy functions as a final testament of the apostle Paul. It has all the characteristics of this popular genre: (a) ethical admonitions of the departing apostle/father to his children in the faith, summarizing his own instructions to be followed in the future with attached eschatological warnings; (b) revelations of the future, predicting the destiny of the church, often as a revelation of the last days and providing a basis for further ethical exhortations. As with 2 Peter and all final testaments, so also 2 Timothy is ascribed to the departing leader years after his death. The personal statements, travel plans, greetings, and other epistolary features also give 2 Timothy more characteristics of a Pauline letter than Titus or 1 Timothy.

[16]Other examples of ancient farewell speeches are: Gen 47:29-49:33; Josh 22–24; Dt 31–33; 1 Chr 28–29; Tob 14:3-11; *T12Patr; 1 Enoch* 91-104; 4 Ezra 14:8-36; *2 Bar* 78–86; *Jub* 10; 20-22; 30-36; *Adam and Eve* 25–29; Josephus *Ant* 4.8.45-47; Jn 13:31-17:26; *Acts of John* 106–7; *Acts of Peter* 36–39; *Acts of Thomas*

As a testament in epistolary form, 2 Timothy (like 2 Pet) is concerned with intensifying adherence to common values (epideictic rhetoric).[17] Like 2 Peter, it contains the following features of demonstrative rhetoric: (a) the call to remember (2 Tim 1:3,5; 2 Pet 1:13,15; 3:1), (b) the censure of opponents (2 Tim 3; 2 Pet 2) as the negative aspect of praising common values, and (c) autobiographical allusions used to support the thesis of extolling common values (2 Tim 1:11-18; 3:10-11; 4:6-21; 2 Pet 1:12-18). Further details are found in the rhetorical outline.

7. The Original Order of the Pastorals

The original arrangement of the Pastoral Letters was probably Titus, 1 Timothy and 2 Timothy, for the following reasons. First, the lengthy prescript of Titus seems to function as the exordium of all three writings (see outline of Ti for allusions to 1 and 2 Tim).[18] Second, this appears to be the order in the Muratorian Fragment: "one to Titus and two to Timothy" (2nd or 4th cent. AD). Titus also has the earliest papyrus recognition (p^{32} ca. AD 200). Third, the similar contents of Titus and 1 Timothy indicate that they belong together. Furthermore, 1 Timothy adds qualifications for deacons and further community rules, possibly indicating that it is a redaction and expansion of material in Titus. Fourth, 1 Timothy's lack of personal Pauline notes (i.e., insufficient credibility) and the abrupt ending of 1 Tim 6:20-21a

159–60; Farewell dialogue of Socrates in Plato's *Phaedo*. See also: W. Kurz, "Lk 22 and Farewell Addresses" *JBL* 104:2 (1985) 251–68.

[17]A farewell speech extolling common virtues is labeled by Menander (AD 300) as *ho syntaktikos logos* (*Rhetoric* 2.15). Specific examples are the farewell speech of Jesus in Jn 13:31–17:26, Paul's farewell speech in Acts 20:17-38 and the farewell address to Origen by Gregory Thoumaturgos in AD 328. See Kennedy, *NT Rhetoric* 76 and idem, *Classical Rhetoric and Its Christian and Secular Traditions from Ancient to Modern Times* (Chapel Hill, N.C.: Univ. of N. Carolina Press, 1980) 140–41.

[18]Themes found in Ti 1:1-4 that are developed in all three books are: apostleship and servanthood of Paul, faith of God's elect, full knowledge of the truth, godliness, hope of eternal life, *kerygmata*, God's promise before times eternal, God our Savior, my son in the faith, grace and peace from God the Father and our Lord Jesus Christ.

anticipate 2 Timothy. The Muratorian Fragment also combined them. Furthermore, 1 and 2 Timothy seem to telescope into one another. Fifth, as the final testament of Paul it is rhetorically appropriate for 2 Timothy to serve as the climactic summary (peroration) of the Pastoral collection.

8. Why Three?

All three Pastoral Letters were probably written about the same general period of time and function as a single book like the seven letters that open Revelation.[19] There are several plausible reasons for writing three letters. First, a credible testimony (Ti 1:13) must come from "two or *three* witnesses" (1 Tim 5:19/Dt 19:15; cf. 1 Tim 6:12; 2 Tim 2:2). Second, regarding their rhetorical structure, Titus and 1 Timothy are deliberative writings with 1 Timothy expanding upon Titus. As epideictic rhetoric, 2 Timothy functions as a fitting peroration to the corpus, by extolling common virtues and values presupposed in all three. Second Timothy as demonstrative rhetoric seeks to affect the listener in the present with some of the expedient concerns of the future found in Titus and 1 Timothy. Third, most farewell speeches address a designated plurality of listeners, whether it is two or more sons, a gathering of friends, or a nation. As the concluding letter of the Pastorals, 2 Timothy indirectly has Paul the "apostolic father," addressing his two designated "sons in the faith," Titus and Timothy (as well as the implied audience of the church). This designated plurality of listeners (Titus and Timothy) makes Paul's farewell address more than a personal correspondence between Paul and Timothy.

[19]J. D. Quinn, "The Last Volume of Luke: The Relation of Luke-Acts to the Pastoral Epistles," *Perspective on Luke-Acts* 62–75. We do not, however, support Quinn's theory that the author of Luke-Acts wrote the Pastorals.

9. The Rhetorical Structure of the Letters

a. Titus

As a form of deliberative address, the thesis of Titus is concerned with directives on appointing worthy leaders to withstand opposition. The title, "Training for Christian Life,"[20] captures the advisory aim of the book. Key terms relevant to deliberative rhetoric will be underscored or followed by the Greek form in parentheses.[21] The epistolary prescript (1:1-4) also functions as the exordium of all the Pastoral Epistles.

The Rhetorical Structure of Titus

I. Epistolary prescript: exordium	1:1-4
A. Sender (*Ethos*)	
1. Authority of sender conveyed by his apostolic titles (1 Tim 1:1; 2 Tim 2:1)	v 1a
2. The function of his office "to further the faith of God's elect" (cf. 2 Tim 2:10) establishes credibility with his addressee	v 1b
3. The trustworthiness of his work is rooted in its eternal hope (cf. 1 Tim 1:1) that God promised ages ago and has now revealed in Paul's preaching	vv 1c-3a
4. The divine authority of Paul's preaching is confirmed by the "command of God our Savior" (cf. 1 Tim 1:1; 2:3)	v 3b
B. Addressee	
Goodwill of "Titus" secured with epithet "my true child in a *common* faith"	v 4a
C. Salutation	
Ornamental to set reader in a favorable frame of mind (cf. 1 Tim 1:2)	v 4b

[20]Hanson, *The Pastoral Letters* (London, 1966) 106–23 (section on "Titus").

[21]The Revised Standard Version of the Bible has been followed except where we have translated from the Greek. Today's English Version (TEV) has been followed where noted. For helpful interpretive suggestions on difficult verses, we have consulted: R. G. Bratcher, *A Translator's Guide to Paul's Letters to Timothy and to Titus* (London; New York; Stuttgart: United Bible Societies, 1983); Fee, *1 and 2 Timothy, Titus* NIBC (Peabody, Mass.: Hendrickson, 1989); Quinn, *The Letter to Titus.*

II. Proposition	
A. Statement of thesis: appoint worthy leaders to refute the opponents	1:5-9
1. Occasion of the letter: when Paul left Titus in Crete	v 5a
2. Opening directives on the unfinished task of appointing qualified elders	vv 5b-6
3. Supporting reason: because the bishop[22] must manage God's household well by *teaching sound doctrine* and *refuting opponents*	vv 7-9
B. Supporting reason for thesis: the appearance of dangerous false teachers who must be refuted	1:10-16
III. Proof	2:1-3:11
A. Positive advice on teaching what agrees with sound doctrine	2:1-15
1. Topic statement	v 1
2. Exposition of topic: ethical instructions for various groups	vv 2-10
3. Supporting reason: the universal gospel as the theological basis for renouncing evil and leading a godly life	vv 11-14
4. Peroration of topic statement: "exhort and reprove with all authority"	v 15
B. Further positive instructions on godly behavior	3:1-8
1. Topic statement on teaching obedience, honesty, and kindness	vv 1-2
2. First supporting reason: For we were once sinners but are now saved and transformed to be heirs of eternal life	vv 3-8a
3. Second supporting reason: "so that believers may give attention to good works"	v 8b-c
4. Third supporting reason (*advantage*): "These things are good and profitable (*ophelima*) for people"	v 8d
C. Closing negative admonitions against false teachers and their immoralities	3:9-11
1. List of immoral vices to avoid	v 9a

[22]The uninterrupted movement of discussion from elder to bishop (Ti 1:5-7) seems to imply that they are synonymous terms for the same office in this context.

2. Supporting advantage: "for they are unprofitable (*anopheleō*) and useless" (contrast of v 8d)	v 9b
3. Recommended procedure on admonishing a factious person	vv 10-11
IV. Peroration: Personal requests and appeals	3:12-15
A. Personal requests (*pathos*)	vv 12-13
1. Paul's plans to send a fellow-worker (Artemas or Tychicus) to Titus	v 12a
2. His request for Titus to join him in Nicopolis, Achaia	v 12b
3. Paul's request for Titus to return Zenas and Apollos	v 13
B. Personal appeal restating thesis: "let our people learn to apply themselves to good deeds for necessary (*anankaia*) needs so that they are not *unproductive*" (like the opponents)	v 14
C. Greetings *topoi* securing the favor of the sender, addressee, and mutual acquaintances	v 15a
D. Benediction (securing favor): "Grace be with *all* of you"	v 15b

b. 1 Timothy

First Timothy continues the deliberative advice of Titus with further elaboration. Its main concern is providing advice on guarding the faith against false teachers. But successful opposition to false teaching must also be maintained by qualified leaders (bishops, elders, deacons) who will promote sound doctrine and practice. Furthermore, to insure "orthodoxy" and "orthopraxy," the congregations must also be in order (household and community rules). All of these subsequent statements are topics relevant to the thesis of waging a good warfare by keeping the faith (1:18-19; cf. 1:3-7).

The Rhetorical Structure of 1 Timothy

I. Epistolary prescript: proem	1:1-2
A. Sender and addressee	
1. *Ethos* of sender conveyed	v 1
2. Goodwill of addressee secured	v 2a

B. Salutation: (Ornamental to set reader in a favorable frame of mind cf. 2 Jn 3; Ti 1:4b; 2 Tim 1:2b)	v 2b
II. Proposition: Oppose false teachings	1:3-7
A. Occasional directive: "Stay in Ephesus as I urged you on my way to Macedonia" (*GNB*)	v 3a
B. Thesis: "Order certain people to stop teaching false doctrines"	v 3b-4b
C. The stated purpose of Paul's charge—"to arouse love that comes from a pure heart, a clear conscience and a genuine faith" (*GNB*)	v 5
—Descriptions of false teachers who have turned away from the above virtues (v 5)	vv 6-7
III. Refutation of opposing view (i.e., the law as a source of speculation and instruction for Christians, cf. 1:7)	1:8-11
A. Opening premise: the law is good (*kalos*) if used as it was intended to be used	v 8
B. Concluding principle: the law is intended for the lawless not the righteous	v 9-11
--the gospel entrusted to Paul is the basis of "sound doctrine"	v 11
IV. Background narration: Paul's experience of God's grace as a model for others (cf. Gal 1:13ff.)	1:12-17
A. Opening statement: Paul's gratitude to Christ for appointing him as a minister (*ethos*)	v 12
B. Paul's former life and his experience of divine grace recounted (*pathos*)	vv 13-14
C. Confessional statement and personal application	v 15
D. The dual purpose of Paul's salvation:	
1. To demonstrate God's forbearance in redeeming sinners	
2. To provide a pattern for believers after Paul	v 16
E. Doxology to "the king of ages"	v 17
V. Proof	1:18-6:2
A. Recapitulation of thesis	1:18-20
1. Opening address to Timothy whose appointment was confirmed by prophetic utterances	v 18a
2. Thesis stated: "that you might wage a good	

warfare by keeping your faith and a clear conscience'' (military imagery; cf. 6:12) — vv 18b-19a

3. Negative examples of people who have destroyed their faith by not listening to their conscience — vv 19b-20

B. First section on prayer, women, and church leaders — 2:1-3:13

1. First topic: directives on praying for the salvation of all peoples — 2:1-8
   This action is good (*kalon*) and acceptable (*apodekton*) before God (vv 3-4; deliberative appeal) Concluding exhortation on where and how men should pray (v 8)
2. Second topic: the behavior of women in the church[23] — 2:9-15
3. Third topic: qualifications for bishop (*episkopos*; Ti 1:7-9) — 3:1-7
4. Fourth topic: qualifications for deacons — 3:8-13
5. Peroration of first section and introduction to second section — vv 14-16
   a. Paul's travel plans: he hopes to visit Timothy soon but writes the following directives if he is delayed — v 14
   b. Summary of first section: ''I wrote you these things . . . so that you might know how one ought to behave in God's household'' — v 15
      confessional hymn illustrating the mystery of our piety — v 16

C. Second section: false teachings, personal admonitions, and treatment of other believers — 4:1–6:2

1. Topic reiterating proposition (1:3-7) and refutation (1:8-11): a rebuttal of false teachings — 4:1-5
2. Various topics of personal admonitions to Timothy — 4:6-16

[23] It appears that women were involved in the false teachings, which necessitated this ''occasional injunction'' by the author: ''let women be silent in the church.'' For further discussion, see R. and C. Kroeger, ''May Women Teach? Heresy in the Pastoral Epistles,'' *The Reformed Journal* (October, 1980) 14–18. See also S. H. Gritz, *Paul, Women, Teachers, and the Mother Goddess at Ephesus* (New York and London: Univ. Press of America, 1991).

a. The *advantages* of implementing Paul's advice and avoiding wrong behavior — vv 6-11
b. Exhortations on youth, exemplary behavior, preaching, and teaching — vv 12-16
c. Peroration: some positive advice with supporting advantages — vv 15-16

3. Topics on the treatment of other believers — 5:1–6:2
a. General advice on the manner of reproving various members — vv 1-2
b. Advice on widows: honor widows who are really alone — vv 3-16
c. Instruction about elders — 5:17-25
d. Instructions for slaves — 6:1-2a

VI. Peroration — 6:2b-21
A. Opening exhortations: "these things teach and exhort"
B. Recapitulation of indictment on false teachers (cf. 1:3-11; 4:1-5) — 6:2b-10
1. Opening statement on the foolishness of not following sound teaching — vv 3-5
2. Correction of misconception about godliness as a means of gain (cf. 6:5)
C. Reiteration of exhortation to Timothy (cf. 1:18-19; 4:6-16; 5:21)
1. Opening statement: Avoid evil and strive for righteousness and godliness (cf. 4:7) — 6:11
2. Restatement of thesis employing athletic imagery (cf. 1:18b): "Fight the good fight of faith, take hold of eternal life" — v 12
3. Restatement of solemn charge to keep the above commandment (cf. 5:21) — vv 13-14
--amplification on the power and authority of the glorified Christ — vv 15-16
4. Charge to those already rich, recalling admonitions against greed (3:3,8; 6:5-10) — vv 17-19
5. Final restatement of charge to guard the faith and avoid false teaching (recalling 1:3-4, 18-19; 4:7-10; 6:2b-11) — vv 20-21
6. Benediction: "Grace be with you" cf. Ti 3:15b (*pathos* conveyed in its abruptness) — v 21b

c. 2 Timothy

Second Timothy serves as the climactic peroration of the Pastorals. It is the farewell address of the departing apostle and seeks to intensify adherence to the common gospel (epideictic rhetoric). The title, "Character of A Christian Minister,"[24] epitomizes the laudatory aim of the book. Special use of *ethos* (character of author) and *pathos* (emotions conveyed to reader) are evident in this final testament of Paul. Allusions back to the previous letters of Titus and Timothy occur in the Proof and Peroration (as noted).

The Rhetorical Structure of 2 Timothy

I. Epistolary prescript	1:1-2
A. Sender and addressee	1:1-2a
1. *Ethos* of sender conveyed by name, apostolic title, and divine authorization	
2. Goodwill of addressee secured by epithet: "my beloved child"	
B. Salutation (ornamental to set reader in a favorable frame of mind; cf. 2 Jn 3)[25]	
II. Proem:[26] Prayer of thanksgiving	1:3-5
A. *Pathos* conveyed by Paul's prayer-wish for the Timothy's welfare and his desire to visit him	vv 3-4
B. Mention of Timothy's "sincere faith" is to set him in a favorable disposition	v 5
III. Proposition: To intensify adherence to our common gospel	vv 6-18
A. Transition and introduction	vv 6-7
1. Opening exhortation to rekindle God's gift (*charisma*) of ministry	v 6
2. Supporting reason ("for")	v 7
B. Thesis: Remain loyal to our gospel	vv 8-18

[24]A. T. Hanson, *The Pastoral Letters* 76–104.

[25]Such rhetorical devices would indirectly have the same effect on the actual audience of 2 Tim (i.e., the Christian recipients of the Pastorals, not merely "Timothy").

[26]Proem secures the sympathies of the addressee and reminds him of the common faith shared by him and the sender.

1. Opening exhortation to testify and share in the suffering of *the gospel* — v 8
2. Amplification of topic: God's saving activity stated in *the gospel* — vv 9-10
3. Example of Paul's loyalty to the gospel (cf. 1 Tim 2:7) — vv 11-12
4. Concluding exhortations to follow Paul's sound teaching (*logoi*) and guard the entrusted deposit of our faith — vv 13-14

C. Examples of disloyalty and loyalty to our common gospel — vv 15-18

IV. Proof — 2:1–3:17

A. Recapitulation of thesis — 2:1-7

1. Be strong in the grace (*charis*) that is in Christ Jesus (cf. 1:6) — 2:1
2. Entrust the apostolic gospel to faithful men (cf. 1:13-14; Ti 1:5-9; 1 Tim 3) — v 2
3. Share in the suffering of the gospel (cf. 2 Tim 1:8) — v 3
   --amplification of above topic with military, athletic, and agricultural metaphors — vv 4-6
4. Concluding exhortation to consider what was stated with supporting reason (cf. 1:18) — v 7

B. The motives for thesis — 2:8-13

1. Jesus Christ as preached in the gospel — v 8
2. Paul's sufferings for the gospel — vv 9-10
3. Promised blessings for loyalty and endurance (Christian hymn with series of premises and subsequent conclusions) — vv 11-13

C. Amplification of thesis topics: follow sound teaching (*logoi*) and guard the deposit of our faith (1:13-14) — 2:14-19

D. Amplification of thesis topic: those who are disloyal to our common gospel (cf. 1:15) — 3:1-9

E. Amplification of thesis topic: follow the example of Paul's loyalty to the gospel (1:11-12) — 3:10-17

V. Peroration — 4:1-22

A. Reiteration of thesis in Paul's solemn charge to Timothy — 4:1-5

1. Introduction to solemn charge — v 1
2. Exhortation to proclaim the word, be always attentive, reprove, admonish, exhort — v 2

   3. Supporting reason and reiteration of topic: those who are disloyal to the gospel vv 3-5
   4. Concluding exhortations to Timothy v 5

B. Reiteration of thesis topic: Paul's example of loyalty to the gospel (farewell address) 4:6-8
   Both the *ethos* of Paul's noble character and the *pathos* of his endurance for the gospel are conveyed in this genre of a farewell address (cf. Ti 1:3; 1 Tim 2:7; 2 Tim 1:11)

C. Personal appeals (*pathos*) 4:9-22
   1. Personal requests and the mention of people disloyal and loyal to the gospel vv 9-13
   2. Caution enjoined against one who opposed (1 Tim 1:20) the apostolic message (*logoi*, cf. 2 Tim 1:13) vv 14-15
   3. The progress of Paul's trial (*pathos*) vv 16-18
   4. Greetings topoi and more personal requests vv 19-21
   5. Benediction (more elaborate than Titus and 1 Tim; leaves reader in a favorable frame of mind) v 22

10. Summary

In this chapter we discussed the authorship, historical setting, literary character, and rhetorical functions of 1 and 2 Timothy and Titus, labeled the "Pastoral Epistles" since the eighteenth century. The Pauline authorship of the Pastorals is a puzzling issue because external evidence for their use before AD 150 is disputed and a clear gap exists between the explicit claims of the letters and their dissimilarities from the undisputed Pauline writings. These dissimilarities occur in the following areas: chronological, linguistic, doctrinal, and ecclesiastical. When considered together they make a strong case against the Pauline authorship of the Pastoral Epistles.

Adhering to the post-Pauline authorship of the Pastorals, one could date them anywhere between the late-first and mid-second centuries. An early second-century date is plausible because of the advanced forms of heresy (like Ebionite, gnostic, Marcion), developed organizational structure (bishops, elders, deacons), and normative Christian ethics (household and community rules), which are all detected in the Pastorals.

Titus and 1 Timothy share with the Deutero-Pauline writings and the General Epistles many literary forms, such as epistolary features and household and community rules. Their added qualifications for church leaders gives them the appearance of a church manual like the Didache. Because they anticipate future problems and give advice through pareneses, both Titus and 1 Timothy have deliberative functions.

Second Timothy, which is a last testament of the apostle (like 2 Pet), has an epideictic function of extolling common values and censuring common vices. As words of the departing apostle-father to his "son(s) in the faith," Paul is portrayed as imparting his religious and ethical values which are to be practiced by his spiritual descendants in the future.

The order Titus, 1 Timothy, 2 Timothy was probably the original. This was the arrangement in the Muratorian Fragment. Titus 1:1-4 functions as the introduction to all three and belongs with 1 Timothy (which is a further elaboration of the contents of Ti). The abrupt ending of 1 Tim 6:20-21a anticipates 2 Timothy. This final testament of Paul (i.e. 2 Tim) serves as the climactic peroration to the entire corpus. The employment of three Pastoral letters is appropriate rhetorically, legally (2 or 3 witnesses, 1 Tim 5:19), and generically (final testaments are usually addressed to more than one designated individual, e.g., a father to his children, a leader to his nation). As a final testament, 2 Timothy leaves behind a work to continue and a legacy upon which to build.

Bibliography

The Ancient Letter Genre

Black II, C. C. "The Rhetorical Form of the Hellenistic Jewish and Early Christian Sermon: A Response to Lawrence Wills." *Harvard Theological Review* 81 (1, 1988) 1–18.

Bullinger, E. W. *Figures of Speech Used in the Bible Explained and Illustrated.* London, 1898; repr. Grand Rapids: Baker, 1968.

Caird, G. B. *Language and Imagery of the Bible.* Philadelphia: Westminster Press, 1980.

Dahl, N. A. "Letter," *IDBSup* 538–41.

Daube, D. "Rabbinic Methods of Interpretation and Hellenistic Rhetoric." *Hebrew Union College Annual Bulletin* 22 (1949) 239–64.

Deissmann, A. *Light from the Ancient East.* Trans. L. Strachan from 1923 ed. Grand Rapids: Baker, 1978.

Doty, W. G. *Letters in Primitive Christianity.* Philadelphia: Fortress Press, 1973.

Fischel, H. A. *Rabbinic Literature and Greco-Roman Philosophy.* Leiden: E. J. Brill, 1973.

Kennedy, G. A. *New Testament Interpretation Through Rhetorical Criticism.* Chapel Hill and London: The University of North Carolina Press, 1984.

Mack, B. L. *Rhetoric and the New Testament.* GBS. Minneapolis: Fortress, 1990.

Malherbe, A. J. *"Mē Genoito* in the Diatribe and Paul." *HTR* 73 (1/2, 1980) 231–40.

Phillips, G. M. "The Practice of Rhetoric at the Talmudic Academies." *Speech Monographs* 26 (1959) 37–47.

Roetzel, C. J. *Letters of Paul: Conversations in Context.* 3rd ed. Louisville: Westminster/John Knox, 1990.

Seitz, O. J. F. "Letter." *IDB* 4:113–15.

Soulen, R. N. *Handbook of Biblical Criticism*. 2nd ed. Atlanta: John Knox, 1981.

Stowers, S. K. *Diatribe and Paul's Letter to the Romans*. Chico, Calif.: Scholars Press, 1981.

______. "Greek and Latin Letters." *ABD* 4:290–93.

______. *Letter Writing in Greco-Roman Antiquity*. Library of Early Christianity: Vol. 5. Louisville: Westminster/John Knox, 1986.

______. "Paul's Dialogue with A Fellow Jew in Romans 3:1-9." *CBQ* 46 (4, 1984) 707–22.

White, J. L. *Light from Ancient Letters*. Philadelphia: Fortress Press, 1986.

Wuellner, W. "Greek Rhetoric and Pauline Argumentation," *Early Christian Literature and the Classical Tradition,* 177–88. Ed., W. R. Schoedel and R. L. Wilken. Paris: Beauchesne, 1979.

______. "Paul's Rhetoric of Argumentation in Romans." *CBQ* 38 (1976) 330–51.

______. "Where Is Rhetorical Criticism Taking Us?" *CBQ* 49 (3, 1987) 448–63.

Introduction to Paul

Babcock, W. S., ed. *Paul and the Legacies of Paul*. Dallas: Southern Methodist University Press, 1990.

Baruch, M. T. *Hard Sayings of Paul*. Downers Grove, Ill.: InterVarsity, 1989.

Bassler, J. M., ed. *Pauline Theology, Vol. 1: Thessalonians, Philippians, Galatians, Philemon*. Minneapolis: Fortress Press, 1991.

Beker, J. C. *Heirs of Paul: Paul's Legacy in the New Testament and in the Church Today*. Minneapolis: Fortress Press, 1991.

______. *Paul's Apocalyptic Gospel: The Coming Triumph of God*. Minneapolis: Fortress Press, 1982.

______. *Paul the Apostle: The Triumph of God in Life and Thought*. Minneapolis: Fortress Press, 1980.

______. "Paul's Theology: Consistent or Inconsistent?" *NTS* 34 (1988): 364–77.

______. *The Triumph of God: The Essence of Paul's Thought*. Trans. by L. T. Stuckenbruck. Minneapolis: Fortress Press, 1990.

Betz, H. D. "Paul." *The Anchor Bible Dictionary*. 5:186–201. Ed. D. N. Freedman, et al. New York: Doubleday, 1992.

Boring, M. E. "The Language of Universal Salvation in Paul." *JBL* 105 (1986) 269–92.

Branick, V. P. *The House Church in the Writings of Paul.* Collegeville, Minn.: The Liturgical Press, 1990.

Buchanan, G. W. "The Day of Atonement and Paul's Doctrine of Redemption." *NovT* 32 (3, 1990) 236–249.

Campbell, D. A. "The Meaning of *Pistis* and *Nomos* in Paul: A Linguistic and Structural Perspective." *JBL* 110 (4, 1992) 91–103.

Castelli, E. A. *Imitating Paul: A Discourse of Power.* Literary Currents in Biblical Interpretation. Louisville: Westminster/John Knox Press, 1991.

Collins, R. F. *Letters that Paul Did Not Write: The Epistle to the Hebrews and the Pauline Pseudepigrapha.* Collegeville, Minn.: The Liturgical Press, 1988.

Cosgrove, C. H. "Justification in Paul: A Linguistic and Theological Reflection." *JBL* 106 (1987) 653–70.

Davies, W. D. *Jewish and Pauline Studies.* Philadelphia: Fortress Press, 1984.

Ellis, E. E. *Paul's Use of the Old Testament.* Grand Rapids: Baker, 1991.

Fiorenza, E. S. *In Memory of Her: A Feminist Theological Reconstruction of Christian Origins.* New York: Crossroad, 1983.

Fitzmyer, J. A. *Paul and His Theology: A Brief Sketch.* 2nd ed. Englewood Cliffs, N.J.: Prentice Hall, 1989.

Flanagan, N. *Friend Paul: His Letters, Theology, and Humanity.* Collegeville, Minn.: The Liturgical Press, 1988.

Francis, F. O. and Sampley, J. P. *Pauline Parallels.* Rev. ed. Minneapolis: Fortress Press, 1988.

Gaston, L. *Paul and the Torah.* Vancouver: University of British Columbia Press, 1987.

Gillman, F. M. *Women Who Knew Paul.* Collegeville, Minn.: The Liturgical Press, 1992.

Hammerton-Kelly, R. G. *Sacred Violence: Paul's Hermeneutic of the Cross.* Minneapolis: Fortress Press, 1992.

Hooker, M. D. and Wilson, S. G., ed. *Paul and Paulinism: Essays in Honor of C. K. Barrett.* London: SPCK, 1982.

Hübner, H. *Law in Paul's Thought.* Edinburgh: T. & T. Clark, 1984.

Jewett, R. *A Chronology of Paul's Life.* Philadelphia: Fortress Press, 1979.

Johnson, S. E. *Paul the Apostle and His Cities.* Good News Studies: Vol. 21. Collegeville, Minn.: The Liturgical Press, 1987.

Kaylor, R. D. *Paul's Covenant Community: Jew and Gentile in Romans.* Atlanta: John Knox, 1988.

Keck, L. E. *Paul and His Letters.* 2nd ed. rev. and enl. Proclamation Commentaries. Minneapolis: Fortress Press, 1988.

Kennedy, G. A. *New Testament Interpretation Through Rhetorical Criticism.* Chapel Hill and London: The University of North Carolina Press, 1984.

Kreitzer, L. J. *Jesus and God in Paul's Eschatology.* JSNTSup 19. Sheffield: JSOT Press, 1987.

Lapide, P. and P. Stuhlmacher, *Paul, Rabbi, and Apostle.* Trans. L. W. Denef. Minneapolis: Augsburg, 1984.

Lüdemann, G. *Paul, Apostle to the Gentiles: Studies in Chronology.* Trans. F. S. Jones. Philadelphia: Fortress Press, 1984.

MacDonald, D. R. *The Legend and the Apostle: The Battle for Paul in Story and Canon.* Philadelphia: Westminster Press, 1983.

MacDonald, M. Y. *The Pauline Churches: A Socio-historical Study of the Institutionalization in the Pauline and Deutero-Pauline Writings.* New York and Cambridge: Cambridge University Press, 1988.

Mack, B. L. *Rhetoric and the New Testament.* Minneapolis: Fortress Press, 1990.

Malherbe, A. J. *Paul and the Popular Philosophers.* Minneapolis: Fortress Press, 1989.

Marrow, S. M. *Paul: His Letters and Theology.* Mahwah, N.J.: Paulist Press, 1986.

Mauser, U. "Paul The Theologian." *HBT* 11 (2, 1989) 80–106.

May, D. M., ed. *Pauline Theology, Vol. 2: 1 and 2 Corinthians.* Minneapolis: Fortress Press, 1993.

Meeks, W. A. *The First Urban Christians: The Social World of the Apostle Paul.* New Haven and London: Yale University Press, 1983.

______. ed. *The Writings of St. Paul.* New York: W. W. Norton & Co., 1972.

Munro, W. *Authority in Paul and Peter: The Identification of a Pastoral Stratum in the Pauline Corpus and 1 Peter.* SNTSMS 45. Cambridge and New York: Cambridge University Press, 1983.

Murphy-O'Connor, J. "Pauline Studies." *RB* 97 (2, 1990) 286–296 and 98 (1, 1991) 145–151.

Neumann, K. J. *The Authenticity of the Pauline Epistles in the Light of Stylostatistical Analysis.* SBLDS 120. Atlanta: Scholars Press, 1990.

Neyrey, J. H. *Paul, in Other Words: A Cultural Reading of His Letters.* Louisville: Westminster/John Knox Press, 1990.

O'Toole, R. F. *What Is a Christian? A Study in Pauline Ethics.* Collegeville, Minn.: The Liturgical Press, 1990.

Pagels, E. H. *The Gnostic Paul: Gnostic Exegesis of the Pauline Letters*. Philadelphia: Fortress Press, 1975; paperback ed., Philadelphia: Trinity Press International, 1992.

Patte, D. *Paul's Faith and the Power of the Gospel: A Structural Introduction to the Pauline Letters*. Philadelphia: Fortress Press, 1983.

Plevnik, J. *What are They Saying About Paul?* Mahwah, N.J.: Paulist Press, 1986.

Räisänen, H. *Paul and the Law*. Philadelphia: Fortress Press, 1986.

Roetzel, C. J. *Letters of Paul: Conversations in Context*. 3rd ed. Louisville: Westminster/John Knox, 1990.

Sanders, E. P. *Paul and Palestinian Judaism: A Comparison of Patterns of Religion*. Minneapolis: Fortress Press, 1977.

______. *Paul, the Law, and the Jewish People*. Minneapolis: Fortress Press, 1983.

Schenke, H.-M. "Four Problems in the Life of Paul Reconsidered." In *The Future of Early Christianity: Essays in Honor of Helmut Koester*. Edited by B. A. Pearson, 319–328. Minneapolis: Fortress Press, 1991.

Schreiner, T. R. "The Abolition and the Fulfillment of the Law in Paul." *JSNT* 35 (1989) 47–74.

Schweitzer, A. *Paul and His Interpreters: A Critical History*. Trans. W. Montgomery. London: Black, 1912.

Segal, A. F. *Paul the Convert: The Apostolate and Apostasy of Saul the Pharisee*. New Haven: Yale University Press, 1990.

Stendahl, K. *Paul Among the Jews and Gentiles and Other Essays*. Philadelphia: Fortress Press, 1976.

Stockhausen, C. L. *Letters in the Pauline Tradition: Ephesians, Colossians, 1 Timothy, 2 Timothy, Titus*. Collegeville, Minn.: The Liturgical Press, 1988.

Stowers, S. K. "Paul on the Use and Abuse of Reason." In *Greeks, Romans, and Christians: Essays in Honor of Abraham J. Malherbe*. Edited by D. L. Balch, et. al., 305–317. Minneapolis: Fortress Press, 1990.

Theissen, G,. *Psychological Aspects of Pauline Theology*. Philadelphia: Fortress Press, 1987.

Tomson, P. J. *Paul and the Jewish Law: Halakha in the Letters of the Apostle to the Gentiles*. CRINT. Sec. 3: Jewish Traditions in Early Christian Literature 1. Assen—Maastricht: Van Gorcum; Minneapolis: Fortress Press, 1990.

Wedderburn, A. J. M. *Baptism and Resurrection: Studies in Pauline Theology Against Its Graeco-Roman Background*. WUNT 44. Tübingen: J.C.B. Mohr (Paul Siebeck), 1987.

Westerholm, S. *Israel's Law and the Church's Faith: Paul and His Recent Interpreters*. Grand Rapids: Eerdmans, 1988.

Wiles, M. *The Interpretation of St. Paul's Letters in the Early Church*. London: Cambridge University Press, 1967.

Wright, N. T. *The Climax of the Covenant: Christ and the Law in Pauline Theology*. Edinburgh: T. & T. Clark; Minneapolis: Fortress Press, 1991.

Wuellner, W. "Greek Rhetoric and Pauline Argumentation." *Early Christian Literature and the Classical Tradition,* 177–88. Ed. W. R. Schoedel and R. L. Wilken. Paris: Beauchesne, 1979.

Yarbrough, L. O. *Not Like the Gentiles: Marriage Rules in the Letters of Paul*. SBLDS 80. Atlanta: Scholars Press, 1985.

Galatians

Barclay, J. M. G. *Obeying the Truth: A Study of Paul's Ethics in Galatians*. Edinburgh: T & T Clark, 1988; Minneapolis: Fortress Press, 1991.

Barrett, C. K. *Freedom and Obligation: A Study of the Epistle to the Galatians*. Philadelphia: Westminster, 1985.

______. "Galatians as an 'Apologetic Letter': *Galatians: A Commentary on Paul's Letter to the Churches in Galatia*, by H. D. Betz." *Int* 34 (1980) 414–417.

Betz, H. D. *Galatians: A Commentary of Paul's Letter to the Churches in Galatia*. Hermeneia. Philadelphia: Fortress Press, 1979.

______. "In Defense of the Spirit: Paul's Letter to the Galatians as a Document of Christian Apologetics." *Aspects of Religious Propaganda in Judaism and Early Christianity*. Ed., E. Schüssler Fiorenza, 99–114. Notre Dame: University Press, 1976.

______. "The Literary Composition and Function of Paul's Letter to the Galatians." *NTS* 21 (1975) 353–79.

______. "Spirit, Freedom, and Law: Paul's Message to the Galatian Churches. *SEÅ* 39 (1974) 145–60.

______. "Galatians, Epistle to the." *The Anchor Bible Dictionary*. 2:872–875. Ed. D. N. Freedman. New York: Doubleday, 1992.

Brinsmead, B. H. *Galatians—Dialogical Response to Opponents*. SBLDS 65. Chico, Calif.: Scholars Press, 1982.

Bruce, F. F. *Commentary on Galatians*. NIGTC. Grand Rapids: Eerdmans, 1982.

______. "Galatian Problems: II. North or South Galatians?" *BJRL* 52 (1969/70) 243–46.

Burton, E. D. *A Critical and Exegetical Commentary on the Epistle of Paul to the Galatians*. ICC. Edinburgh: T. & T. Clark, 1921.

Cosgrove, C. H. *The Cross and the Spirit: A Study in the Argument and Theology of Galatians*. Macon, Ga.: Mercer University Press, 1989.

Dolamo, R. T. "Rhetorical Speech in Galatians." *Theologia Viatorum* (Sovenga, South Africa) 17 (1989) 30–37.

Duncan, G. S. *The Epistle of Paul to the Galatians*. New York: Harper & Row, 1934.

Dunn, J. D. G. "The Theology of Galatians: The Issue of Covenantal Nomism." In *Pauline Theology, Vol. 1: Thessalonians, Philippians, Galatians, Philemon*. Edited by J. M. Bassler, 125–146. Minneapolis: Fortress Press, 1991.

Fung, R. Y. K. *The Epistle to the Galatians*. NICNT. Grand Rapids: Eerdmans, 1988.

Guthrie, D. *Galatians*. NCB. London: Thomas Nelson & Sons, 1969.

Hays, R. B. "Christology and Ethics in Galatians: The Law of Christ." *CBQ* 49 (1987) 268–290.

______. *The Faith of Jesus Christ: An Investigation of the Narrative Substructure of Galatians 3:1–4:11*. SBLDS 56. Chico, Calif.: Scholars Press, 1983.

Hester, J. D. "The Rhetorical Structure of Galatians 1:11–2:14." *JBL* 103 (2, 1984) 223–33.

______. "The Use and Influence of Rhetoric in Gal 2:1-14." *TZ* 42 (1986) 386–408.

Howard, G. *Paul: Crisis in Galatia. A Study in Early Christian Theology*. SNTSMS 35. 2nd. ed. Cambridge; New York: Cambridge University Press, 1990.

Jewett, R. "The Agitators and the Galatian Congregation." *NTS* 17 (1971) 198–212.

Krentz, E., et al. *Galatians, Philippians, Philemon, 1 Thessalonians*. Augsburg Commentary on the NT. Minneapolis: Augsburg, 1985.

Lightfoot, J. B. *The Epistle of St. Paul to the Galatians*. 10th ed. London: Macmillan, 1890.

Longenecker, R. N. *Galatians*. WBC 41. Dallas: Word, 1990.

Lührmann, D. *Galatians*. A Continental Commentary. Trans. by O. C. Dean. Minneapolis: Fortress Press, 1992.

Lull, D. J. " 'The Law Was Our Pedagogue': A Study in Gal 3:19-25." *JBL* 105 (1986) 481–98.

______. *The Spirit in Galatia: Paul's Interpretation of Pneuma as Divine Power*. SBLDS 49. Chico, CA: Scholars Press, 1980.

Mitchell, S. "Galatia." *The Anchor Bible Dictionary*. 2:870–872. Ed. D. N. Freedman. New York: Doubleday, 1992.

Munck, J. *Paul and the Salvation of Mankind*. Trans. F. Clarke. Orig. ed. 1959. Atlanta: John Knox, 1977.

Räisänen, H. "Paul's Conversion and the Development of His View of the Law." *NTS* 33 (1987) 404–19.

Ramsay, W. M. *A Historical Commentary on St. Paul's Epistle to the Galatians*. New York: G. P. Putnam's Sons, 1900.

Schmithals, W. *Paul and the Gnostics*. Trans. J. Steely. Nashville: Abingdon, 1972.

Schweizer, E. "Slaves of the Elements and Worshipers of Angels: Gal 4:3,9 and Col 2:8,18,20." *JBL* 107 (1988) 455–68.

Smit, J. "The Letter of Paul to the Galatians: A Deliberative Speech." *NTS* 35 (1989) 1–26.

Stanley, C. D. " 'Under A Curse': A Fresh Reading of Gal 3.10-14." *NTS* 36:4 (1990) 481–511.

Thielman, F. S. *From Plight to Solution: A Jewish Framework to Understanding Paul's View of the Law in Galatians and Romans.* NovTSup 61. Leiden: Brill, 1989.

Thornton, T. C. G. "Jewish New Moon Festivals, Gal 4:3-11 and Col 2:16." *JTS* 40 (1989) 97–100.

Williams, S. K. "The Hearing of Faith: *akoē pisteos* in Gal 3." *NTS* 35 (1989) 82–93.

______. "Justification and the Spirit in Galatians." *JSNT* 29 (1987) 91–100.

______. "*Promise* in Galatians: A Reading of Paul's Reading of Scripture." *JBL* 107 (1988) 709–20.

Winger, J. M. *By What Law? The Meaning of Nomos in the Letters of Paul*. SBLDS 128. Atlanta: Scholars Press, 1992.

Paul's Corinthian Correspondence

Baird, W. R. "Letters of Recommendation: A Study of 2 Cor 3:1-3." *JBL* 80 (1961) 166–72.

Balch, D. L. "Backgrounds of 1 Cor VII: Sayings of the Lord in Q; Moses As an Ascetic *Theios Aner* in 2 Cor 3." *NTS* 18 (1972) 351–64.

Barrett, C. K. *The First Epistle to the Corinthians*. HNTC. (New York: Harper and Row, 1968) 12–17.

______. "Paul's Opponents in II Corinthians." *NTS* 17 (1971) 233–54.

______. *The Second Epistle to the Corinthians*. HNTC. New York: Harper & Row, 1973.

Bartchy, S. S. *Mallon Chresai: First Century Slavery and the Interpretation of 1 Corinthians 7:21*. Missoula, Mont.: Scholars Press, 1973.

Bates, W. H. "The Integrity of 2 Corinthians," *NTS* 12 (1965) 56–59.

Beasley-Murray, G. R. *Baptism in the New Testament*. London: Macmillan, 1962.

Betz, H. D. and M. M. Mitchell, "Corinthians, First Epistle to the." *The Anchor Bible Dictionary*. 1:1139–1148. Ed. D. N. Freedman. New York: Doubleday, 1992.

______. "Corinthians, Second Epistle to the." *The Anchor Bible Dictionary*. 1:1148–1154. Ed. D. N. Freedman. New York: Doubleday, 1992.

Betz, H. D. "2 Cor 6:14–7:1: An Anti-Pauline Fragment?" *JBL* 92 (1973) 88–108.

______. *2 Corinthians 8 and 9*. Hermeneia. Philadelphia: Fortress Press, 1985.

Broneer, O. "Corinth: Center of Paul's Missionary Work in Greece." *BA* 14 (1951) 78–96.

______. "The Apostle Paul and the Isthmian Games." *BA* 25 (1962) 2–31. "Corinth, A Brief History of the City and A Guide to the Excavations," American School of Classical Studies, Athens, revised 1972.

Callan, T. "Prophecy and Ecstasy in Greco-Roman Religion and 1 Corinthians." *NovT* 27 (22, 1985) 125–40.

Castelli, E. A. "Interpretations of Power in 1 Corinthians." *Semeia* 54 (1991) 197–222.

Chance, J. B. "Paul's Apology to the Corinthians." *PeRelSt* 9 (1, 1982) 146–55.

Collins, G. G. "Power Made Perfect in Weakness: 2 Cor 12:9-10." *CBQ* 33 (1971) 528–37.

Conzelmann, H. *1 Corinthians: A Commentary on the First Epistle to the Corinthians*. Hermeneia. Philadelphia: Fortress Press, 1975.

Dahl, N. A. "Paul and the Church at Corinth." In N. A. Dahl, *Studies in Paul*, 49–55. Minneapolis: Augsburg, 1977.

Dunn, J. D. G. "2 Cor III.17- 'The Lord is Spirit.' " *JTS* 21 (1970) 309–20.

Ellis, E. E. "Paul and His Co-workers." *NTS* 17 (1971) 437–53.

______. "II Cor v. 1-10 in Pauline Eschatology." *NTS* 62 (1960) 211–24.

Engberg-Pedersen, T. "The Gospel and Social Practice According to 1 Corinthians." *NTS* 33 (1987) 557–84.

______. "1 Corinthians 11:16 and the Character of Pauline Exhortation." *JBL* 110 (1991) 679–89.

Fee, G. D. *Paul's First Letter to the Corinthians*. NIC. Grand Rapids: Eerdmans, 1987.

______. "II Corinthians vi.14-vii.1 and Food Offered to Idols," *NTS* 23 (1977) 140–61.

______. *1 Corinthians*. NIC. Grand Rapids: Eerdmans, 1987.

Finegan, J. "Corinth." *IDB* 1:683–4.

Fiorenza, E. S. "Rhetorical Situation and Historical Reconstruction in 1 Corinthians." *NTS* 33 (1987) 386–403.

Fitzgerald, J. T. *Cracks in an Earthen Vessel. An Examination of the Catalogues of Hardships in the Corinthian Correspondence*. SBLDS 99. Atlanta: Scholars Press, 1988.

______. "Paul, the Ancient Epistolary Theorists, and 2 Corinthians 10–13." In *Greeks, Romans, and Christians: Essays in Honor of Abraham J. Malherbe*. Edited by D. L. Balch, et al., 190–200. Minneapolis: Fortress Press, 1990.

Frederickson, D. "Pentecost: Paul the Pastor in 2 Corinthians." *WW* 11 (2, 1991) 208–214.

Furnish, V. P. *II Corinthians*. AB 32A. Garden City, NY: Doubleday, 1984.

______. "The Ministry of Reconciliation." *CurTM* 4 (1977) 204–18.

______. *Theology and Ethics in Paul*. Nashville: Abingdon, 1968.

Georgi, D. "Corinthians, First Letter to the." *IDBSup* 181.

______. *The Opponents of Paul in 2 Corinthians*. Philadelphia: Fortress Press, 1985.

______. *Remembering the Poor. The History of Paul's Collection for Jerusalem*. Nashville: Abingdon, 1992.

Gundry, R. H. *Soma in Biblical Theology, with Emphasis on Pauline Anthropology*. NTSMS 29. Cambridge and New York: Cambridge University Press, 1976.

Hay, D. M., ed. *Pauline Theology, Vol. 2: 1 and 2 Corinthians*. Minneapolis: Fortress Press, 1993.

Hill, A. E. "The Temple of Asclepius: An Alternative Source for Paul's Body Theology?" *JBL* 99 (3, 1980) 437–39.

Hock, R. *The Social Context of Paul's Ministry: Tentmaking and Apostleship*. Philadelphia: Fortress, 1980.

Hodgson, R. "Paul the Apostle and First Century Tribulation Lists." *ZNW* 74 (1/2, 1983) 59–80.

Holladay, C. R. "1 Corinthians 13: Paul as Apostolic Paradigm." In *Greeks, Romans, and Christians: Essays in Honor of Abraham J. Malherbe*. Edited by D. L. Balch, et al., 80–98. Minneapolis: Fortress Press, 1990.

Holmberg, B. *Paul and Power: The Structure of Authority in the Primitive Church as Reflected in the Pauline Epistles*. Philadelphia: Fortress Press, 1978.

Hughes, P. E. *2 Corinthians*. NIC. Grand Rapids: Eerdmans, 1962.

Hurd, J. C. *The Origin of 1 Corinthians*. Second ed. Macon, Ga.: Mercer University Press, 1983.

Jewett, R. *Paul's Anthropological Terms. A Study of Their Use in Conflict Settings*. Leiden: E. J. Brill, 1971.

______. "The Redaction of 1 Corinthians and the Trajectory of the Pauline School." *JAARS* 44 (1978) 389–444.

Judge, E. A. "St. Paul and Classical Society." *JAC* 15 (1972) 19–36.

______. "St. Paul and Socrates." *Interchange* 14 (1980) 106–16.

Käsemann, E. "The Pauline Doctrine of the Lord's Supper." in idem, *Essays on New Testament Themes*, 108–35. Trans. W. Montague. London: SCM, 1964; Philadelphia: Fortress Press, 1982.

Kee, D. "Who Were the 'Super-Apostles' of 2 Corinthians 10–13?" *RestQ* 23 (1980) 65–76.

Klijne, J. J. "We, Us and Our in I and II Corinthians." *NovT* 8 (1966) 171–79.

MacDonald, M. Y. "Women Holy in Body and Spirit: The Social Setting of 1 Corinthians 7." *NTS* 36 (1990) 161–181.

Marshall, P. *Enmity in Corinth: Social Conventions in Paul's Relations with the Corinthians*. Tübingen: J. C. B. Mohr (Paul Siebeck), 1987.

Martin, R. P. *2 Corinthians*. WBC. Dallas: Word, 1986.

May, D. M., ed. *Pauline Theology, Vol. 2: 1 & 2 Corinthians*. Minneapolis: Fortress Press, 1993.

Mullins, T. Y. "Paul's Thorn in the Flesh." *JBL* 76 (1957) 299–303.

Murphy-O'Connor, J. "Corinth." *The Anchor Bible Dictionary*. 1:1134–1139. New York: Doubleday, 1992.

______. "The Corinth that Saint Paul Saw." *BA* 47:3 (1984) 147–59.

______. *St. Paul's Corinth, Texts and Archaeology*. Wilmington, Del.: Michael Glazier, 1983.

______. *The Theology of the Second Letter to the Corinthians*. New Testament Theology. Cambridge: Cambridge University Press, 1991.

Mussies, G. *Dio Chrysostom and the New Testament*. Leiden: E. J. Brill, 1972.

Neyrey, J. H. "Body Language in 1 Corinthians: The Use of Anthropological Models for Understanding Paul and his Opponents." Edited by J. H. Elliott, 127–170. *Semeia: Social Scientific Criticism of the New Testament and Its Social World* 35 (1986).

Nickle, K. *The Collection, A Study in Paul's Strategy*. SBT 48 (Naperville, IL: Alec R. Allenson, 1966).

Plank, K. A. "Resurrection Theology: The Corinthian Controversy Reexamined." *PerRelSt* 8 (1, 1981) 41–54.

Schithmals, W. *Gnosticism in Corinth: An Investigation of the Letters to the Corinthians*. Trans. J. Steely. Nashville: Abingdon, 1971.

______. *The Office of the Apostle in the Early Church*. Trans. J. Steely. Nashville: Abingdon, 1969.

Spencer, A. B. "The Wise Fool (and the Foolish Wise): A Study of Irony in Paul." *NovT* 23 (1981) 349-60.

Tannehill, R. C. *Dying and Rising with Christ: A Study in Pauline Theology*. BZNW 32. Berlin: Topelmann, 1967.

Taylor, N. H. "The Composition and Chronology of Second Corinthians." *JNTS* 44 (1991) 67–87.

Theissen, G. *The Social Setting of Pauline Christianity. Essays on Corinth*. Trans. J. Shutz. Philadelphia: Fortress, 1982.

Thielman, F. "The Coherence of Paul's View of the Law: The Evidence of First Corinthians." *NTS* 38:2 (1992) 235–253.

Thrall, M. E. "The Problem of II Cor vi.14–vii.1 in Some Recent Discussion." *NTS* 24 (1977) 132–48.

______. "Super-Apostles, Servants of Christ, and Servants of Satan." *JSNT* 6 (1980) 42–57.

Travis, S. H. "Paul's Boasting in 2 Cor 10–12." In *Studia Evangelica*. Edited by E. A. Lingston, 6:527–32. Berlin: Akademie-Verlag, 1973.

Willis, W. *Idol Meat in Corinth: Pauline Argument in 1 Corinthians 8 and 10*. SBLDS 68. Chico, Calif.: Scholars Press, 1985.

Wilson, R. McL. "How Gnostic Were the Corinthians?" *NTS* (1972–3) 65–74.

Wire, A. C. *The Corinthian Women Prophets: A Reconstruction through Paul's Rhetoric*. Minneapolis: Fortress Press, 1990.

Wiseman, J. R. "Ancient Corinth: The Gymnasium Area." *Arch* 22 (1969) 216–25.

Romans

Barrett, C. K. *The Epistle to the Romans*. HNTC. New York: Harper & Row, 1957.

Bornkamm, G. "The Letter to Romans as Paul's Last Will and Testament." In K. Donfried, ed. *The Romans Debate*, 17–31. Minneapolis: Augsburg, 1977.

Campbell, W. S. "Why Did Paul Write Romans?" *ExpT* 85 (1974) 264–69.

Crafton, J. A. "Paul's Rhetorical Vision and the Purpose of Romans: Toward a New Understanding." *NovTest* 32 (4, 1990) 317–339.

Cranfield, C. E. B. *Romans: Critical and Exegetical Commentary.* 2 vols. ICC. Edinburgh: T. & T. Clark, 1975, 1979.

Cranfield, C. E. B. " 'The Works of the Law' in the Epistle to the Romans." *JSNT* 43 (1991) 89–101.

Davies, W. D. *Paul and Rabbinic Judaism: Some Rabbinic Elements in Pauline Theology.* London, 1948; 4th ed., Philadelphia: Fortress Press, 1980.

Dodd, C. H. *The Epistle of Paul to the Romans.* MNTC. New York: Harper & Row, 1932.

Donfried, K. P. "A Short Note on Romans 16," *JBL* 89 (1970), 441–49.

______., ed. *The Romans Debate.* Minneapolis: Augsburg, 1977.

______., ed. *The Romans Debate.* Rev. ed. Peabody, Mass.: Hendrickson, 1991.

Dunn, J. D. *Romans, Chapters 1–8.* Vol. 38A. WBC. Dallas: Word, 1988.

______. *Romans, Chapters 9–16.* Vol. 38B. WBC. Dallas: Word, 1988.

Edwards, J. R. *Romans.* New International Biblical Commentary. Peabody, Mass.: Hendrickson, 1992.

Elliott, N. *The Rhetoric of Romans. Argumentative Constraint and Strategy and Paul's Dialogue with Judaism.* JSNTSupp 45. Sheffield: JSOT, 1990.

Gamble, H. *The Textual History of the Letter to the Romans.* Grand Rapids: Eerdmans, 1977.

Guerra, A. J. "Romans: Paul's Purpose and Audience with Special Attention to Romans 9–11." *RevBib* 97 (2, 1990) 219–237.

Heil, J. P. *Paul's Letter to the Romans: A Reader-Response Commentary.* Mahwah, NJ: Paulist Press, 1987.

Hultgren, A. J. *Paul's Gospel and Mission, The Outlook from His Letter to the Romans.* Philadelphia: Fortress Press, 1985.

Karris, R. J. "Rom. 14:1–15:13 and the Occasion of Romans." In *Romans Debate* (1977) 75–99.

Käsemann, E. *Commentary on Romans.* Trans. G. Bromiley. Grand Rapids: Eerdmans, 1980.

______. *New Testament Questions of Today.* Trans. W. Montague. Philadelphia: Fortress Press, 1969.

______. *Perspectives on Paul.* Trans. M. Kohl. Philadelphia: Fortress Press, 1971.

Klein, G. "Paul's Purpose in Writing the Epistle to the Romans." In *Romans Debate* (1977) 32–49.

______. "Romans, Letter to." *IDBSup* 753–54.

Lüdemann, G. *Paul, Apostle to the Gentiles: Studies in Chronology.* Trans. F. S. Jones. Philadelphia: Fortress Press, 1984.

MacDonald, J. I. H. "Was Romans xvi a Separate Letter?" *NTS* 16 (1969–70) 369–72.

Malherbe, A. J. "*Mē Genoito* in the Diatribe and Paul." *HTR* 73 (1/2, 1980) 231–40.

______. *Moral Exhortations, A Greco-Roman Sourcebook*. Philadelphia: Westminster, 1986.

Manson, T. W. "St. Paul's Letter to the Romans—and Others." *BJRL* 31 (1948) 224–40.

Minear, P. S. *The Obedience of the Faith*. SBT 19. London: SCM, 1971.

Munck, J. *Paul and the Salvation of Mankind*. Trans. F. Clarke, Orig. ed., 1959. Atlanta: John Knox, 1977.

Petersen, N. R. "On the Ending(s) to Paul's Letter to Rome." *The Future of Early Christianity: Essays in Honor of Helmut Koester*. Edited by B. A. Pearson, 337–347. Minneapolis: Fortress Press, 1991.

Porter, S. E. "The Argument of Romans 5: Can a Rhetorical Question Make a Difference?" *JBL* 110 (4, 1991) 655–677.

Räisänen, H. *Paul and the Law*. Philadelphia: Fortress Press, 1986.

Ramsay, W. M. *St. Paul The Traveller and Roman Citizen*. London, 1897; Grand Rapids: Baker, 1962.

Sanday, W. and Headlam, A. C. *The Epistle to the Romans*. ICC. Edinburgh: T. & T. Clark, 1905.

Sanders, E. P. *Paul and Rabbinic Judaism: A Comparison of Patterns of Religions*. Philadelphia: Fortress Press, 1977.

Sanders, J. A. "Torah and Christ." *Int* 29 (4, 1975) 372–90.

Sandmel, S. *The Genius of Paul*. New York: Farrar, Strauss and Cudahy, 1958.

Schoeps, H. J. *Paul, The Theology of Paul in the Light of Jewish Religious History*. Trans. H. Knight. Philadelphia: Westminster, 1961.

Stendahl, K. *Paul Among Jews and Gentiles and Other Essays*. Philadelphia: Fortress Press, 1976.

Stowers, S. K. *The Diatribe and Paul's Letter to the Romans*. Chico, Calif.: Scholars Press, 1981.

______. "Paul's Dialogue with A Fellow Jew in Romans 3:1-9." *CBQ* 46 (4, 1984) 707–22.

Wedderburn, A. J. M. *The Reasons for Romans*. Edinburgh: T & T Clark; Minneapolis: Fortress Press, 1991.

______. " 'Like an Ever-rolling Stream': Some Recent Commentaries on Romans." *SJT* 44 (3, 1991) 367–380.

Wuellner, W. "Paul's Rhetoric of Argumentation in Romans." In *Romans Debate* (1977) 152–74.

Philippians and Philemon

Bartchy, S. S. "Philemon, Epistle to the." 5:305–310. *The Anchor Bible Dictionary*. Ed. D. N. Freedman, et al. New York: Doubleday, 1992.

Beare, F. W. *A Commentary on The Epistle to the Philippians*. 2nd ed London, 1969.

Bruce, F. F. *Philippians*. San Francisco: Harper and Row, 1983.

______. *Philippians*. New International Biblical Commentary. Peabody, Mass.: Hendrickson, 1989.

______. "St. Paul in Rome (2): The Epistle to Philemon." *BJRL* 48 (1965–66) 90.

Church, F. F. "Rhetorical Structure and Design in Paul's Letter to Philemon." *HTR* 71 (1/2, 1978) 17–33.

Fitzgerald, J. T. "Philippians, Epistle to the." *The Anchor Bible Dictionary*. 5:318–326. Ed. D. N. Freedman, et al. New York: Doubleday, 1992.

Gunther, J. *St. Paul's Opponents and Their Background: A Study of Apocalyptic and Jewish Sectarian Teachings*. Leiden: E.J. Brill, 1977.

Hawthorne, G. F. *Philippians*. WBC. Dallas: Word Books, 1983.

Hendrix, H. L. "Philippi." *ABD* 5:313–17.

Hurst, L. D. "Re-Enter the Pre-Existence of Christ in Philipians 2.5-11?" *NTS* 32 (1986) 449–57.

Jewett, R. "Conflicting Movements in the Early Church as Reflected in Philippians." *NovT* 12 (1970) 367–90.

Jonas, H. *The Gnostic Religion*. 2nd ed. Boston: Beacon Press, 1963.

Kim, C.-H. *Form and Structure of the Familiar Greek Letter of Recommendation*. SBLDS 2. Missoula, Mont.: Scholars Press, 1972.

Knox, J. *Philemon Among The Letters of Paul*. 2nd ed. Nashville: Abingdon, 1959.

______. "Philemon and the Authenticity of Colossians." *JR* 18 (1938) 144–60.

Lewis, L. A. "An African American Appraisal of the Philemon-Paul-Onesimus Triangle." *Stony the Road We Trod: African American Biblical Interpretation*. 232–246. Ed. C. H. Felder. Minneapolis: Fortress Press, 1991.

Lightfoot, J. B. *St. Paul's Epistle to the Philippians*. London: Macmillan, 1913.

Lohse, E. *Colossians and Philemon*. Hermeneia. Trans. W. Poehlmann et al. Philadelphia: Fortress Press, 1971.

Martin, R. P. *Philippians*. Grand Rapids: Eerdmans, 1976.

———. *Carmen Christi, Philippians 2:5-11.* Rev. ed. Grand Rapids: Eerdmans, 1983.

O'Brien, P. T. *Colossians, Philemon*. Word Biblical Commentary. Dallas: Word Books, 1982.

———. *The Epistle to the Philippians. A Commentary on the Greek Text.* NIGTC. Grand Rapids: Eerdmans, 1991.

Patzia, A. G. *Ephesians, Colossians, Philemon.* NIBC. Peabody, Mass.: Hendrickson, 1991.

Perkins, P. "Philippians: Theology for the Heavenly Politeuma." In *Pauline Theology, Vol. 1.* Edited by J. M. Bassler, 89–104. Minneapolis: Fortress Press, 1991.

Soards, M. L. "Some Neglected Theological Dimensions of Paul's Letter to Philemon." *PRS* 17 (3, 1990) 209–219.

Schmithals, W. *Paul and the Gnostics*. Trans. J. Steely. Nashville: Abingdon, 1972.

Wanamaker, C. A. "Philippians 2.6-11: Son of God or Adamic Christology?" *NTS* 33 (1987) 179–93.

Wong, T. "The Problem of Pre-Existence in Philippians 2,6-11." *ETL* 62 (1986) 267–82.

White, J. "The Structural Analysis of Philemon." 1–47. SBLASP. Missoula, Mont.: Scholars Press, 1971.

White, L. M. "Morality between Two Worlds: A Paradigm of Friendship in Philippians." In *Greeks, Romans, and Christians: Essays in Honor of Abraham J. Malherbe*. Edited by D. L. Balch, et al., 201-215. Minneapolis: Fortress Press, 1990.

Thessalonians

Bailey, J. "Who Wrote 2 Thessalonians?" *NTS* 25 (1979) 131–45.

Beare, F. "Thessalonians, Second." *IDB* 4:626.

Best, E. *The First and Second Epistles to the Thessalonians*. London: Black, 1972.

Boers, H. "The Form Critical Study of Paul's Letters. 1 Thes As A Case Study." *NTS* 22 (1975–76) 140–58.

Bruce, F. F. *1 and 2 Thessalonians*. WBC. Dallas: Word Books, 1982.

Collins, R. F., ed. *The Thessalonian Correspondence*. BETL 87. Leuven: Leuven University Press; Peeters, 1990.

Frame, J. *Epistles of Paul to the Thessalonians*. ICC. Edinburgh: T. & T. Clark, 1912.

Hendrix, H. L. "Thessalonica." *The Anchor Bible Dictionary*. 6:523–527. Ed. D. N. Freedman. New York: Doubleday, 1992.

______. "Thessalonians, First and Second Epistles to the." *The Anchor Bible Dictionary*. 6:515–523. Ed. D. N. Freedman. New York: Doubleday, 1992.

Holland, G. S. *The Tradition That You Received from Us: 2 Thessalonians in the Pauline Tradition*. HUT 24. Tübingen: JCB Mohr (P. Siebeck), 1988.

Hughes, F. W. *Early Christian Rhetoric and 2 Thessalonians*. JSNTSup 30. Sheffield: JSOT Press, 1989.

Jewett, R. "Enthusiastic Radicalism and the Thessalonian Correspondence." *SBL 1972 Proceedings* 1:181–232.

______. *The Thessalonian Correspondence: Pauline Rhetoric and Millenarian Piety*. Facets and Foundations, NT. Philadelphia: Fortress Press, 1986.

Johanson, B. C. *To All the Brethren. A Text-Linguistic and Rhetorical Approach to 1 Thessalonians*. ConBNT 16. Stockholm: Almquist & Wiksell International, 1987.

Krodel, G. "The 'Religious Power of Lawlessness' (*Katechon*) as Precursor of the 'Lawless One' (*Anomos*) 2 Thess 2:6-7." *CurrTheoMiss* 17 (6, 1990) 440–446.

Lührmann, D. "The Beginnings of the Church at Thessalonica." In *Greeks, Romans, and Christians: Essays in Honor of Abraham J. Malherbe*. Edited by D. L. Balch, et al., 237–249. Minneapolis: Fortress Press, 1990.

Malherbe, A. " 'Gentle As A Nurse,' the Cynic Background of 1 Thes 2." *Nov Test* 12 (2, 1970) 203–217.

______. *Paul and the Thessalonians: The Philosophic Tradition of Pastoral Care*. Philadelphia: Fortress Press, 1987.

Marshall, I. H. *1 and 2 Thessalonians*. NCBC. Grand Rapids: Eerdmans, 1983.

Morris, L. *The First and Second Epistles to the Thessalonians*. Grand Rapids: Eerdmans, 1959. Rev. ed., 1991.

Olbricht, T. H. "An Aristotelian Rhetorical Analysis of 1 Thessalonians." In *Greeks, Romans, and Christians: Essays in Honor of Abraham J. Malherbe*. Edited by D. L. Balch, et al., 216–236. Minneapolis: Fortress Press, 1990.

Pearson, B. "1 Thes 2:13-16: A Deutero-Pauline Interpolation." *HTR* 64 (1971) 79–94.

Richard, E. "Contemporary Research on 1 (& 2) Thessalonians." *BTB* 20 (3, 1990) 107–115.

Schmidt, D. "The Authenticity of 2 Thessalonians: Linquistic Argument." *SBL 1983 Seminar Papers* 289–96.

Sumney, J. L. "The Bearing of a Pauline Rhetorical Pattern on the Integrity of 2 Thessalonians." *ZNTW* 81 (3/4, 1990) 192–204.

Wanamaker, C. A. "Apocalypticism at Thessalonica." *Neot* 21 (1987) 1–10.

______. *The Epistle to the Thessalonians. A Commentary on the Greek Text.* NIGTC. Grand Rapids: Eerdmans, 1990.

Williams, D. J. *1 and 2 Thessalonians.* New International Biblical Commentary. Peabody, Mass.: Hendrickson, 1992.

Colossians and Ephesians

Abbott, T. *Epistles to the Ephesians and Colossians.* ICC. Edinburgh: T. & T. Clark, 1897.

Arnold, C. E. "Colossae." *ABD* 1:1089–1090.

______. *Ephesians: Power and Magic: the Concept of Power in Ephesians in Light of Its Historical Setting.* SNTSMS 63. Cambridge and New York: Cambridge University Press, 1989.

Barth, M. *Ephesians.* 2 vols. Anchor Bible 34, 34A. New York: Doubleday, 1974.

Cannon, G. E. *The Use of Traditional Material in Colossians.* Macon, Ga.: Mercer University Press, 1983.

Cope, L. "On Rethinking the Philemon-Colossae Connection." *BR* 30 (1985) 45–50.

Francis, F. O. and Meeks, W. A. *Conflict at Colossae.* Rev. ed. SBS 4. Missoula, Mont.: Scholars Press, 1975.

Furnish, V. P. "Colossians, Epistle to the." *The Anchor Bible Dictionary.* 1:1090–1096. Ed. D. N. Freedman. New York: Doubleday, 1992.

______. "Ephesians, Epistle to the. *The Anchor Bible Dictionary.* 2:535–542. Ed. D. N. Freedman. New York: Doubleday, 1992.

Goodspeed, E. J. *The Meaning of Ephesians.* Chicago: University of Chicago Press, 1933.

Gunther, J. *St. Paul's Opponents and Their Background: A Study of Apocalyptic and Jewish Sectarian Teachings.* Leiden: E. J. Brill, 1977.

Harris, M. J. *Colossians and Philemon.* Exegetical Guide to the Greek NT. Grand Rapids: Eerdmans, 1991.

Knox, J. "Philemon and the Authenticity of Colossians." *JR* 18 (1938) 144–60.

Lincoln, A. T. *Ephesians.* WBC 42. Dallas: Word, 1990.

Lohse, E. *Colossians and Philemon.* Hermeneia. Trans. W. Poehlmann et al. Philadelphia: Fortress, 1971.

MacDonald, M. Y. *The Pauline Churches: A Socio-historical Study of Institutionalization in the Pauline and Deutero-Pauline Writings.* New York and Cambridge: Cambridge University Press, 1971.

Martin, C. J. "The *Haustafeln* (Household Codes) in African American Biblical Interpretation: 'Free Slaves' and 'Subordinate Women.' " *Stony the Road We Trod: African American Biblical Interpretation.* 206–231. Ed. C. H. Felder. Minneapolis: Fortress Press, 1991.

Mayerhoff, E. T. *Der Brief an die Colosser mit vornehmlicher Berücksichligung der drei Pastoralbriefe.* Ed., J. L. Mayerhoff. Berllin, 1838.

Mitton, C. L. *Ephesians.* New Century Bible Commentary. Grand Rapids: Eerdmans, 1976.

O'Brien, P. T. *Colossians, Philemon.* Word Biblical Commentary. Dallas: Word, 1982.

Patzia, A. G. *Ephesians, Colossians, Philemon.* New International Biblical Commentary. Peabody, Mass.: Hendrickson, 1991.

Petersen, N. R. *Rediscovering Paul.* Philadelphia: Fortress Press, 1985.

Pokorny, P. *Colossians: A Commentary.* Trans. S. S. Schatzmann. Peabody, Mass.: Hendrickson, 1991.

Sampley, J., et al. *Ephesians, Colossians, 2 Thessalonians, The Pastoral Epistles.* Proclamation Commentaries. Philadelphia: Fortress Press, 1978.

Sanders, E. P. "Literary Dependence in Colossians." *JBL* 85 (1966) 28–45.

Schweizer, E. *The Letter to Colossians: A Commentary.* Trans. A. Chester. Minneapolis: Augsburg, 1982.

Taylor, W. F. and J. H. P. Reumann. *Ephesians; Colossians.* Augsburg Commentary on the NT. Minneapolis: Augsburg, 1985.

Yamauchi, E. "Sectarian Parallels. Qumran and Colossae," *BSac* 121 (1964) 141–52.

Hebrews

Attridge, H. *Hebrews.* Hermeneia. Minneapolis: Fortress Press, 1989.

______. "Paraenesis in a Homily (*logos paracleseos*): The Possible Location of, and Socialization in, the 'Epistle to the Hebrews.' " *Semeia* 50 (1990) 211–226.

______. "Hebrews, Epistle to the." *The Anchor Bible Dictionary.* 3:97–105. Ed. D. N. Freedman, et al. New York: Doubleday, 1992.

Bruce, F. F. " 'To the Hebrews' or 'To the Essenes,' " *NTS* 9 (3, 1963) 217–32.

______. *The Epistle to the Hebrews.* NICT. Rev. ed. Grand Rapids: Eerdmans, 1990.

Carlston, C. E. "Commentaries on Hebrews: A Review Article." *ANR* 1 (2, 1990) 27–45.

D'Angelo, M. R. *Moses in the Letter to the Hebrews*. SBLDS 42. Missoula, Mont.: Scholars Press, 1979.

Dey, L. K. K. *The Intermediate World and Patterns of Perfection in Philo and Hebrews*. SBLDS 25. Missoula, Mont.: Scholars Press, 1975.

Ellingworth, P. *Commentary on Hebrews*. NIGTC. Grand Rapids: Eerdmans, 1993.

Hagner, D. A. *Hebrews*. NIBC. Peabody, Mass.: Hendrickson, 1990.

Horton, F. L. *The Melchizedek Tradition: A Critical Examination of the Sources to the Fifth Century A.D. and in the Epistle to the Hebrews.* SNTSMS 30. Cambridge and New York: Cambridge University Press, 1976.

Hughes, G. *Hebrews and Hermeneutics: The Epistle to the Hebrews as a New Testament Example of Biblical Interpretation*. SNTSMS 36. Cambridge and New York: Cambridge University Press, 1979.

Hurst, L. "How 'Platonic' Are Heb 8:5 and 9:23f?" *JTS* 34 (1, 1983) 156–68.

Hurst, L. D. *The Epistle to the Hebrews. Its Background of Thought*. SNTSMS 65. Cambridge and New York: Cambridge University Press, 1990.

Jobes, K. H. "Rhetorical Achievement in the Hebrews 10 'Misquote' of Psalm 40." *Biblica* 72 (3, 1991) 387–396.

Kistermaker, S. J. *Exposition of the Epistle to the Hebrews*. New Testament Commentary. Grand Rapids: Baker, 1984.

Kobelski, P. J. *Melchizedek and Melchiresa'*. CBQMS 10. Washington, D.C.: Catholic Biblical Association, 1981.

Lane, W. L. *Hebrews 1–8*. WBC 47A. Dallas: Word, 1991.

Manson, W. *The Epistle to the Hebrews*. London: Hodder and Stoughton, 1951.

Moffatt, J. *Epistle to the Hebrews*. International Critical Commentary. Edinburgh: T. & T. Clark, 1924.

Montefiore, H. *A Commentary on the Epistle to the Hebrews*. London: Black; New York: Harper & Row, 1964.

Peterson, D. *Hebrews and Perfection: An Examination of the Concept of Perfection in the 'Epistle to the Hebrews.'* SNTSMS 47. Cambridge and New York: Cambridge University Press, 1982.

Smith, R. H. *Hebrews*. Augsburg Commentary on the NT. Minneapolis: Augsburg, 1984.

Spicq, C. *L'Epitre aux Hebreux*. Paris, 1952.

Thompson, J. W. *The Beginnings of Christian Philosophy: The Epistle to the Hebrews*. CBQMS 13. Washington, D.C.: Catholic Biblical Association, 1982.

Westcott, B. F. *The Epistle to the Hebrews*. London: Macmillan, 1889.

Wild, R. A. "The Warrior and Prisoner: Some Reflections on Ephesians 6:10-20." *CBQ* 46 (1984) 284–298.

Williamson, R. *Philo And the Epistle to the Hebrews*. Leiden: E. J. Brill, 1970.

Wilson, R. McL. *Hebrews*. NCB Commentary. Grand Rapids: Eerdmans, 1987.

Witherington, B. "The Influence of Galatians on Hebrews." *NTS* 37 (1, 1991) 146–152.

Yadin, Y. "The Scrolls and The Epistle to the Hebrews," *Aspects of the Dead Sea Scrolls*, 36–55. Eds. Ch. Rabin and Y. Yadin. Jerusalem: Magnes, 1958.

The Pastoral Letters

Bratcher, R. G. *A Translator's Guide to Paul's Letters to Timothy and to Titus*. London; New York; Stuttgart: United Bible Societies, 1983.

Brown, R. E. "*Episkōpe* and *Episkopos*: the NT Evidence." *TS* 41 (1980) 322–38.

Dibelius, M. and Conzelmann, H. *The Pastoral Epistles*. Hermeneia. Trans. P. Buttolph, et al. Philadelphia: Fortress Press, 1972.

Easton, B. S. *Pastoral Epistles*. New York: Scribner's Sons, 1948.

Ellis, E. E. "The Authorship of the Pastoral Epistles: A Resume and Assessment of Recent Trends." In idem, *Paul and His Recent Interpreters*, 49–57. Grand Rapids: Eerdmans, 1961.

Fee, G. D. *1 and 2 Timothy, Titus*. Good News. San Francisco: Harper & Row, 1984.

______. *1 and 2 Timothy, Titus*. New International Biblical Commentary. Peabody, Mass.: Hendrickson, 1989.

______. "Issues in Evangelical Hermeneutics, Part III: The Great Watershed—Intentionality & Particularity: 1 Timothy 2:8-15 as a Test Case." *Crux* 26 (4, 1990) 31–37.

Fiore, B. *The Function of Personal Example in the Socratic and Pastoral Epistles*. AnBib 105. Rome: Biblical Institute Press, 1986.

Grayston, K. and Herdan, G. "The Authorship of the Pastorals in the Light of Statiscal Linguistics." *NTS* 6 (1959) 1–15.

Gritz, S. H. *Paul, Women, Teachers, and the Mother Goddess at Ephesus. A Study of 1 Timothy 2:9-15 in Light of the Religious and*

Cultural Mileau of the First Century. Lanham, Md.; New York; London: University Press of America, 1991.

Guthrie, D. *The Pastoral Epistles and the Mind of Paul*. London: Tyndale, 1956.

______. *The Pastoral Epistles*. 2nd. ed. Grand Rapids: Eerdmans, 1990.

Hanson, A. T. *The Pastoral Epistles*. NCB. Grand Rapids: Eerdmans, 1982.

______. *The Pastoral Letters*. Cambridge: University Press, 1966.

Harrison, P. N. *The Problem of the Pastorals*. London: Oxford University Press, 1921.

Hultgren, A. J. and Aus, R. *I-II Timothy, Titus, II Thess*. Augsburg Commentary NT. Minneapolis: Augsburg, 1984.

Karris, R. J. *The Pastoral Epistles*. New Testament Message 17. Wilmington, Del.: Michael Glazier, 1979.

______. "The Background and Significance of the Polemic of the Pastoral Epistles." *JBL* 92 (1973) 549–64.

Kelly, J. N. D. *A Commentary on the Pastoral Epistles*. Harper NT Commentary New York: Harper & Row, 1963.

Knight, G. W. *Commentary on the Pastoral Epistles*. NIGTC. Grand Rapids: Eerdmans, 1993.

______. *The Faithful Sayings in the Pastoral Letters*. Grand Rapids: Baker, 1979.

Kroeger, R. and C. "May Women Teach? Heresy in the Pastoral Epistles." *The Reformed Journal* (October 1980) 14–18.

McEleney, N. J. "The Vice Lists of the Pastoral Epistles." *CBQ* 36 (1974) 203–19.

Meirer, J. B. "*Presbyteros* in the Pastoral Epistles." *CBQ* 35 (1973) 323–45.

Metzger, B. M. "A Reconsideration of Certain Arguments Against the Pauline Authorship of the Pastoral Epistles." *ExpT* 70 (1958–59) 91–94.

Moule, C. F. D. "The Problem of the Pastoral Epistles: A Reappraisal." *BJRL* 47 (1965) 430–52.

Murphy-O'Connor, J. "2 Timothy Contrasted with 1 Timothy and Titus." *RevBib* 93:3 (1991) 403–418.

Prior, M. *Paul the Letter-Writer and the Second Letter to Timothy*. JSNTSup 23. Sheffield: JSOT Press, 1989.

Rogers, P. "The Pastoral Epistles as Deutero-Pauline." *ITQ* 45 (1978) 248–60.

Quinn, J. D. "The Last Volume of Luke: The Relation of Luke-Acts to the Pastoral Epistles." In C. H. Talbert, ed. *Perspective on Luke-Acts* 62–75. Danville, Va.: Association of Baptist Professors of Religion, 1978.

______. *The Letter to Titus. A New Translation with Notes and Commentary and An Introduction to Titus, I and II Timothy, The Pastoral Epistles*. AB 35. New York; London: Doubleday, 1990.

______. "Paraenesis and the Pastoral Epistles: Lexical Observations Bearing on the Nature of the Sub-Genre and Soundings on its Role in Socialization and Liturgies." *Semeia* 50 (1990) 189–210.

______. "The Pastoral Epistles." *BibToday* 23 (4, 1985) 228–38.

Schweizer, E. *Church Order in the NT*. SBT 32. London: SCM, 1961.

Verner, D. C. *The Household of God. The Social World of the Pastoral Epistles*. SBLDS 71. Chico, Calif.: Scholars Press, 1983.

Wilson, S. G. *Luke and the Pastoral Epistles*. London: SPCK, 1979.

"Dr. Charles B. Puskas's *The Letters of Paul* addresses the basic questions of each Pauline letter and provides the background and literary information necessary for the reader to see more easily the arguments and their relevance for then as well as now. This volume would make a fine companion to any theological exposition of these letters."

—Robert F. O'Toole, S.J.
Pontifico Istituto Biblico
Rome

"If one is looking around for an introduction to the Pauline letters, this one is certainly worth considering. It contains the usual coverage of historical and literary questions as well as a clear treatment of rhetorical criticism. The book contains useful outlines of the epistles that follow the structures of rhetorical criticism, and valuable comparisons of the Deutero-Paulines and the undisputed letters of Paul."

—Calvin J. Roetzel
Arnold Lowe Professor of Religious Studies
Macalaster College
Saint Paul